MAKING MATTERS

MAKING MATTERS

Craft, Ethics, and New Materialist Rhetorics

LEIGH GRUWELL

UTAH STATE UNIVERSITY
Logan

© 2022 by University Press of Colorado

Published by Utah State University Press
An imprint of University Press of Colorado
245 Century Circle, Suite 202
Louisville, Colorado 80027

 The University Press of Colorado is a proud member of
the Association of University Presses.

The University Press of Colorado is a cooperative publishing enterprise supported,
in part, by Adams State University, Colorado State University, Fort Lewis College,
Metropolitan State University of Denver, Regis University, University of Alaska Fairbanks,
University of Colorado, University of Northern Colorado, University of Wyoming, Utah
State University, and Western Colorado University.

∞ This paper meets the requirements of the ANSI/NISO Z39.48-1992 (Permanence of
Paper).

ISBN: 978-1-64642-254-8 (paperback)
ISBN: 978-1-64642-255-5 (ebook)
https://doi.org/10.7330/9781646422555

Library of Congress Cataloging-in-Publication Data

Names: Gruwell, Leigh, author.
Title: Making matters : craft, ethics, and new materialist rhetorics /
  Leigh Gruwell.
Description: Logan : Utah State University Press, [2022] | Includes
  bibliographical references and index.
Identifiers: LCCN 2021059132 (print) | LCCN 2021059133 (ebook) | ISBN
  9781646422548 (paperback) | ISBN 9781646422555 (ebook)
Subjects: LCSH: Rhetoric—Social aspects. | Rhetoric—Moral and ethical
  aspects. | Materialism—Moral and ethical aspects. | Online social
  networks—Political aspects. | Craftivism. | Feminism and rhetoric.
Classification: LCC P301.5.S63 G78 2022 (print) | LCC P301.5.S63 (ebook)
  | DDC 808–dc23/eng/20220217
LC record available at https://lccn.loc.gov/2021059132
LC ebook record available at https://lccn.loc.gov/2021059133

Cover photograph © Rafa artphoto / Shutterstock

For Mikko. I made this while I was making you.

CONTENTS

ACKNOWLEDGMENTS

I am indebted to many friends, mentors, colleagues, family members, and those in between. This book project, unrecognizable as it may be, is rooted in my graduate programs at Miami University and Florida State University. Courses with Michael Neal, Kathi Yancey, Cindy Lewiecki-Wilson, LuMing Mao, Jim Porter, and Michele Simmons stay with me still: I am grateful to have learned from such incredible scholars. I am especially thankful for the mentorship and warmth of Kristie Fleckenstein, whose support of a slightly overwhelmed and very young feminist rhetorician inspires my teaching today, and Heidi McKee, whose long-ago research methods class has shaped my career in ways neither of us could have imagined. I am also fortunate to have studied with Kate Ronald, whose work not only defined the field of feminist rhetorics but also deeply informed my own professional outlook. Kate deserves more praise than I am capable of writing, but attentive readers will see her in many places throughout this book. Finally, Jason Palmeri is undoubtedly the best advisor, mentor, and friend I have had at every stage of my professional life. I only wish every young scholar could have the chance to work with someone as generous and patient as him. This book would not have been possible without these mentors; they have challenged me in the very best ways.

My time at Florida State and Miami was made all the better by the company of other very smart people: I am lucky to have worked alongside (or just nearby) Chanon Adsanatham, Dominic Ashby, Lisa Blankenship, Erin Brock Carlson, Bridget Gelms, Kevin Rutherford, and Jonathan Rylander. Jonathan Bradshaw and Dustin Edwards deserve a special thanks, both for their friendship and for kindly offering their feedback on parts of this book. Rory Lee, whose love for wrestling is only eclipsed by his love of his family, has offered me more than a decade of laughter and support. His friendship has only been paralleled by Morgan Leckie, my favorite person to get lost in late-night conversations with. There is no question I would not be the thinker and writer I am without her wisdom and humor. Finally, I've learned so much from

Natalie Szymanski over the last decade-plus, but I am perhaps most grateful for her unending lessons in strength. I thank her for loving me all these years.

I am grateful for the many colleagues at Auburn who have been kind enough to share their expertise and support: Julia Charles, Kate Craig, Emily Friedman, Derek Ross, Chad Wickman, and Susan Youngblood have all been unselfish friends and cheerleaders. Ashley Ludewig is not only a beloved colleague but exceptional workout buddy, baker, and all-around lovely human who has effortlessly become a part of my family. I also am lucky to have found both a friend and a collaborator just down the hall in Charlie Lesh. I don't think this book would have been possible without his wit, camaraderie, and endless pep talks.

Additionally, I want to thank the team at Utah State University Press, especially Rachael Levay, whose consistent support of this project made this book much better than I ever expected it to be. This book is also deeply indebted to the anonymous reviewers who provided profoundly generative feedback on earlier versions of this manuscript. I know this labor is not nearly as visible as it should be, but I thank them here for their time and guidance.

I also want to acknowledge the many peoples who have built and protected the lands and places where this book was written. I live and work on the ancestral home of the Muscogee (Creek) Indians. Auburn University, my employer, is a land-grant university whose initial endowment was funded by the seizure and sale of Indigenous land and whose continued prosperity was made possible by the forced labor of enslaved Black men, women, and children. Making this state safe for its Black and Indigenous citizens begins with recognizing their integral role in creating and maintaining it; I am grateful for the chance to do so here.

These acknowledgments would not be complete without noting those who loved me first: my family. My Oma and Opa inspired a love of learning, reading, and language in me. It is because of them that I first saw myself as a writer. My sister, Melissa, who has always been able to make me laugh, has also shown me the value of an open heart. My mom, Mary, has never not been proud of me. Now that I too am a mother, I realize what a gift it was to have her standing beside me from the start. Last, my greatest thanks goes to the family I have built for myself: my husband, Veikko, and my son, Mikko, who challenge me to make the world they deserve every day.

MAKING MATTERS

Introduction

RHETORIC IN THE MAKING

Ada Lovelace's story is by now a familiar one. The woman who is often described as the mother of computer programing was born of unique privilege in early nineteenth-century England. The daughter of mathematician Lady Byron and poet Lord Byron, a teenage Lovelace began working closely with engineer Charles Baggage on his analytical engine machine, and she quickly recognized its capacity to perform tasks beyond basic calculations. By her twenties, Lovelace had written what was, essentially, an algorithm for the machine to perform and just like that, the framework for modern-day computing was born (Fuegi and Frances 2003; Plant 1997). A lesser-known feature of Lovelace's story, however, is that her mathematical breakthrough was inspired, at least in part, by the Jacquard loom, a machine that automated weaving. A technological innovation in its own right, the Jacquard loom used punch cards—much like those used by the earliest computers—to store binary data that could create patterns for weaving (Burgess, Gollihue, and Pigg 2018; Fuegi and Frances 2003; Harlizius-Klück 2017; Plant 1997). For Lovelace, the similarities between computing and weaving seemed much more natural than they might to modern-day readers: as she explained it, "the Analytical Engine *weaves algebraical patterns* just as the Jacquard-loom weaves flowers and leaves" (qtd. in Fuegi and Frances 2003, 17; emphasis original). That is, at least as Lovelace saw it, the craft of weaving and the craft of coding were simply different sides of the same coin.

Lovelace's story highlights how the digital and physical are not as distinct as our everyday usages of those terms might imply. Rather, from its very origins, the digital has been rooted in and inspired by the physical: as Angela M. Haas (2007) notes, "digital" does not only refer to computer technologies but also "to our fingers, our digits, one of the primary ways (along with our ears and eyes) through which we make sense of the world and with which we write into the world" (84). Just look to the language of computing to see evidence of its material, woven roots: "Terms such as texture, pattern, layering, links, nodes, sampling, net,

https://doi.org/10.7330/9781646422555.c000

network, web, web weaver, and threads belong to a lexicon employed in both weaving and computing" (Gabriel and Wagmister 1997, 335). Although the increasing ubiquity of digital technologies might indicate that the material is less and less relevant, Lovelace's story suggests otherwise: The physical bleeds into the digital and vice versa, to the point where any distinctions between them erode entirely. Thus, to fully understand *how* we make, both online and offline, we must look to what we make with (and what, in turn, makes us).

That making happens not as the result of a single, independent actor but through the entanglements of actors (both human and other-than-human) is made plain by the work of the weaver at the loom (or the programmer at the keyboard), says Sadie Plant (1997). In both scenarios, she observes, "the user and the used are merely the perceptible elements, the identifiable components which are thrown up by—and serve also to contain—far more complex processes. The weaver and the loom, the surfer and the Net: none of them are anything without the engineerings which they both capture and perpetuate" (77). That is, individuals only become recognizable as such through the relationships they enter, and the larger outcomes they serve: the punch card, for example, is useless on its own, and only becomes significant as it encounters the loom, or the computer. Making, in other words, is just as relational as it is material.

For rhetoricians, then, the story of Ada Lovelace might serve as the perfect illustration of how other-than-human *things* become rhetorical in concert with humans as well with other nonhumans. Indeed, this has become an ever-more pressing question for the field. Though this material turn goes by many names—"object-oriented rhetoric" (Barnett 2015; Reid 2012), "posthuman rhetoric" (Boyle 2016; Dobrin, 2015), and "new materialism/ist" (Gries 2015; Micciche 2014) appear most often—it results from a fundamental interest in the question of rhetoric's materiality. This scholarship, which I refer to as *new materialist rhetorics*, argues that rhetoric is not an exclusively human product; rather, it emerges from the entanglements of actors, human or otherwise. Through its foregrounding of the material, this work has expanded the purview of rhetorical studies, producing important and provocative scholarship attuning us to "the non discursive (or not exclusively discursive) things that occasion rhetoric's emergence" (Barnett and Boyle 2016, 3). Considering rhetoric in these terms—that is, as neither entirely discursive nor entirely human—raises crucial questions about who or what counts as a rhetorical agent. Agency, in new materialist rhetorics, is not limited to humans alone but also extends to nonhumans, as rhetoric emerges from their complex and varied encounters. New materialist rhetorics thus productively orient the field toward an understanding of agency as distributed among assemblages of human and nonhuman actors, offering particularly valuable insights as the interdependencies between humans and nonhuman writing technologies become increasingly visible. Just as Lovelace's machine demonstrated almost two hundred years ago, materiality matters.

There is another lesson rhetoricians might take away from Lovelace's story, however: While her innovative approach to computing suggests that making is a relational, material practice, it also points to the ways that power can structure, infuse, and inform that making. Lovelace's accomplishments are remarkable given the narrow role of women in nineteenth-century England. While Lovelace was no doubt a very privileged woman—her race, socioeconomic background, and high level of education certainly afforded her many resources—she also faced challenges. Most notably, she suffered from poor health throughout her life, "walking with crutches until the age of seventeen, and endlessly subject to the fits, swellings, faints, asthmatic attacks, and paralyses which were supposed to characterize hysteria," as Plant (1997) describes it (29).[1] She also chafed against her role as mother, dismissing her three children as "irksome *duties* & nothing more" (quoted in Plant 1997, 28; emphasis original). Navigating the world through her ill, female body and the expectations that followed it, Lovelace faced the intersection of power and materiality every day.

The same power dynamics that shaped Lovelace's life also, inevitably, shaped the machines Lovelace was inspired by and the machines her innovations made possible. Who gets to use these machines—the looms, the smartphones, the laptops—and for what reasons? Who, or what, do these machines serve, and who or what do they exclude? What do these machines make possible? These are important questions that new materialist rhetorics are well positioned to grapple with, even if this scholarship has yet to fully explore how power is interwoven within the material entanglements that make rhetoric possible. New materialist rhetorics foreground the complex of human and nonhuman agents that undergird any rhetorical act, but its current formulations tend to overlook the power inequities that persist within many of the assemblages that make rhetoric possible, even though power—like rhetoric itself—is complex, networked, and emergent.

The stakes are as high now as they were for Lovelace: While new composing technologies make the material, ecological nature of rhetorical agency ever more apparent, they also raise important questions about how to theorize the political implications of such a radically reconfig-ured rhetorical agency. How, for example, do we account for power relations when agency is distributed between and emerges from affini-ties and ecologies? How do material things participate in inequitable relations and rhetorical outcomes? What are our ethical obligations as co-actors in an agentic assemblage? How, from a new materialist per-spective, does political change occur? These are not mere hypotheticals: even a small sampling of recent cases suggests that the increasingly vis-ible co-constituency of humans and nonhumans presents weighty ethical questions. Consider, for example, the political implications of an insur-ance company making use of wearable technology like Fitbit to gather health data from policyholders, rewarding "good" bodies with reduced premiums (Barlyn 2018); or of algorithmically authored bots spread-ing "fake news" and, arguably, shaping election results (Guilbeault and Woolley 2016; Mayer 2018); or of Google's search results for phrases like "black girls" returning racist, sexist, and even pornographic con-tent (Noble 2018). New materialist rhetorics might see these instances as evidence of rhetoric's fluidity, a demonstration of how rhetorical agency results from human-machine encounters. But these examples also starkly demonstrate how these encounters are interlaced with, and sometimes work in service of, power relationships that can further mar-ginalize already-marginalized people and communities.

It is essential, then, that new materialist rhetorics take up the difficult task of accounting for how power structures the material entanglements that make rhetoric possible, and to articulate what ethical rhetorical practice might look like in the face of such a radical reframing of rheto-ric. To begin this work, I propose we begin exactly where Lovelace did: by looking to craft. Defined broadly as material practices of making, craft easily accepts the new materialist claim that rhetoric is fundamen-tally material. Like new materialist rhetorics, craft also understands that rhetorical action is not the product of a singular, human actor but rather a result of assemblages of varied human and nonhuman actors. Importantly, however, craft also calls attention to the emplaced, embodied qualities of rhetorical actors and the power relationships they must navigate. Craft's ability to illuminate the interdependence of materiality, power, and rhetorical action is thus significant for new materialist rhetorics.

Throughout this book, I explore how craft and new materialist rheto-rics might inform one another in order to better account for the power relationships to which rhetoric is inextricably bound, and to recognize their ethical implications. While it shares new materialism's interest in the rhetoricity of nonhuman things, craft recognizes the way that power is located in, produced by, and may be upended through materiality, and thus centers the ethical and political significance of the building, reordering, or disruption of assemblages. Even in its digital manifestations, craft foregrounds the material conditions from which rhetoric emerges. Accordingly, I suggest, we might imagine new materialist rhetorics as inherently *crafty*. Recasting new materialist rhetorics as craft recognizes rhetoric as a material practice that is both structured by power and carries significant ethical weight. This argument centers on what I am calling *craft agency*, which accepts the new materialist position that rhetorical agency results from the material intra-actions of diverse agents, human and otherwise. Craft agency, however, sees the assemblages that make rhetoric possible as intensely political, and thus locates ethical practice in the cultivation of reciprocal entanglements between agents that are both co-constitutive and materially specific. A means of grounding new materialism in the ethical and political considerations that are so central to craft, craft agency clarifies how power circulates and sometimes stagnates within assemblages of actors and provides tools to rectify that uneven distribution.

This book, then, explores how craft agency might articulate a clearer ethical and political framework for new materialist rhetorics. To better understand how new materialist rhetorics might be imagined as craft, I historicize and locate the concept of craft both within rhetorical history (chapter 2) and in the field of writing studies, specifically (chapter 6), so that we might have a clearer basis from which to integrate craft into our disciplinary frameworks and activities. I center my investigation around specific case studies: craftivism, the fibercraft website Ravelry, and the 2017 Women's March. These instances all highlight how a material, ecological understanding of rhetorical agency can still enact political change. The craft agency at work in these locations offers a model of how to create more equitable relationships through and with the embodied people and the material things that we interact with every day, specifically by modeling craft agency's ethics of entanglement. The pages that follow are my attempt to demonstrate how we humans work with and alongside things—nonhuman, sometimes digital, sometimes material—to enact change and craft our world.

Chapter 1, "Craft Agency: An Ethics for New Materialist Rhetorics," explores in depth the theoretical framing on which the rest of the book relies and more thoroughly details the concept of craft agency. I begin by outlining the current state of new materialist scholarship, noting particularly its implications for refiguring rhetorical agency. Because new materialist rhetorics insist that agency is an emergent, fluid happening, many have criticized it as being ill-equipped to support political action or ethical practice. Yet, feminist scholarship (both in rhetorical studies and new materialism more widely) has a deep body of scholarship that has productively highlighted how materiality is bound to power relations. To reconcile the capacious sense of rhetorical agency articulated by new materialist rhetorics with the robust theories of power central to feminist scholarship, I propose relying on craft. Craft—like new materialist rhetorics—sees rhetoric as material and questions the viability of the traditionally bounded, causal rhetorical agent. Craft, however, understands the political significance of such an approach to agency, and can thus provide the robust ethical framework that new materialist rhetorics have yet to fully articulate.

From there, chapter 1 turns to the book's key argument and introduces craft agency. Craft agency describes how agency emerges from the material intra-actions of human and nonhuman, digital and material, entities. While craft agency recognizes the agency of nonhuman things, thus decentering humans, it also does not absolve humans of agentic responsibilities; it instead locates that responsibility in practices that foster reciprocal, equitable entanglements. By imagining new materialist rhetorical agency as craft agency, then, we are better equipped to locate an ethics of new materialism as well as imagine its political potentials.

Chapter 2, "Crafting History, Crafting Rhetoric: Locating Craft Agency," historicizes my attempts to recast new materialist rhetorics as craft. This chapter builds on the foundational concepts presented in the introduction and chapter 1, offering a detailed examination of the historical and theoretical origins of craft. Craft has always been politically significant, despite the tendency to dismiss it as domestic, amateurish frivolity. Craft foregrounds the relationships that make *making* possible, and, importantly, it recognizes those relationships as both human and nonhuman. For craft, the (re)arranging of material relationships often results in meaningful change. New materialist rhetorics, then, are craft, and reframing them as such only further emphasizes their political potential and ethical significance.

This relationship alone is not my sole reason for situating new materialist rhetorics as craft, however: Craft has notable and persistent ties to rhetorical theory. I thus devote the second half of chapter 2 to exploring how the interrelated concepts of *techne*, *mêtis*, and *kairos* all frame rhetoric as a situated, contingent craft that depends on a rich awareness of materiality, including and exceeding individual (human) bodies. Foundational to the earliest formulations of rhetoric, techne, mêtis, and kairos are all grounded in responsivity, openness, and relationality, and value materiality while recognizing the body as a site of political resistance and ethical action. These terms thus inform an understanding of rhetoric's inherent craftiness and further suggest the need for new materialist rhetorics to adopt the ethics of craft agency.

I begin my in-depth exploration of specific instances of craft agency with chapter 3, "Craftivism and the Material Specificity of Rhetorical Action," which investigates craftivism, a recently coined term that describes the convergence of craft and activism. Through the deliberate cultivation of embodied, emplaced relationships with specific (nonhuman) composing tools and technologies, craftivists from the nineteenth century through today demonstrate the political potentials of craft agency. Often emerging from the lived experiences and practices of marginalized peoples, craftivism draws attention to the material intra-actions that can both create power inequities and the conditions for their reversal. Craftivism sees power as the result of entanglements between human and nonhuman actors and demonstrates how attention to assemblages can create meaningful political changes. In short, craftivism is fundamentally interested in the development, maintenance, and even refusal of material alliances for political goals.

Craftivism, I suggest, is a useful starting point for addressing criticisms of new materialist rhetorics because it not only functions from the position that rhetorical action is a product of complex intra-actions between a network of human and nonhuman actors, but also does so with an explicitly activist agenda that positions the body itself as a material interface. Through its insistence on dismantling the strict divisions between material agents, craftivism practices what I call an ethics of entanglement, which helps articulate how new materialist rhetorics might adopt coalitional politics. Through analysis of specific craftivist acts, I demonstrate how we might retheorize new materialist rhetorics as a means of restructuring power in productive and ethical ways.

I build from this focus on embodied materiality in chapter 4, "Manifesting Material Relationships Online through Ravelry," and explore what a politically attuned new materialist rhetoric might look like in spaces that, ostensibly, don't appear to be material at all: internet communities. Here, I turn to Ravelry, a digital crafting community for knitters, crocheters, and other fiber artists. With nearly eight million members—the vast majority of whom are women—Ravelry is both a social network and database, where users write, share, and edit patterns. Ravelry and its users are notable for their sophisticated awareness of materiality, as digital practices reflect and are reflected in "real life."

Drawing on surveys and interviews with users as well as an analysis of the site's interface, I argue that Ravelry demonstrates digital materiality in action, where the intra-actions between bodies, objects, and locations are made visible and are the condition for rhetorical agency.

Ravelry's radical digital materiality, I argue, can serve as a basis for theorizing what a politically aware, ethical new materialist rhetoric might look like online. While Ravelry is by no means a feminist utopia (users are overwhelming white, for example), the kind of relationships that emerge on Ravelry serve as a starting point for imagining craft agency online and challenge traditional understandings of what counts as political. Like craftivism, Ravelry highlights the necessity of craft agency's ethics of entanglement, but also demonstrates how that ethics depends on a reciprocity that dismantles boundaries between self and other, human and nonhuman, digital and material.

In chapter 5, "The Women's March, Digital-Material Assemblages, and Embodied Difference," I examine the worldwide Women's March protests that followed the inauguration of Donald Trump as US president in January 2017. The Women's March serves as an example of how an assemblage of co-constructed digital and material actors can perform political work. Organized through digital tools, the Women's March led to physical demonstrations worldwide, and its associated digital and physical artifacts (such as signs, pussyhats, social media posts, and bodies) make visible how craft agency's ethics of entanglement collapses agential boundaries. What's more, the Women's March demonstrates how the construction, maintenance, and disruption of these boundaries is intensely political. As such, the 2017 Women's March illustrates how the orchestration of physical and digital space, as well human and non-human actors, can make a significant political intervention.

The Women's March, however, did face criticism: Many trans women and women of color argued the march failed to listen to and include their voices and thus reproduced an exclusionary version of cis white feminist activism that ignores embodied difference. In this chapter, then, I argue that both the successes and failures of the Women's March signal the significance materiality holds for ethical, politically focused rhetoric. While the Women's March demonstrates the promise of a richly conceived materiality that values both digital and physical artifacts, it also serves as a warning that overlooking material differences will endanger any attempt at political action and the reciprocal ethics of entanglement it is grounded in.

I conclude with chapter 6, "Rescuing Craft for Writing Studies." In this final chapter, I turn to the discipline as a whole, exploring how craft and craft agency might inform the work of the field, including our pedagogical, administrative, and scholarly activities. While craft was once a central term for the field, particularly during its maturation in the 1970s, writing studies has largely abandoned craft, casting it as a rhetorical artifact of process and expressivist pedagogies. Yet craft remains a productive metaphor for highlighting how composing is a material practice that results from the commingling of various human and nonhuman agents. I argue that a reclamation of craft, one that imagines it in these robustly rhetorical terms, can help secure an intellectual and disciplinary agenda for writing studies, one that redirects the field away from the focus on subjectivity that has for too long relegated writing studies (and writing itself) to its merely managerial or skills-based position within the university. An embrace of craft, and craft agency, instead moves us toward the interrogation of the agential intra-actions that make rhetoric possible and can thus ensure our disciplinary practices are attuned to the immediacies of the material constraints that structure educational and political life.

These chapters offer what I hope is a compelling reimagining of both new materialist rhetorics and craft that highlights their ethical and political possibilities. Grounded in craft's insistence that ethics lies in the material entanglements that enable rhetorical action, I believe that new materialism can productively interrogate and dismantle the powerful rhetorical assemblages that result in the continued marginalization of historically disenfranchised groups. The intentional structuring of affinities that is visible in craft practices and communities models a new materialist approach that gives materiality its due while also remaining vigilant to its political possibilities. Likewise, new materialist rhetorics offer craft the theoretical positioning to directly articulate the role of nonhumans as well the complex account of ecological agency that is always implicit in craft and can accordingly help to dismantle some of the craft community's more persistent problems; namely, its gendered, raced, and classed dimensions. Together, then, craft and new materialist rhetorics can generate an approach to rhetorical agency that recognizes the ethical and political consequences of forming, dissolving, or rearranging assemblages of various human and nonhuman actors.

Ada Lovelace might thus offer one final lesson to rhetoricians: When we acknowledge that making is not just material but also relational, and thus ethical, we create the conditions for new ways of being. Teshome Gabriel and Fabian Wagmister note that "weaving, as a practice, is a matter of linkage—a connectedness that extends the boundaries of the individual. . . . Computer technology also opens up the possibility of a digital weaving that acknowledges this sense of connection" (Gabriel and Wagmister 1997, 337), but I would argue that the interrelatedness they describe is inherent to all making. Making, that is, "connects and reconnects bodies, tools, and surroundings in ways that create new ways of moving and being" (Burgess, Gollihue, and Pigg 2018, sec 3.2, para. 3). What is most revolutionary about new materialist rhetorics, then, is not their dissolution of the traditional subject or rhetorical agency itself, but their recognition of the transformative power of relationships. Understanding how these relationships develop, change, and discontinue offers a way toward the creation of more equitable conditions for rhetorical action.

1

CRAFT AGENCY
An Ethics for New Materialist Rhetorics

Rhetoric, as a human enterprise, has never not been political. From its earliest articulations, theorists and practitioners have recognized rhetoric's ability to forge relationships, enact change, and make worlds. But what does it mean to be rhetorical, to traverse and intervene in networks of power, when the capacity for both is not limited to humans alone? Or, to put it more bluntly, "Is the power to disrupt really limited to human speakers?" (Bennett 2010, 106). The question becomes even trickier when we accept that neither humans nor nonhumans have agency, at least not in the traditional, causal sense. New materialist rhetorics offer provocations on both these fronts: not only do they claim that rhetorical agency exceeds the human (that is, they recognize nonhumans as rhetorical agents), but they are also skeptical of the autonomous subject altogether, arguing that individuals—and their rhetorical actions—do not exist prior to their involvements with other agents, whether they be human or nonhuman. As Laurie Gries (2011) argues, "We are not rhetorical agents; we become rhetorical agents just as any other matter becomes rhetorical through intra-actions with other agents" (74). Agents, and rhetorical agency itself, emerge from encounters with other human and nonhuman agents. In such a radical repositioning, it is no wonder that questions of power follow.

Because new materialist rhetorics reject the notion that individual actors can possess agency, some of the most fundamental assumptions about rhetoric as a political practice are upended. How do the mutually constitutive actors that new materialism favors enact change? How does power circulate throughout these agentic networks, and how might it be reoriented in more ethical ways? Who—or what—is responsible for unethical rhetorical practices or inequitable results? What does ethical practice even look like when agency is so thoroughly reimagined?

Even as we accept new materialist approaches that reframe rhetorical agency as "an orchestration of ecological relations" (Boyle 2016, 539) rather than the work of a singular, skilled rhetor, we must also contend

https://doi.org/10.7330/9781646422555.c001

with the reality that the agency co-constitutive agents generate still has meaningful, concrete outcomes. As Marilyn Cooper (2019) explains, "Agents' actions always make a difference; their actions, even though they are not consciously intended, are their own, and awareness of agents as agents is crucial to understanding what comes to matter" (130). An ethics of new materialist rhetorical agency would accordingly recognize the complexities and nuances of rhetorical agency while also acknowledging the deeply political, consequential nature of rhetoric itself. However, new materialist rhetorics have by and large sidestepped questions of power and ethics, ultimately undermining their value in a moment when our entanglements with other actors (human and non-human, digital and material) have become ever more apparent. It is therefore not only possible but imperative that we embrace new materialism's complex account of agency while also practicing an ethics that is attuned to power inequities.

To begin this important work, I suggest we turn to an ostensibly unlikely location: craft. Craft is a material, process-oriented practice that takes seriously the entanglements of humans and nonhumans. Craft—understood as material practices of making—shares new materialist rhetorics' insistence that agency emerges from intra-actions between human and nonhuman, digital and material, entities. Importantly, however, it also calls attention to the ethics of *how* we make the tangled webs that make rhetoric possible. Craft foregrounds the alliances that enable any act of making: As Kristin Prins (2012) notes, craft "implies a complex of relationships between a maker's identity, her interactions with others, and the things she makes" (145). Those relationships are mediated by and located in the material, which craft recognizes as both capacious and specific. That is, materiality for craft both encompasses a broad spectrum of "things" (including bodies, technologies, objects, environments, and more) while simultaneously acknowledging how the locations and identities of those things are unique (and thus, likely subject to varied markers of difference). Most importantly, craft always regards the material as mutable. It is in this mutability that craft finds its political possibilities, as the (re)arranging of entanglements among material actors can result in meaningful change. Accordingly, craft sees our participation in these entanglements as a profoundly ethical concern.

Craft is both a verb and a noun; it describes material practices of making as well as the material results of that making. Craft thus values both process and product, even if those products are understood as provisional. Craft also recognizes how the various actors that participate in these practices of making are themselves constructed through their mutual engagement. Like new materialist rhetorics, craft understands agency as not simply causal, effected by a singular, self-determined agent, but as the product of the intra-actions between varied rhetorical actors, including humans and nonhumans. Craft, however, also understands how those intra-actions are mediated through the specificity of materiality and sees in that materiality political potential and ethical significance. Through craft, for example, marginalized communities can foster social ties, which can then crystalize into more durable activist networks that advocate for and even create change. Likewise, a new materialist perspective can enrich our understanding of craft, providing the theoretical framing and language to name the complex networks of power that persist within craft communities. Juxtaposing craft and new materialist rhetorics, then, may help articulate the political and ethical complexities of rhetoric as an ecological, emergent, material practice.

As early as 2005, Karlyn Kohrs Campbell argued that new materialist rhetorical agency "emerges in artistry or *craft*" (2; emphasis mine). I suggest we take Campbell's suggestion seriously and further explore the implications of positioning new materialist rhetorics as craft. Doing so not only directs our attention to the material assemblages from which rhetoric emerges, but it also demands a focus on the political and ethical implications of such an understanding of agency. This position, which I term *craft agency*, insists that ethics is located in the entanglements that create agents and rhetoric itself. Grounded in feminist intellectual traditions and practices, craft agency sees agents as both wide-ranging and materially specific; it thus advocates for a reciprocal ethics of entanglement aimed at equalizing power relationships and making social change. The goal of this book, then, is to examine how craft might model an ethics and politics of new materialist rhetorics, and to imagine its possibilities as such.

In what remains of this chapter, I sketch out the theoretical framing for my investigation of craft agency. I begin by defining the contours of new materialist rhetorics in more detail, focusing specifically on its implications for rhetorical agency, ethics, and political action. New materialist rhetorics emerge from the larger critical turn toward the material, which positions agency as both collective and more-than-human. For rhetoric, the consequences of such a conceptual shift are massive: no longer the product of independent human agents, rhetoric is instead a continual process that emerges from the intra-actions of human and nonhuman agents (who themselves are in a continual process of becoming through their intra-actions). Yet, new materialist rhetorics as a whole have struggled to fully articulate the ethics of this extensive reimagining of agency, especially when it comes to accounting for the power relations that structure rhetorical action. Notably, these questions are central to another area of rhetorical scholarship: feminist rhetorics, which have been largely ignored by new materialist rhetorics, despite their shared interests in troubling traditional models of rhetorical agency and figuring rhetoric as a robustly material practice. Indeed, feminist thinking has been quite influential in new materialism more broadly and has been especially useful in articulating the political stakes of new materialist agency. In order to unite the politically attuned mechanisms of feminist rhetorics with the expansive account of rhetorical agency offered by new materialist rhetorics, then, I turn to craft. Particularly in its feminist formulations, craft proves a rich conceptual framework for theorizing a new materialist approach to rhetorical agency that also remains attentive to power relations. This provides the grounding for a more comprehensive discussion of craft agency, which articulates a new materialist agency that is emergent, material, and most notably, politically consequential.

NEW MATERIALISM AND THE CHALLENGE OF AGENCY

New materialist rhetorics emerge from a larger posthumanist scholarly turn that upends long-held assumptions of humans as bounded, privileged subjects. Theorists like Karen Barad (2007), Jane Bennett (2010), Ian Bogost (2012), and Bruno Latour (2005) are perhaps most readily aligned with this newfound fascination with the material: While these authors all have specific and differing approaches, their work shares a concern with ontology, often explicitly in contrast with constructivist orientations—such as postmodernism—that posit reality is generated primarily or entirely through language.[1] The constructivist emphasis on discursivity is flawed, new materialists argue, because it overlooks the function of *things*—rain storms, iPhones, computer code, street signs—in world-making, inappropriately privileging humans. Instead, as Bogost (2012) puts it, "humans are elements, but not the sole elements, of philosophical interest" (6). We, in other words, must confront the twin insights that humans (and human language) are not the only actors of consequence, and that *being* is just as valid a line of inquiry as *meaning*. Accordingly, new materialists insist on a "flat ontology" that "suggests that there is no hierarchy of being" (Bogost 2012, 22) and positions humans and nonhumans as equal participants in world-making, even if the details of their participation in that process differ.

Moving away from a human-centered epistemology toward an object-inclusive ontology presents many conceptual challenges, but perhaps none so sizable as agency. If *being* and *doing* are no longer solely human enterprises, then how should we account for the actions and existence of nonhuman things? One particularly influential answer is found in Bennett's (2010) notion of "thing-power," which she describes as "the curious ability of inanimate things to animate, to act, to produce effects dramatic and subtle" (9). When we acknowledge the "vitality" of non-humans, Bennett argues, we must recognize agency as not located in humans alone, but instead "as differentially distributed across a wider range of ontological types" (9). In other words, a new materialist perspective is deeply invested in understanding nonhumans as legitimate and often powerful actors in their own right, in concert with either each other or with humans.

What's more, for new materialists, agency is not a discrete quality possessed by individual subjects. New materialism understands agency not as the result of an individual (human) actor but instead the product of encounters between co-constitutive human and nonhuman agents. New materialist agency, Bennett (2010) argues, "always depends on the collaboration, cooperation, or interactive interference of many bodies and forces" (21). Agency is emergent, arising from entanglements between agents, human or otherwise. Indeed, new materialists are skeptical of bounded agents altogether and contend that agents are only discernible as such through their interactions with other agents. Even the word "interaction" itself is unable to reflect the complex agency new materialists imagine: As Barad (2007) notes, *interaction* is inadequate because it "assumes that there are separate individual agencies that precede their interaction" (33). She instead introduces the term "intra-action," which better "*signifies the mutual constitution of entangled agencies. . . .* The notion of intra-action recognizes that distinct agencies do not precede, but rather emerge through, their intra-action" (33; emphasis original). Not all new materialists make use of Barad's specific language of intra-action, but I highlight it here because it succinctly captures the difficulties of new materialist agency. Through this book, I rely on this term as a useful shorthand, but my use of intra-action is meant to signal to the larger new materialist perspective on agency, not just Barad's specifically.

Thinking of agency in this way—as an ever-unfolding process of intra-actions—necessitates a shift in emphasis from individual agents to the larger assemblages that they inhabit. Originating in the work of Deleuze and Guattari, the concept of *assemblage* is valued by new materialists because it highlights the dynamic agential groupings from which agency emerges; assemblage emphasizes that agency is not singular but plural. While individual actors may all possess some degree of "vitality," to use Bennet's term, agency itself is collective, the result of intra-actions between varied (human and nonhuman) actors rather than individuals. Thus, argues Barad (2007), "the primary ontological units are not 'things' but phenomena—dynamic topological reconfigurings/entanglements/relationalites/(re)articulations of the world" (141). Agency is not a question of the subject, then, but of the capacities afforded within and among assemblages, which both create and are created by agential intra-actions.

Given this intense interest in redefining materiality and agency, it is no wonder that one especially influential strain of new materialist scholarship has emerged in the form of feminist materialisms. The material has always held special importance for feminist theory, which has historically engaged materiality in two related but distinct ways: first, the materiality of the (gendered) body, and second, the economic, labor, and historical conditions that (re)produce gender and inequity. This latter formation has its roots in Marxist theory and is what "materialist feminism" has traditionally signaled. Materialist feminism recognizes how gendered oppression is the result of divisions of labor (in capitalist modes of production or otherwise). For materialist feminism, the material, especially as it concerns economic relations, is the source of power inequities, but, importantly, it is also the means by which we can address those inequities.[2] Feminist theory's interest in the material is likewise visible through its persistent concern with the body: Because gender is inscribed on and performed through the body, feminist scholars have traditionally identified it as a critical location from which power relations can be traced and resisted. As a result, feminists tend to see the body as integral to knowledge-making processes. Feminist standpoint theory, for example, has offered a compelling account of how bodies and experiences shape both knowing and doing.[3] The body, then, is another fundamental material site for feminists to track how power emerges, is enacted, and even contested.

In short, the material is so significant to feminist theory because it is inextricable from power relations—power relations that feminists seek to disrupt and redistribute more equitably. This interest in dismantling oppressive power structures may appear to be a fundamentally *humanist* orientation that is at odds with new materialism's posthuman objectives. As Katherine Behar (2016) incisively observes, for example, some posthumanist work leaves little room for feminist inquiries, as it "seems to relish, in the idea that humans too are objects, a sense of liberation from the shackles of subjectivity" (5). Such a position is inherently problematic from a feminist perspective, she writes, because "all too many humans are well aware of being objects, without finding cause to celebrate in that reality" (5). This is especially true from the perspective of what Armand Towns (2018) terms "Black feminist new materialism" (351), which reminds us that "Black bodies—as chattel, or the Negro (those ontological, epistemological, and biological constructs fabricated for us by the West)—have been situated as *things*, absent of self-determination," (351–352; emphasis original). Feminist materialisms, then, bring an acute awareness of the problems inherent in objectifying bodies and work to extend traditional feminist perspectives on materiality to account not only for different types of agents (human and nonhuman) but also for different types of agential capacities.

Feminist scholars like Bennett, Barad, Rosi Bradoitti, Stacy Alaimo, Elizabeth Grosz, and Susan Hekman have become notable figures in the world of new materialism, producing work that both stresses "the material interconnections of human corporeality with the more-than-human world, and . . . [acknowledges] that material agency necessitates more capacious epistemologies." (Alaimo 2008, 238). Because feminist theory already has the conceptual tools to address the materiality of power (and to conceive of power as an amorphous, systemic phenomenon), feminist materialism has been successful in defining the ethical stakes of new materialism and has accordingly become an influential facet of new materialist scholarship as a whole.

NEW MATERIALIST RHETORICS

Feminism is not the only intellectual tradition to take up the challenges of new materialism: rhetoric scholars have been eager to reconcile new materialism's insistence on decentering individual humans and their actions with rhetoric's traditionally humanist orientation. Scholars such as Scot Barnett, Casey Boyle, Gries, and many others have worked to define *new materialist rhetorics*, which upend the assumption that "human beings alone determine the scope and possibilities of rhetoric" (Barnett and Boyle 2016, 4) and assert that rhetoric is lively, material, and emergent. New materialist rhetorics invite questions about the rhetorical function of things, and in so doing dispute accounts of rhetorical agency that posit humans (and human language) as the sole originators of rhetorical action. Much work in new materialist rhetorics has thus been devoted to developing new theoretical models of rhetorical agency that include but also exceed the human. In these accounts, rhetorical agency is not simply the causal product of the autonomous classical subject, nor is it solely the result of the various discourses that interpellate the fractured, postmodern subject. Instead, new materialist rhetorics see rhetorical agency as unfolding from the intra-actions of entities, either human or nonhuman. As Gries (2011) argues, "Rhetorical agency is a distributed process that emerges out of fluctuating intra-actions between human and material agents" (80). Rhetorical agency is not something that any individual agent can possess; rather, it originates in the dynamic ecologies that varied agents inhabit.

Accordingly, new materialist rhetorics are less interested in understanding the actions of individual agents (indeed, they would dispute the individual agent even exists) but instead are concerned with mapping the agential groupings that make rhetoric possible. *Assemblage* helps new materialist rhetorics articulate the "collective world-making process" that results from agential intra-actions (Gries 2019, 334). While rhetoricians have also made use of other metaphors—such as "ecologies" (Boyle 2016; Stormer and McGreavy 2017) or "networks" (Sheridan, Ridolfo, and Michel 2012)—to describe the fluid agential collectives of new materialism, the point is the same: agency emerges from lively intra-actions of "entities that are mutually influencing each other and bending space as a consequence of their divergent activities" (Gries 2015, 75). Assemblages are unpredictable, as "they are constantly territorializing and deterritorializing as participating actors come and go and as various forces, from both within and beyond, work to stabilize and destabilize them" (Gries 2019, 335), but it is this unpredictability that gives assemblages their political value, as at their best, they are able to "[open] up new ways of thinking, seeing, and living" (Arola and Arola 2017, 211). Even as the concept of assemblage acknowledges its own volatility, new materialists have embraced it because it shifts the scale of rhetorical inquiry from the bounded, independent agent to the wider matrix of intra-actions that give rise to rhetoric.

This understanding of rhetorical agency informs the more capacious descriptions of rhetoric that new materialists favor: Rhetoric is "the art of being between: of between things and yet also being their means of connection" (Barnett and Boyle 2016, 5); "a distributed, material process of becoming in which divergent consequences are actualized with time and space" (Gries 2015, 7); and "a continuous exercise of tendencies" (Boyle 2016, 551). Common to all these definitions is a view of rhetoric as expansive, fluid, and not entirely or even primarily human. Thomas Rickert's (2013) description of rhetoric as "ambient" speaks to this complexity, as rhetoric is not a discrete event but instead is "embedded complexly in and through [environments]" (254). Indeed, explains Boyle (2016), rhetoric is perhaps better imagined as *practice*, a repetitive engagement that "[exercises] an ecology's tendencies and develops, over time, further capacities for that ecology" (546). In the new materialist view, rhetoric is a process, not a product; an ever-unfolding situated entanglement.

One of the most notable contributions of new materialist rhetorics, then, is their methodological implications. Most discussions of new materialist rhetorical methodology build from the principle of symmetry, a deliberate methodological move that flattens any distinction between humans and nonhumans. From this perspective, any rhetorical investigation should not focus solely on or even privilege human rhetorical activity but instead should attempt to account for the presence of nonhumans as well. Clay Spinuzzi (2015) explains that a symmetrical methodology is not "dehumanizing" (23), as some critics may charge, but rather serves to "[focus] us on the associations among various humans and nonhumans. . . . It's not that nonhumans become humans or vice versa, it's that *these differences in qualities are no longer what we're investigating*" (35; emphasis original). A methodology based on symmetry has obvious consequences for rhetoric scholars, as it adjusts our attention from individual (human) actors and texts toward the associations between all agents in a given ecology. Put differently, a methodology of symmetry asks rhetoricians to flatten the traditional hierarchies that place human actors over all others, and to describe the processes of rhetorical becoming that become visible as a result.[4]

New materialist rhetorics are provocative: not only do they challenge dominant paradigms that assert the constructive nature of language (as opposed to the material and ontological existence of things), but they also undermine the very humanist orientation of rhetoric. Insisting on the materiality of rhetoric may indeed "herald something of a historic crisis for rhetoric" (Barnett 2015, 82), but it also presents significant opportunities at a time when digital composing technologies are forcing us to revise long-held assumptions about rhetoric and rhetorical agency. Indeed, it is no coincidence, I suggest, that new materialist rhetorics have emerged alongside the increasing ubiquity of digital composing technologies. That so much new materialist rhetorical scholarship has found a home in digital and multimodal corners of the field further attests to this relationship. Scholars such as Cynthia Selfe, Gail Hawisher, Patricia Sullivan, and James E. Porter have long recognized composing technologies as rhetorical and have productively worked to trouble the idea that the bounded human agent is solely responsible for rhetorical practice. New materialism offers a promising new theoretical base from which to continue investigating how rhetoric emerges from the entanglements of human writers and nonhuman writing technologies.

Such a major theoretical shift, however, is bound to present questions and even attract criticism. For new materialist rhetorics, there has been significant concern regarding the ethical implications of repositioning of the human. It is not uncommon, as Christian Lundberg and Joshua Gunn (2005) note, for the "question of rhetorical agency . . . [to meld] the ontological (what?) with the ethical (how?)" (86). When agency is not confined to an individual human rhetor but is instead disbursed across a complex and unstable network, it is difficult to ascribe responsibility for unethical or irresponsible rhetorical practices and the power inequities that can result. How, from a new materialist perspective, do we account for bad rhetorical acts? Who—or what—is responsible for unethical relationships or outcomes? Cooper (2011), for example, expressed concern that contemporary approaches to agency—both postmodern and new materialist—"[leave] us with no basis for assigning responsibility for actions" (438). Kristie Fleckenstein (2005) raises similar questions, asking how posthuman agential fluidity might challenge how we gauge rhetorical ethics: "If we have no stable boundaries, no stable reality, and no stable subject, how do we judge whose 'voice,' as well as whose reality, resonates with the greatest ethical authority, the greatest 'good character'?" she asks (325). These criticisms all center around a shared concern of how to conceptualize ethical rhetorical practice when rhetorical agency—and the rhetorical agent themself—is so thoroughly complicated. Scholars have also wondered how this radical reconfiguration of rhetoric and rhetorical agency might play out pedagogically, especially since rhetorical education has long been justified on the basis that it prepares students to imagine themselves as rhetors capable of participating in civic life: "What shall we, as teachers, say to our students about their potential and obligations with respect to becoming rhetorical agents?" Cheryl Geisler (2005) writes in response to new materialist accounts of rhetorical agency (111). Such questions emerge from the fear that new materialist rhetorics are not sufficiently attuned to power and are accordingly ill-equipped to theorize or enact political change, either in the classroom or beyond.

There are many possible explanations for these concerns. One likely culprit is the methodological principle of symmetry I described above. A deliberate methodological decision to flatten the traditional hierarchy that privileges human agents over all else, symmetry is meant to account for the complexities of new materialist rhetorical agency. As a methodological move, however, symmetry focuses our attention in one direction and, consequently, away from others. Specifically, while a symmetrical methodology may help researchers recognize the many actors, human and otherwise, that constitute rhetorical practice, it also presents the risk of obscuring the power relations that structure the intra-actions of those agents. Researchers who choose to enact a symmetrical methodology must take care to not mistake the flattening of the ontological hierarchy for the flattening of existing power relations. As Ehren Pflugfelder (2015) reminds us, "Though humans and nonhumans are on a level playing field to begin with, a flat ontology does not necessarily mean that all things are *perpetually equal* but that they have no innate inequality" (120–121; emphasis original). In other words, while a methodology of symmetry asks researchers to recognize the coequal rhetorical vitality of both human and nonhuman actors, it does not simultaneously suggest that those actors exist independently of the power dynamics that construct, flow through, and concentrate within agentic assemblages. Symmetrical methodologies that fail to make this important distinction can render new materialist rhetorics vulnerable to charges that they are either uninterested or unable to theorize power.

New materialist rhetorics have also likely attracted such criticisms because they frequently elide other intellectual traditions that parallel (and predate) new materialism, especially the complex accounts of agency found in Indigenous thought and decolonial scholarship. Zoe Todd (2016), for example, argues that long before the arrival of "the trendy and dominant Ontological Turn" (7), Indigenous thinkers have for millennia engaged "with sentient environments, with cosmologies that enmesh people into complex relationships between themselves and *all* relations, and with climates and atmospheres as important points of organization and action" (6–7; emphasis original). That is, while Western epistemologies have only recently started to take the proposition of agency as diffuse, material, and more-than-human seriously, "indigenous peoples have never forgotten that nonhumans are agential beings engaged in social relations that profoundly shape human lives," writes Kim TallBear (2015, 234). Our entanglements with nonhumans have always been visible to Indigenous thinkers; accordingly, Indigenous knowledges have also developed a robust and nuanced ethical framework for understanding our obligations as coactors. Jerry Lee Rosiek and Jimmy Snyder (2020) explain that because "many Indigenous studies scholars have taken nonhuman agency as a given in their social and philosophical analysis . . . [they thus] have more experience working out its practical and performative implications (e.g., through protocols for working with places and land, protocols for acknowledging the stakes of nonhuman entities in deliberative processes, ceremonies that acknowledge reciprocal ethical relations with nonhuman agents, a vocabulary that frames nonhuman entities as agential and ethically significant)" (3). The question of forging ethical intra-actions with nonhuman actors is, in other words, not a new one for Indigenous thinkers.

Despite the many important contributions of Indigenous knowledges, new materialist scholarship tends "to treat AngloEuropean theory as the only body of work relevant to ontological questions about nature and culture," thereby "[reproducing] colonial ways of knowing and being by further subordinating other ontologies" (Sundberg 2014, 42). New materialism's penchant for ignoring Indigenous thought is an act of colonial violence that "brings new materialism itself into an unwitting alliance with the very imperialism of the Western sovereign subject that it avowedly strives to undo" (Ravenscroft 2018, 357). Even worse, perhaps, is Eurocentric new materialist scholarship that engages with Indigenous knowledges in only the most shallow or cursory of ways. As Todd (2016) warns, white scholars who "sashay in and start cherry-picking parts of Indigenous thought that appeal to them *without engaging directly in (or unambiguously acknowledging) the political situation, agency, legal orders and relationality of both Indigenous people and scholars* . . . become implicit in colonial violence" (18; emphasis original). As a result of such practices—not to mention "legacies of cultural appropriation, genocide, and outright theft" (Grant 2017, 62)—new materialism becomes incapable of addressing power because it is ultimately just another expression of colonializing power that erases, claims credit for, and/or tokenizes contributions that have long been central to Indigenous communities and decolonial scholarship.

Notably, however, many researchers working with/in Indigenous knowledge traditions have articulated concrete methods that new materialist scholars might use to ethically intra-act with this work. In writing studies specifically, many of these efforts have emerged from the cultural rhetorics subfield,[5] which aims to position "rhetorics as always-already cultural and cultures as persistently rhetorical" (Powell et al. 2014, sec 2.1, para. 2) and, thus, seeks to move the field beyond the traditional Greco-Roman rhetorical canon to value *all* rhetorical traditions and practices. In order to create space that allows for the flourishing of all intellectual traditions, then, Indigenous studies scholars within and beyond our field have advocated practices such as storytelling (Cushman et al. 2019; Powell et al. 2014; Riley-Mukavetz 2020; Schulz 2017) as well as protocols for developing reciprocal relationships with places and land (Clary-Lemon 2019; Powell et al. 2014; Riley-Mukavetz 2020; Rosiek and Sydner 2020). Additionally, many cultural rhetorics and Indigenous studies scholars encourage critical citation practices (Clary-Lemon 2019; Todd 2016; Willey 2016). Citation in this sense goes beyond "simple ethical practices of having read widely and diversely," explains Jennifer Clary-Lemon (2019, sec. 3, para. 3) and is instead a matter of listening and honoring: Citation should both acknowledge "particular intellectual ancestors, past and present" (sec. 3, para. 3) and function as "gifts that we carry forward," she writes (sec. 3, para. 4). From this perspective, citation is a matter of constructing assemblages. Constructing those assemblages ethically, according to decolonial and Indigenous scholars, means looking both within and beyond the academy to highlight and build textual and material relationships with epistemic partners and forebearers.

These arguments have all informed my work in this book, which seeks to cultivate ethical intra-actions with Indigenous thinkers and practitioners principally through my citational practices. As Clary-Lemon (2019) incisively notes, "We are always choosing who we work with, but increasingly . . . we need to be clear about why we make the choices we do about who we draw from, and why" (sec. 1, para. 5). I take her point here seriously: Scholars of new materialism are especially obligated to consider their position as simultaneous products and producers of citational assemblages. I also recognize that to many readers, I will fall short of this goal. Indeed, this book relies heavily on the work of many white/ European scholars, which is undoubtedly a result of my position as a white woman who was trained and currently exists within an overwhelmingly white discipline that still largely ignores Indigenous knowledges. I also am aware of the risks of appropriating knowledge traditions that are not mine and further enacting colonializing violence. At the same time, however, I do not wish to contribute to the continued erasure of Indigenous thinking in new materialist scholarship. As another self-described "white settler scholar," Dustin Edwards (2020) has argued, cultivating "nonappropriative solidarity" with Indigenous knowledges means "listening to and dwelling with the persistence of colonial erasures while also contemplating possible paths of mutuality in the shared project of working toward collective flourishing." (64). To that end, I seek to practice throughout this book what Juanita Sundberg (2014) describes as "walking alongside other epistemic worlds" (35) by highlighting how new materialist rhetorics might listen to and learn from the diverse cosmologies and practices that compromise Indigenous knowledges—even if I inevitably stumble along the way.

Indeed, I believe that the risks of continuing to disregard Indigenous knowledges are far too high for new materialist rhetorics; specifically, it makes it difficult to answer the question of what ethical practice looks like under a new materialist framework. It is essential, however, that rhetoricians understand how power circulates, accumulates, and is reoriented within the agentic assemblages that make rhetoric possible. Indigenous knowledges offer valuable insights for rhetoricians undertaking in such work. With these insights in mind, then, I am also interested in exploring yet another knowledge tradition that has been largely ignored in new materialist rhetorics: feminist theory.[6] Although there is little question that feminist thought has been quite influential in new materialist scholarship more broadly, our field's engagement with new materialism doesn't reflect this influence. That is, despite the robust feminist traditions within both rhetorical studies and new materialisms more widely, *new materialist rhetorics* specifically have failed to engage substantively with feminist thought and scholarship. This omission is striking, especially given their shared emphases on relationships, collective agency, and the material. Yet, feminist rhetorics have always foregrounded the material and the relational in a way that's attuned to power and political action. New materialist rhetorics, then, might make use of the rich conceptual tools offered by feminist rhetorics in order to more productively interrogate, theorize, and account for power relations.

FEMINIST RHETORICS: MATERIALISM MADE NEW AGAIN

Well before rhetoric's current material turn, feminist rhetorics[7] have highlighted the materiality of rhetorical practice. Because, as Elizabeth Fleitz (2015) notes, the "material conditions of women's lives, from their bodies to their living situations, have historically had a major influence on their ability to be literate and produce rhetoric," feminist rhetoricians have always recognized the material as an indispensable aspect of rhetoric (36). Like feminist thought more broadly, feminist rhetorics often manifest this interest in the material through a particular attentiveness to the body, asking how the physical body shapes how we both perform and study rhetoric (Banks 2003; Fleckenstein 2009; Jack 2009; Johnson et al. 2015; Ratcliffe 2002; Royster and Kirsch 2012). The body, from the perspective of feminist rhetorics, is a useful tool for recognizing (and resisting) how power emerges, especially for those in possession of bodies that are raced, gendered, or otherwise read in a way that limits their rhetorical power. Scholarship on nineteenth-century women's rhetoric, for example, has examined in depth the relationship between women's bodies and their rhetorical practices, particularly in terms of gaining access to public space (Buchanan 2005; Johnson 2002; Mattingly 2002; Royster 2000). Even as we acknowledge how bodies structure and are structured by the environments, technologies, and discourses that surround them, the body functions for feminist rhetorics as a politically significant concept because it so starkly demonstrates how power and materiality are co-constitutive. Feminist rhetorics, then, not only have a robust tradition of valuing materiality (especially the materiality of the body), but also of recognizing how materiality functions as a key location from which power emerges, persists, and may even be upended.

Feminist rhetorics' robust theoretical account of materiality and power can serve as a productive complement to new materialist rhetorics, especially because both share an interest in complicating traditional humanist accounts of agency. Feminist rhetorics recognize that rhetorical agency is not confined to an individual human actor but instead is networked, relational, and nonhuman. In the introduction to their edited collection *Feminist Rhetorical Resilience*, for instance, Elizabeth Flynn, Patricia Sotirin, and Ann Brady offer resilience as a way of describing feminist rhetorical agency: "We find resilience to be a significant feminist alternative to traditional conceptions of rhetorical agency in that the pregiven nature of rhetors, resources, exigences, or change is replaced by a conception of dynamic creativity, reshaping possibilities, opportunities, meanings, and subjects. Resilience as feminist rhetorical agency is thus a relational dynamic, responsive in and to contexts, creating and animating capacities and possibilities" (Flynn, Sotrin, and Brady 2012, 7–8). Even if it is not explicitly rooted in any new materialist scholarship, this discussion sounds remarkably similar to new materialist descriptions of agency—for example, contrast it against Barad's (2007) description of agency as found in "the dynamic intra-play of indeterminacy and determinacy [that] reconfigures the possibilities and impossibilities of the world's becoming" (225). Flynn, Sotirin, and Brady's concept of resilience, however, emerges from feminist rhetorical scholarship, which (well before the field's current material turn) has imagined rhetorical agency as both relational and material.

In 1995, for example, Lisa Ede, Cheryl Glenn, and Andrea Lunsford asserted that feminist rhetorics present significant challenges to the traditional bounded rhetorical agent: "From [a feminist position] . . . the angles of the rhetorical triangle—speaker, hearer, text—become shape-shifters, three-dimensional and elastic points of contact, of location" (Ede, Glenn, and Lunsford 1995, 441). Similarly, Kathleen Boardman and Joy Ritchie's 1999 review of feminism's presence (and absence) within composition concludes by arguing for "notions and accounts of agency that exceed limited ideas of the determined subject" (Boardman and Ritchie 1999, 603)—a recognition, in other words, that a feminist approach to rhetorical agency will locate it beyond the classical individual subject. In her 2005 book *Radical Feminism, Writing, and Critical Agency*, Jacqueline Rhodes compares the textual practices of 1960s radical feminists to modern-day feminists online, claiming that both groups demonstrate how rhetorical agency emerges from temporary moments of identification within discursive and material networks (Rhodes 2005). Together, this work (and the work of many others) suggests that feminist rhetorics have long been comfortable framing rhetorical agency as intra-active, collaborative, and emergent.

This refusal to locate rhetorical agency in bounded subjects alone is undoubtedly related to feminist rhetorics' willingness to identify nonhuman actors as partners in the production of rhetorical agency. Objects, for feminist rhetoricians, have a long and rich history as rhetorical artifacts, from needlework samples (Goggin 2002) to quilts (Banks 2006; Rohan 2004) to American Indian wampum belts (Haas 2007). Importantly, much of this scholarship emerges from the recognition that traditional alphabetic literacy practices, typically, have been denied to women, people of color, and other historically marginalized groups. As Maureen Daly Goggin (2002) argues, valuing language alone "limits *what* may count and *who* may count in the production and circulation of cultural *doxa*" (313; emphasis original). Objects, then, are not just tools with which to enact rhetorical agency; they are co-constitutive of rhetorical practice. Seen from the perspective of feminist rhetorical history, then, rhetoric has always been material, emerging from intra-actions between and among human and nonhumans. Importantly for new materialist rhetorics, however, feminist rhetorics also highlights how those intra-actions are both mediated by and the product of power relations.

Long before rhetoric began to embrace new materialism, then, our discipline has productively interrogated materiality. By focusing on how power is created, maintained, and disassembled through material locations (including and exceeding the body), feminist rhetorics help to articulate the political value of a new materialist approach. Feminist thought asks us to consider how, through the material, power is exercised and contested, and ethical actions and consequences unfold. It is remarkable, then, that new materialist rhetorics have yet to engage with feminist perspectives in much depth, especially given the influence that feminist thought has had in new materialist scholarship more broadly.

Laura Micciche's (2014) article "Writing Material" shares this concern, pointedly criticizing new materialist rhetorics' inattention to feminist rhetorics. She argues that much scholarship in new materialist rhetorics represents "a longing for theory unfettered by the distraction of pesky subjects and their unruly bodies. The aversion to diverse fleshiness is reaffirmed by the overrepresentation of men among the sources that tend to drive this research. . . . [Meanwhile, some advocates] substitute talk of bodies, identities, and differences with the materiality of texts. In the grips of this approach, writing becomes an effect of tools and technologies, an activity that is unteachable, a ghostly production, and the province of theory and men" (491). Micciche points to a critical oversight that plagues much work in new materialist rhetorics: without a consideration of the body as a material artifact, new materialist rhetorics are bound to obscure or even ignore entirely the political weight of materiality, undermining its radical potentials to become a means of excluding or even further oppressing those in possession of bodies that are marked in a way that limits their power.

New materialist rhetorics must contend with these concerns in a meaningful way if they are to realize their full potential. Indeed, I suggest, it is precisely because of their promise that new materialist rhetorics must address these concerns about their political capacities and ethical implications. Because power itself is both systemic and material, new materialist rhetorics' embrace of materially attuned, systems-level thinking in fact make them well-suited for the task of addressing and rectifying power inequities. A handful of scholars have already made this point, noting that new materialist rhetorics offer valuable tools for articulating the complexities of feminist rhetorical agency. Sarah Hallenbeck (2012) has argued persuasively that feminist historiographers ought to incorporate new materialist methodologies in order to "shift our understanding of our subjects away from the *people* or *groups* we typically study to encompass instead the entire network in which these rhetors acted" (21; emphasis original). Megan McIntyre (2015) makes a similar argument, suggesting that new materialism's assemblage thinking "allows [feminist rhetoricians] to better account for how real-world change is often affected: political and cultural changes are the results of a myriad of extended, messy, sometimes inexplicable interventions" (26). The systemic, persistent nature of power demands an ecological perspective focused not on individual actors but rhetorical assemblages—a perspective articulated clearly by new materialist scholarship. What we need, then, is to embrace new materialism's interest in the material but to do so in a way that also sees the material as always and inevitably political.

A CRAFT AGENCY FOR NEW MATERIALIST RHETORICS

New materialist rhetorics productively foreground the role of material things in rhetorical action without privileging a particular class of the material (such as human or object). I want to emphasize, however, that while the material in new materialist rhetorics encompasses a wide variety of material things and processes, including, but not limited to (human and other organic) bodies, technologies, places, economic resources, and histories, it is also necessary to understand how those material things and processes produce, maintain, and disrupt power relations. Thus, the new materialist approach to rhetoric I envision would seek to highlight the vast assortment of co-constitutive material actors that populate an assemblage while at the same time recognizing how those material actors are produced by unique and dynamic sets of intra-actions that result in differing levels of access to power. In other words, while new materialist rhetorics recognize all agents as material, they should also recognize that materiality as political.

Acknowledging the agency or vitality of nonhumans implicit in this understanding of new materialist rhetorics does not mean that we must abandon our concern for humans, or the power relations that result in human oppression. Researchers may still inquire about human matters and advocate for social justice while also recognizing that agency is not singularly human or pursuing a more symmetrical account of the nonhuman—after all, argue Barnett and Boyle (2016), the "posthuman turn . . . need not be an antihuman one" (6). Many of the central tenets of new materialism suggest that human interests are inextricable from nonhuman interests and in fact argue that it is this enmeshment with the material world that makes a new materialist perspective necessary. As Bennett (2010) argues, "a [new materialist] attentiveness to matter and its power will not solve the problem of human exploitation or oppression, but it can inspire a greater sense of the extent to which all bodies are kin in the sense of inextricably enmeshed in a dense network of relations. And in a knotted world of vibrant matter, to harm one section of the web may very well be to harm oneself. Such an enlightened or expanded notion of self-interest is *good for humans*" (13; emphasis original). In other words, according to Bennett, new materialism is well-suited to account for the complexities of power: no longer merely the product of discourse, power is instead material and fluid, the result of intra-actions between humans, nonhumans, and the assemblages they constitute. Diana Coole and Samantha Frost echo this argument, noting that "no adequate political theory can ignore that importance of bodies in situating empirical actors within a material environment of nature, other bodies, and the socioeconomic structures that dictate where and how they find substance, satisfy their desires, or obtain the resources necessary for participating in political life" (Coole and Frost 2010, 19). From this perspective, new materialism is not a barrier to, but instead essential for, any project that aims to identify and more equally distribute access to power across *all* bodies.

How, then, might rhetorical theory articulate a new materialist agency that is sensitive to its political consequentiality? Craft can serve as a productive, if unexpected, framework for understanding the political significance of new materialist agency. Indeed, I argue that new materialist rhetorics are inherently crafty, and by bringing this craftiness to light, we can better recognize the ethical and thus political capacities of new materialist rhetorics. Craft, especially in its feminist formulations, shares new materialism's insistence that rhetoric and rhetorical agency are material and relational. However, because craft sees materiality as inherently political, it recognizes that building, dismantling, or abstaining from particular intra-actions is an ethical practice. I term this process *craft agency* and suggest that it can begin the important work of articulating how new materialist agency can also work to identify, resist, or even rectify power inequities.

Craft is a deceptively complex concept that recognizes the importance of becoming, together: Like new materialism, it understands that agency emerges from intra-actions between humans and nonhumans. Craft, however, also acknowledges how these intra-actions—as grounded in and a product of materiality—are a function of power dynamics. Thus, craft foregrounds the ethical implications of rhetorical assemblages. Because craft helps to articulate the complex ethical dimensions of this kind of ecological agency, I suggest that situating new materialist rhetorics as craft will productively emphasize the material and the relational in a way that's attuned to power, ethics, and political action.

While craft may appear to be an almost-ubiquitous or even banal concept, there is a great deal of disagreement about what exactly *craft* means, or what even counts as *craft*. Craft functions as an important concept in the work of artists, historians, designers, classicists, archeologists, creative writers, and many others—but each of these fields define craft in differing ways. Most discussions about craft, however, emerge from the recognition that craft centers around "the process of working, of *making*" (Fariello 2011, 23; emphasis original). This observation is my starting point, as I embrace a deliberately capacious understanding of craft in order to fully mine its relevance to new materialist rhetorics. Craft, as I use it throughout this book, denotes material, process-oriented practices of making that foreground the intra-actions between humans, objects, and their environments. For craft, these intra-actions—as material manifestations of power—are always political, and thus, craft understands relationships as the condition for rhetorical practice. While craft draws attention to the materiality of rhetorical practice, it often manifests in the overtly relational terrain of the digital. Indeed, craft refuses altogether the strict distinctions between *digital* and *material*. Because it calls us to consider the conditions that render intra-actions—and therefore rhetoric itself—possible, craft can provide a clearer ethical grounding for new material rhetorics.

Despite these possibilities, new materialist rhetorics have yet to thoroughly or explicitly explore how craft, as a philosophy and as a practice, might inform rhetoric's material turn. This does not mean that craft has been absent from recent writing studies scholarship, however: several notable pieces have taken up craft in an attempt to clarify the ethical stakes of the relationships between people, objects, and the world around them. Unsurprisingly, perhaps, it is multimodal and digital scholarship, which has long understood rhetoric as a material (or at least materially mediated) practice, that has produced these engagements with craft. For example, Prins (2012) claims that approaching writing as craft highlights its material, relational nature. Although her argument is located specifically in the first-year composition classroom, it is easy enough to imagine how her approach to craft "as a particular set of actions and relationships between people and between people and things" (145) might inform an ethics of new materialist rhetorics. Jeff Rice's 2016 book *Craft Obsession* also considers the question of craft and its relationship to rhetoric. While Rice's focus is less on craft itself and more on the social networks that sustain the craft beer community, he does suggest that craft might help articulate how change occurs across new materialist networks. For Rice, craft operates as "the space where objects interact with humans and other objects to produce a network of relationships" (xiii) and, thus, functions as affective, aesthetic delivery.

Perhaps the most compelling account of craft to emerge from multimodal scholarship is found in Jody Shipka's (2011) *A Composition Made Whole*. In this book, Shipka argues for an expansive approach to multimodality, one that includes but also exceeds the digital, so that we might "trace the multiple spaces in which and time as which composing occurs, and attend as well to embodied activity, and co-practice" (39). Although Shipka does not name this argument *craft* explicitly, nor does she directly position her work as new materialist, her insistence on understanding "the highly distributed, complexly mediated, multimodal dimensions of all communicative practice" (29) is undoubtedly aligned with craft as I articulate it here. Shipka's work—as well as that of other scholars of multimodality such as Anne Frances Wysocki or Jonathan Alexander and Jacqueline Rhodes—serves as a compelling case for the value of craft in a new materialist rhetorical framework.

Another area of the field that has also been receptive to craft is feminist rhetorics—likely, perhaps, given feminist rhetorics' tendency to locate rhetorical agency in the entanglements between human and non-humans, as described above. Scholars like Goggin, Liz Rohan, Susanne Kesler Rumsey, and Vanessa Kraemer Sohan have engaged with craft in depth, exploring its rhetorical dimensions and demonstrating how craft can be a crucial site for locating the rhetorical practices of marginalized groups. Yet, these investigations of craft tend to center around relatively isolated craft artifacts and practices, focusing on how specific instances of craft (such as quilting or needlepoint) might be positioned as rhetorical rather than exploring how craft might inform rhetoric itself. Instead, I argue that new materialist rhetorics might recast themselves as craft, not only in order to articulate their complex materiality but also to acknowledge the ethical contours and political consequences of that materiality more fully.

My understanding of craft is informed by a recent surge of feminist scholarship devoted to tracing the social, political, and rhetorical implications of craft (Bratich and Brush 2011; Goggin and Tobin 2009; Parker 1984; Turney 2009). Craft has a fraught history, simultaneously evoking connotations of creativity, discipline, frivolity, virtue, and, perhaps above all, domesticity. These romanticized, nostalgic, or even uncritical understandings of craft persist in many ways today, particularly as we find ourselves at yet another point of technological change. Indeed, William Kurlinkus (2014) argues that craft emerges as "a stabilizing design god term during periods of technological flux" (50) and its use thus speaks to anxieties about our relationship to the material as much as it designates actual material practices. Craft's status as "an inherently nostalgic word" in fact serves new materialist rhetorics well: Because craft so often designates "*an ecology of technological values at tension with one another*" (Kurlinkus 2014, 52; emphasis original), deliberately situating new materialist rhetorics as craft asks us to consider the values—the ethical positioning—that new materialism invokes. That is, if craft emerges from the "constant interplay between tacit knowledge and self-conscious awareness," where "the tacit knowledge [serves] as an anchor, [and] the explicit awareness [serves] as a critique and corrective," as Richard Sennett (2008)[8] claims (50), then craft functions as a reflective, generative practice—a *techne*—that forces consideration of not just the *how* but the *to what end?* of new materialist rhetorics.

Craft is not idle leisure or mere aesthetics, then. Rather, it is better understood as a process of world-making, a *poesis*. Craft locates its generative capacities in its ability to forge generative entanglements not just between various humans, but between humans, objects, technology, and their environments. That is, craft's fundamentally inventive nature is realized not through individual actors, but through the various intra-actions that craft makes possible. For craft, these actors are decidedly not solely human: as David Gauntlett (2012) argues in his book *Making is Connecting*, craft is characterized by "a connection between humans and handmade objects and nature" (25). Craft calls attention to the material conditions of making: knitters know, for example, that the same pattern knit with yarns of different weights or textures can yield very different results. What's more, craft's homespun, amateur spirit—one that "does *not* rely on hierarchies of experts and elites to be validated" (Gauntlett 2012, 218; emphasis original)—serves as an argument for the democratization of making. Craft holds that creation, whether it be of household goods, art, or rhetoric, should not be limited to powerful assemblages alone, although it also acknowledges that power often shapes who and what can participate in that creation. As such, craft illustrates how materiality is both the cause of and solution to power inequities: While power differentials are generated and maintained through material assemblages, they can also be rectified through the creation of new or different material assemblages. Craft, in short, recognizes that agency results from intra-actions between human and nonhuman entities, but because it also highlights the material conditions that make those intra-actions possible, it is particularly attuned to the political nature, and therefore the ethical significance, of such a complex account of agency.

Craft agency, as I use it, depends upon a distinction between agent and agency, recognizing the need for "a decisive analytical cut between *agency*, understood as the production of effect or action, and the *agent* as the presumed origin of effect or action" (Lundberg and Gunn 2005, 88; emphasis original). Agency (or the capacity for agency) does not reside within the agent. Rather, agency is, as Cooper (2019) writes, "a relation of agents" (137). Lundberg and Gunn (2005) offer one particularly useful illustration of this symbiosis in their description of a Ouija board, noting that "while the exercise of agency takes place in the movement of the planchette, the status and possibly even the existence of the agent who originates the action is undecidable" (84). The success of a game of Ouija does not depend on assigning responsibility for who or what moves the planchette—if knowing is even possible—but rather the agential effects that emerge from the intra-actions between the players, the board, and the planchette. The Ouija board example demonstrates how we might conceive of agency without relying on the "intentionality or autonomy" of individual agents (K. Campbell 2005, 5). Craft agency, instead, conceives of agents as "points of articulation" (K. Campbell 2005, 5) or "choreographers" (Sheridan, Ridolfo, and Michel 2012, 107) who negotiate their entanglements between other human and nonhuman agents in order to effect rhetorical outcomes.

Craft thus shares new materialist rhetorics' view of agency as fundamentally relational: that is, it understands that agency manifests through the intra-actions of diverse material agents, even if craft scholarship does perhaps not explicitly articulate this. Indeed, it is for this reason that craft likewise stands to benefit from a coupling with new materialist rhetorics, which would help craft more directly name the agential complexities that it implies. Importantly, though, craft recognizes how these agents are always governed by power, which is inevitably embedded in, circulating throughout, and the product of the intra-actions that are the condition for rhetorical agency. I term this dynamic *craft agency*, which captures the complexity of both new materialist and craft conceptions of agency in order to create a politically viable, ethically responsive model of rhetorical action. Craft agency centers around the material intra-actions from which rhetorical agency emerges and posits that agents' ethical obligations and political commitments lie in the entanglements formed with other agents. Since rhetorical agency exceeds individual agents, craft agency asserts that a politically viable model of new materialist rhetoric should locate ethical practice in our responsibility *to* others rather than our responsibility *for* individual actions.

CRAFTING AN ETHICS FOR NEW MATERIALIST RHETORICS

While the decoupling of agent and agency accounts for the complexity of rhetorical assemblages, it also results in one of the most pressing tensions facing new materialist rhetorics: the question of accountability. If individual agents do not possess agency, who or what do we hold responsible in instances of unethical rhetoric? How do we—as teachers, scholars, colleagues, and citizens—ensure our rhetorical practices, and the intra-actions that enable them, are ethical? After all, as Cooper (2019) notes, "agents' actions always make a difference," even if those actions are "neither produced by their conscious intentions nor a matter of free will" (130). Craft agency acknowledges these concerns and presents a framework for ethical rhetorical action in the absence of a stable, autonomous subject. Craft centers process, both in terms of making and in terms of becoming: through intra-actions between various humans and nonhumans, actors construct each other as they engage in the act of making. As Joanne Turney (2009) explains, "Craft can be understood through practice as process, as a series of learned gestures. The implication is that maker and object are one" (153). By focusing on process in this way, craft forces us to consider who and what we make *with*—and how, in turn, those co-actors make us. Janis Jefferies' (2016) assessment of craft ethics captures this dynamic clearly: "The ethical implications of how we make relations and connections between us is to place an emphasis on becoming with," she writes. For her, to craft "is to engage with continuous working and re-working, making and re-making, crafting and re-crafting experience as a means of care" (30). Craft demands a consideration of the agents we are responsible to, and as such, it locates ethical action in the assemblages we alternatively work to create, alter, or even fracture altogether; craft, in other words, calls for an ethics of entanglement.

This understanding of ethics is consistent with rhetorical approaches to ethics, which scholars typically frame as responsibility to others, even if those others have traditionally been defined as humans. Porter (1998), for example, describes "rhetorical ethics" as a "set of implicit understandings between writer and audience about their relationship" (68) that confronts the "*should* of writing activities" (69; emphasis original). Similarly, John Duffy (2017) contends that "writing involves ethical decisions because every time we write . . . we propose a relationship with others, our readers" (229). For rhetoricians, ethics are the result of a series of collaborative negotiations. It is not enough to say that rhetorical ethics are communal, however. Developing shared norms means "acknowledging differences, including exposing the hidden or obscured differences that often end up dominating" (Porter 1998, 153). Such an approach to ethics—one based on "a process of mutual recognition"—inevitably "throws fiercely maintained boundaries of self and other into question" (Micciche 2005, 179). In other words, ethics are found not in discrete subjects but instead in the various intra-dependencies that agents construct between themselves and others. Ethics are interactive, situational, and, above all, relational: Rather than a strict code governing independent subjects, they are instead located in the encounters between agents. Importantly, then, the dialogic process of ethical doing already assumes a permeable agent rather than a fixed, bounded subject. Like craft ethics, then, rhetorical ethics goes well beyond merely finding commonalities among diverse agents and instead insists on recognizing those agents as co-constitutive.

Both new materialist rhetorics and craft insist on dismantling the assumption that we are somehow separate and independent actors, and instead locate agency in the complex intra-actions that produce agents. It follows that ethics would emerge from this liminal space. If, as Nathan Stormer and Bridie McGreavy argue, "rhetoric's ontology, approached ecologically, considers *qualities of relations* between entities" (Stormer and McGreavy 2017, 3; emphasis original), then it is easy enough to define an ethics of new materialist rhetorics in similarly relational terms. As Barad (2007) argues, "Ethics is about accounting for our part of the entangled webs we weave" (384). While Barad doesn't expand on the craft metaphor of weaving that she invokes, I argue that craft is in fact the ideal framework for understanding the ethics of new materialist agency. Craft agency locates an ethics for new materialist rhetorics within the intra-actions that construct permeable, fluid agents. Instead of jettisoning the question of accountability altogether, craft agency thus turns on the distinction between responsible *for* and responsible *to*; ethics are not a matter of responsibility *for* individual actions, but rather a matter of responsibility *to* other agents and the intra-actions that create the conditions for rhetorical agency. If agency is not contained within or possessed by individual subjects, if it instead emerges from our intra-actions with both human and nonhuman things, then it is perhaps more accurate to locate responsibility not in discrete, causal actions but in the assemblages that we produce (as they simultaneously produce us).

Although craft agency situates ethics in the encounters that form various agents, thus acknowledging ways that agents can bleed into and inform one another, it does not deny the material specificity of those agents. In other words, although craft agency locates ethics in intra-actions, it also recognizes those intra-actions as bound by material differences. Cooper (2019) details this distinction in her book *The Animal Who Writes*, noting that while rhetorical ethics demand "responding in a way that acknowledges entanglement, becoming, and the creating of possibilities for being and becoming," they also require "recognizing others not only as entities that act but also as individualizing entities, concrete others who have opinions and beliefs grounded in their own experiences and perceptions and meanings constructed in their bodies" (156). As Cooper explains, because writing "always has real effects on others, because it always changes the world by creating new possibilities," it is inescapably ethical (221). Craft agency takes this acknowledgment one step further, arguing that any act of *making*—the practices of belonging in assemblages comprised human and nonhuman entities—is fundamentally ethical.

Assemblages can produce good or bad outcomes, which is why they present "a collective ethical obligation," write Kristin Arola and Adam Arola (Arola and Arola 2017, 210). They argue that Indigenous knowledges provide a productive framework to evaluate the ethics of assemblages, suggesting that all co-actors in assemblages are called to reflect on the consequentiality of their participation. For Arola and Arola, a good assemblage is not just generative, "responding to situations and enacting new functions," but is also intensely focused on power relations, "always considering, 'Whom does this assemblage benefit?'" (211). Instead of adopting a cynical perspective on the possibility of political action in a new materialist framework, then, craft agency holds that tracing the intra-actions that bind agents—and from which agency emerges—can identify power imbalances within rhetorical assemblages, and, either through the creation of new intra-actions or the dismantling of existing ones, work to correct those imbalances. This approach to agency also locates ethics within our attunement to the possibilities brought about by our intra-actions with human and nonhuman actors; through this "ongoing responsiveness to the entanglements of self and other, here and there, now and then," actors can either build resilient coalitions or fracture existing affinities in order to cultivate change (Barad 2007, 394). Importantly, such entanglements are always understood as material, located between bodies, things, places, and histories. Craft agency thus presents a reciprocal ethics of entanglement that recognizes that "the ethical is bound up in the material" (Sheridan, Ridolfo, and Michel 2012, 126), and it is only through materiality that solidarity and political change can emerge.

Although craft agency unravels the autonomous subject, it does not preclude the possibility of ethical action or of political change. Indeed, it insists that it is only once we recognize the co-constitutive, intra-active nature of agents that we can fully account for the complexities of power. By acknowledging that agency is material, networked, and embodied, craft agency thus offers a viable politics for new materialist rhetorics. Craft agency answers the call for what Joanna Zylinska (2014) describes in her book of the same name as a "minimal ethics for the Anthropocene." Craft agency is intensely self-aware and is based on "an ethics that makes sense—and that *senses its own making*" (16; emphasis original). Craft agency is precisely the "embedded and embodied practice" Zylinska demands, as it presents a clear means of "a material working out of the relations between entities and of their varying forces"

(32). Situating new materialist rhetorics as craft, and new materialist rhetorical agency as craft agency, thus forces attention to both the assemblages we make together and the assemblages that in turn make us.

Throughout the rest of this book, I will explore how craft agency functions as a material practice of forging, disassembling, or reorganizing entanglements between humans and nonhumans. By recasting new materialist rhetorics as a craft, I argue, we can more clearly articulate how the diverse material assemblages that create rhetoric can be both ethically aware and politically effective. The chapters that follow build from and expand this definition of craft agency, exploring specific instances of craft that illustrate the material, networked, and embodied nature of agency. In the end, the various locations and manifestations of craft that I highlight all offer a framework for new materialist theories and practices that are situated in an ethics of entanglement and geared toward a politics of coalition building.

2
CRAFTING HISTORY, CRAFTING RHETORIC
Locating Craft Agency

As any teacher or scholar of rhetoric can attest, rhetoric is a slippery, even loaded word. While it can be used to invoke eloquence or expressiveness, it is perhaps more frequently associated with guile or duplicity. Common usage tends to frame rhetoric as dangerous, exploitative, or devious. Consider the first listing for the term "rhetorical" in the *Oxford English Dictionary*, which notes its use is "frequently somewhat depreciative" (OED 2019). These connotations are not confined to modern usage, either: Classical Greek texts offer ample illustrations of rhetoric's fraught nature. In his *Gorgias*, Plato famously dismissed rhetoric as "cookery," mere "flattery" rather than real art (463b–463c). Despite its ability to signal productive, inventional practices, then, rhetoric too often becomes shorthand for deception and artifice.

Craft is a paradoxical word as well. Like rhetoric, its multiplicity of meanings can quickly become contradictory. Used as a noun, craft can alternately describe processes of making (as in "the craft of woodworking") or the material results of those processes ("crafts for sale"). Craft can also be used as a verb, a way to signal *doing* ("crafting a syllabus," "crafted by hand"). Craft has negative implications as well, particularly in its adjectival form, *crafty*. At turns, *crafty* can describe artistry, denote skillfulness or cleverness, or, perhaps most commonly, signal guile, cunning, or trickery. Craft practices, in fact, have long been understood as a means of deception: in Homer's *Odyssey*, for example, Penelope warded off potential suitors by continually weaving and un-weaving Laertes' shroud. The craft of weaving, in this case, "suggested a talent for deception" (Mueller 2010, 2).[1] Rhetoric and craft thus share a common incongruity: both clever and deceitful and almost always powerful, instances of either can invite suspicion and misgivings.

It is perhaps no surprise, then, that both rhetoric and craft often occupy the less privileged position in well-tread binary pairs: rhetoric versus literature; craft versus art. As disadvantaged terms, rhetoric and

https://doi.org/10.7330/9781646422555.c002

craft quickly accumulate connotations of vacuity, femininity, and duplicity. Yet, the connection between the two goes well beyond their shared disrepute. Indeed, there are important and substantial overlaps between craft and rhetoric throughout classical Greek thought, even if these overlaps have yet to be fully explored. As we begin to acknowledge how agency emerges from varied assemblages of human and nonhuman actors, it may then be wise to map the deep historical ties that exist between rhetoric and craft. Understanding rhetoric's inherent craftiness, I argue, not only historicizes the current material turn that positions rhetoric as a material, embodied, responsive process, but provides a grounding for the craft agency I theorize throughout this book.

In this chapter, then, I explore the connections between craft and rhetoric, arguing that just as craft is rhetorical, rhetoric is crafty. Making this interdependence more explicit results in a more robust account of rhetoric's material dimensions, stressing how agency emerges from the intra-actions of human and nonhuman actors. Importantly, however, craft helps rhetoric articulate the ethical implications and political consequences of the intra-actions that make it possible. By unpacking the deep ties between rhetoric and craft, I argue, we can embrace a new materialist position where actors recognize not just their co-constituency, but their mutual interests, ethical obligations, and political potentials.

I begin with a discussion of the history of craft, highlighting how craft's complicated history—both as a mechanism of control as well as a means of resistance—informs current understandings of craft. Craft values the same kind of mutually constitutive material intra-actions that characterize new materialist rhetorics, but craft frames the forging of these material entanglements as a fundamentally ethical process. Accordingly, I suggest, rhetoric might benefit from reimagining itself as crafty. In order to begin this rethinking, I examine the persistent, if largely unexplored, presence of craft in rhetorical history, particularly in relation to the three interrelated concepts of *techne*, *mêtis*, and *kairos*. While techne is by no means an unfamiliar concept to rhetoricians, here I situate it directly within the emplaced, embodied nature of mêtis and kairos, which highlight the contingent materiality of rhetorical practice and figure this character as a means to reorient normative or inequitable power structures. Notably, however, mêtis and kairos both have long associations with the feminized craft of weaving; that is, they are both literally and figuratively craft practices. Framing techne in this way—as explicitly fueled by the craftiness of mêtis and kairos—is not just crucial to understanding rhetoric's rich, networked materiality, but also demonstrates the political possibilities and ethical significance of that materiality. It is through techne, in other words, that rhetoric's full craftiness becomes apparent and that craft agency is made possible.

CRAFTING HISTORY

Craft is an expansive and complex concept. Because of this capaciousness, my goal in this chapter is not to provide a comprehensive history of craft or to categorize specific practices or products as craft but rather to try to define its most salient features in its contemporary manifestations, particularly as they relate to new materialist rhetorics. The overview of craft that follows is thus limited and, admittedly, focused primarily on Western understandings of craft and craft practices. Yet, even this somewhat reductive sketch demonstrates how craft values material entanglements among co-constitutive human and nonhuman agents and sees those entanglements as essential to rhetorical agency. Seen from this perspective, craft might function as a "god term"—as Kurlinkus (2014) suggests—for new materialist rhetorics, as it invites us to reflect on our relationship to materiality as well as the ethical implications and political possibilities that result.

While craft practices are as old as humanity itself, contemporary understandings of craft are almost always linked in some way to the work of John Ruskin and William Morris, who are credited as the minds behind the Arts and Crafts movement of the late nineteenth and early twentieth century. Ruskin and Morris were skeptical of industrialization, not only because of its potential to temper creativity, but also because of its tendency to alienate workers from the products of their labor (Crawford 1997; Gauntlett 2012). Such Marxist sentiments were at the center of the Arts and Crafts movement, which celebrated the individual laboring to produce honest, unique, and functional goods. In part, a goal of the movement was to undo the strict binary that separated art from craft, a division that is often rooted in designers' economic and/ or social status (Crawford 1997; Parker 1984). The belief behind the Arts and Crafts movement was that "craft skills were valued for their own careful, individual, handmade beauty, not because they were supposed to be the skills of an expert elite," and that all people—poor and elite alike—stand to benefit from the making and enjoyment of art, design, and craft (Gauntlett 2012, 49). The democratizing spirit of the Arts and Crafts movement thus worked to trouble class boundaries, even as a strongly moralistic attitude often lay behind advocates' desire for easily accessible design. Champions of the movement valued creative work as "the means by which human beings could connect with nature, with their own sense of self, and with other people" (Gauntlett 2012, 47), and, as a result, "proponents believed that good design and beautiful objects would raise the moral tone of society" (Parker 1984, 179). For the Arts and Crafts movement, craft carried the potential to create a world where people value each other as much as the objects they interact with.

Through these rather lofty goals, the Arts and Crafts movement called attention to the economic and social conditions that determine whether a particular practice is deemed "art" or mere "craft." While the movement was particularly alert to class distinctions—likely owing to the fact that many members were socialists (Crawford 1997, 15; Parker 1984, 179)—the Arts and Crafts movement also helped "women to recoginse the value of their work" (Parker 1984, 185), prompting many to consider how the hierarchical distinction between art and craft is gendered as well as classed. Historically, women's practices of making, particularly domestic ones, have been devalued as craft, while men's practices of making are elevated to art (Edwards 2006; Goggin and Tobin 2009; Kurtyka 2016, Parker 1984; Turney 2009). As a result, the cultural and rhetorical significance of women's craft has been widely trivialized or overlooked entirely. Anthropologist Cathy Lynne Costin (2015) identifies this dynamic at work even in preindustrial cultures: While "there is no universal division of labor in craft production" (271)—that is, there is no inherently feminine craft—"many crafts are feminine endeavors when domestic, but are adopted by men when they are commercialized" (273). The art/craft hierarchy is thus in many ways tied to the public/private binary that positions women, and women's work, firmly within the domestic sphere. Women's labor is deemed "craft," and the interrelated art/craft and public/private hierarchies became self-perpetuating, as women were generally excluded from professional organizations and opportunities to pursue art beyond the home (Parker 1984).

The relationship between craft and femininity is thus mutually constitutive: craft practices reinforce restrictive notions of femininity, while femininity reinforces restrictive notions of craft. In her influential book *The Subversive Stitch*, Rozsika Parker (1984) traces this dynamic through embroidery specifically, charting its role "in the creation of femininity" (16). Domestic handcrafting practices such as sewing, needlepoint, or knitting served to cement normative notions of womanhood well into the twentieth century, particularly among middle- and upper-class Western white women (MacDonald 1988; Parker 1984; Turney 2009). Women and girls who were privileged enough to be educated received instruction in these crafts in order to instill the womanly traits of "discipline and obedience" (Turney 2009, 13) as well as "patience" (Parker 1984, 83). Because domestic crafts were so often "the means of educating women into the feminine ideal, and of proving that they have attained it" (Parker 1984, ix), their association with specific notions of womanhood—virtuousness, gentility, submissiveness, familial devotion—lingers today.

Importantly, however, these notions of craft are tied specifically to middle- and upper-class white femininity, as these women had the financial resources and leisure time to pursue what was considered naturally feminine craftwork in the home. Less privileged women found themselves in a different position in regard to craft, which was either undertaken out of financial necessity or imposed as a means of enforcing the upper- and middle-class feminine sensibilities that were associated with domestic crafts. Building from the Arts and Crafts movement's insistence that good design and craftsmanship are inherently moral, progressive education advocates turned to craft as a "hands-on educational method" valued "for its potential to 'uplift' entire populations," including poor women and formerly enslaved Black people (Fariello 2011, 35).[2] Throughout the nineteenth century, for example, embroidery was used as a way to properly domesticate and feminize working-class women (Parker 1984, 173). Many other working-class women undertook craft both within and beyond the home as a means of earning money or making limited household resources stretch (Hackney 2006; MacDonald 1988). It is in these conditions that craft's "negative connotations—such as femininity, queerness, and amateurism—as well as undesired associations with poor and working-class people, oppressed minority populations, people of color, and Third World populations" (Roberts 2014) are at least partially grounded, as craft became either a mechanism of control meant to impart some ephemeral notion of propriety to oppressed populations, or a representation of the thriftiness necessitated by limited economic means. Craft's gendered history, then, is conflicted, relying on and perpetuating traditional notions of feminine refinement as well as undertones of poverty and its perceived moral failures.

Yet, just as craft's gendered features worked to confine women, craft also provided a space for resistance. As Parker (1984) argues, domestic crafts such as embroidery can "lead women to an awareness of the extraordinary constraints of femininity, providing at times a means of negotiating them, and at other times provoking the desire to escape the constraints" (11). Indeed, the long history of women's activism through craft—a history I explore in detail in the next chapter—suggests that women have used craft to subvert its own limiting connotations, as well as to advocate for themselves and others. With few outlets for political action, craft, even when denigrated, offered women opportunities for creative expression, community-building, and protest. Scholars have identified knitting circles, for example, as important locations for raising political consciousness among women (Bratich and Brush 2011; MacDonald 1988; Turney 2009). Thus, although craft has been used to perpetuate economic, gendered, and raced inequities, it simultaneously offers marginalized groups the tools to resist those inequities, in instances as wide-ranging as advocating for women's suffrage (Borda 2002; Parker 1984), making the AIDS crisis visible (Blair and Michel 2007), or resisting the violence and censorship of Chilean dictator Augusto Pinochet (Strycharz 2014). Craft, then, has held a conflicting place in the lives of oppressed groups, especially women, poor people, and people of color.

With this complex history in mind, feminist artists and scholars from varied fields have sought to reclaim and rehabilitate craft, finding in it a way to push against more traditional definitions of art, a history of women's subversive political activities, and, perhaps most notably, a means of redefining femininity. Many situate this recent re-emergence of craft within a larger movement, sometimes termed *new domesticity*, a phenomenon rooted in a "longing for more authentic, meaningful life in an economically and environmentally uncertain world" (Matchar 2013, 5). Despite the sometimes-romanticized ideals of preindustrial life that characterize the language of new domesticity, advocates insist it is at heart a political stance, comprised of "men and women who have chosen to make family, community, social justice and the health of the planet the governing principle of their lives" (Hayes 2010, 13). As an outgrowth of this movement, contemporary crafters often see their work as explicitly political, whether it be to reject rigid, gendered boundaries between public and private spaces (Bratich and Brush 2011; Turney 2009), repudiate capitalist demands for mass consumption (Bratich 2010; Gauntlett 2012), or as a means of direct protest (Greer 2008; Pentney 2008).

This feminist reconsideration of craft has not gone unnoticed by rhetorical scholars, who have identified women's craft practices as an important location for rhetorical recovery work. Recognizing that many women have historically been denied access to traditional, text-based literacies, feminist rhetoricians have examined how women's craft practices—such as needlework (Goggin 2002; Gradea 2014), quilting (Rohan 2004; Rumsey 2009; Sohan 2015), sewing (Foss 1996), and scrapbooking (Rohan 2004)—provide rich evidence of women's rhetorical activities across time and cultures. While most feminist rhetorical craft scholarship is focused on the past, some scholarship also examines how contemporary craft can function as feminist rhetorical practice. Much of this work has examined the explicitly political practices of craftivism—a phenomenon I explore in more detail in the next chapter (Bellower and Berrones 2015; Goggin 2015)—but it has also examined more mundane craft practices such as crafting within a sorority (Kurtyka 2016). Together, such scholarship emphasizes the inextricable nature of rhetoric, power, and materiality; the rhetorical practices of marginalized peoples emerge along with the material conditions that result from and reflect power relationships. This scholarship has been important not just in terms of widening the scope of rhetoric to account for the rhetorical activities of women and other systemically disempowered groups, but also because it calls attention to ways in which contemporary crafters and scholars alike recognize craft as a mechanism to undo the very gender roles and societal relations that craft has, in the past, been used to reinforce.

The feminist resurgence of craft has not been without criticism, however. Many concerns center around craft's persistent raced and classed dimensions, which continue to render craft as the province of middle- to upper-class white women. Elizabeth Groeneveld (2010) locates craft's contemporary revival within a broader third-wave feminist movement that (like new domesticity) sought to reclaim domestic practices considered to be feminine without recognizing the exclusionary nature of those practices.[3] She argues that many of these third-wave reconsiderations of craft failed "to acknowledge the class dynamics inherent in crafting cultures," which only reflected "a broader lapse within some branches of third-wave feminism, when it comes to engaging critically with the intersecting of race, class, age, ability, and gender" (270). Craft and domesticity, as articulated by third-wave feminism, are "marked by privilege" because they are simply "not available to everyone," Groeneveld contends (274). Even if craft practice, historically, often resulted from necessary frugality, most modern-day manifestations of craft position it as "an expensive and leisured practice" (Luckman 2013, 258) that demands "ability and the capacity to indulge long stretches of time and pricy materials" (Hahner and Varda 2014, 307). Accordingly, says Laura Portwood-Stacer (2013), leisure craft assumes "a certain privileged class position of its participants" (16), inexorably tying itself to middle-class sensibilities.

To further explore the questions of class and labor that these criticisms of contemporary craft invite, many scholars have thus positioned craft as an extension of capitalism (C. Campbell 2005; Dawkins 2011; Krugh 2014). While an Arts and Crafts perspective on craft may situate it as an antidote to the alienation of labor that followed the Industrial Revolution, modern craft practices have been criticized for relying upon or even reifying capitalist modes of production and consumption (C. Campbell 2005; Carr and Gibson 2016; Gibson 2016). Although craft's professed skepticism of industrial manufacturing in many ways drives its current resurgence, craft has nevertheless become an industry, with presence both at the corporate level with chain retailers like Michaels or Hobby Lobby,[4] as well as through independent producers at various craft fairs or online platforms like Etsy or Ravelry. As Chris Gibson (2016) explains, the craft industry relies on "the logics of cultural capitalism" even as it positions itself as "artisanal" (62). The result, says Nicole Dawkins (2011), is an ambivalent ideology that values "autonomy, choice and self-improvement," and thus, "[speaks] not only to a postfeminist subjectivity but to the central values of neoliberalism" (277). From these perspectives, craft is an essentially conservative practice that works to preserve existing economic structures and is thus unable to perform the radical reordering necessary for feminist politics.

Craft, then, can carry problematic connotations that position it as leisure activity limited to privileged (white and/or wealthy) women. While it is important to emphasize that crafters of color and poor crafters certainly exist and influence the crafting community in important ways—influence I discuss in more detail in the following chapters—contemporary celebrations of craft, especially explicitly "feminist" ones, too often fail to engage with craft's complex raced and classed features. While I attempt to bring these intricacies to the fore throughout this book, I also rely on scholarship and scholarly traditions that do not and may thus perpetuate some of craft's more exclusionary features. This, of course, is not my intention: I instead hope to sketch a vision of craft that is inclusive, generative, and profoundly attuned to the ethics of *who we make with*. In order to begin this difficult work, then, I want to examine in more detail the deep ties between craft and rhetoric. While craft may be inherently rhetorical, rhetoric is likewise inherently crafty, even if our histories and theories have yet to fully acknowledge it. Yet, a close reading of rhetorical history shows that craft has always been there and reminds us that rhetoric—like craft—is a material, emergent, and shared practice.

CRAFTING RHETORIC

Rhetoric has much to gain by acknowledging its inherent craftiness, not only in terms of articulating its complex materiality but also in terms of more fully acknowledging its ethical and political dimensions. While rhetoric has always been crafty—particularly as articulated in Greek thought—rhetorical scholars have yet to fully acknowledge this relationship. In this section, then, I explore craft's ties with rhetoric through the interconnected concepts of techne, mêtis, and kairos, which all recognize the transformative power of intra-actions between human bodies and nonhuman tools, technologies, and environments. Rhetoric is a techne—a craft knowledge—that is made possible by the embodied, relational intelligence of mêtis and kairos, two terms that have lengthy and significant ties to craft. Together, these concepts historicize and ground craft agency, as they locate ethical practice and just outcomes in rhetoric's inherently material and contingent nature; that is, in rhetoric's craftiness.

While craft's presence in rhetorical history is persistent, it is also complex, in part because the same negative connotations that haunt craft today were present in ancient Greek thought, which often posited craft—particularly weaving—as a feminized and even duplicitous activity. As early as Homer, weaving was recognized as an important craft activity for ancient Greek women (Håland 2004; Mueller 2010; Sennett 2008). Through weaving, Greek women created relationships with each other as well as with material objects, even as it was viewed somewhat suspiciously by Greek men who frequently saw weaving—or anything "that is twisted together" as "plotted, arranged and contrived" (Detienne and Vernant 1991, 115). The connection between women and weaving was so durable, suggest Jack Z. Bratich and Heidi M. Brush, that "a distaff, a tool used for weaving, eventually became a kind of verbal shorthand signifying women, women's work, or the woman's side of a family. . . . The tool could linguistically, as synecdoche, stand in for women in general" (Bratich and Brush 2011, 238). Weaving thus functions to identify not just traces of women's domestic labor, or of women themselves, but of women's *rhetorical* activities within Greek tradition. Indeed, Evy Johanna Håland (2004) argues, "In ancient Greek tradition, mostly sources written by men, the sign of the female, first and foremost, is weaving, since women do not speak, they weave" (170). It is likely, I suggest, that rhetoric has failed to fully explore these deep connections to craft because craft—in ancient Greece as today—carries negative connotations of femininity, vacuity, and deceit.

These attitudes toward craft continue to influence contemporary scholars, whose readings of rhetorical history have largely overlooked craft, either because weaving is not recognized as rhetorical or because it is dismissed as mere "women's work." Alan Wace (1948) suggests that not acknowledging the complexities of craft has serious implications. He argues that classics scholars often conflate all textile production with embroidery in translation and thus fail to fully unpack the nuances of textile and craft production. He contends that modern attitudes toward craft are a likely culprit, arguing that translators "are apparently accustomed to seeing their own womenfolk working at embroidery . . . and they assume that the women of the ancients acted likewise" (51).[5] Accordingly, the full range of textile and craft activity—especially that of women—in canonical Greek texts has, in all likelihood, not been adequately represented in translation.

Craft, then, holds a contradictory place in both Greek rhetorical tradition as well as more current scholarly interpretations. While craft's presence is abundant, it is either misrepresented, dismissed as unimportant, or ignored entirely, likely because craft carries the connotation of a feminized, embodied practice that does not conform to more conventional understandings of rhetorical activities. Given that we have inherited a rhetorical tradition that "denounces the body" (Dolmage 2009, 1), it is perhaps inevitable that craft's place in rhetoric has not been more thoroughly explored. However, as the field increasingly embraces new materialist approaches that figure rhetoric as a situated, dynamic unfolding between human and nonhuman bodies, craft offers a productive location from which to explore this relationship. Craft is not only stubbornly persistent throughout rhetorical history, but it also recognizes the contingent, political nature of individual (human and nonhuman) bodies. It is well past time for rhetoric to contend with its own craftiness.

Specifically, I argue that rhetoric's relationship with craft is best articulated through techne, mêtis, and kairos, which all frame rhetoric as a situated practice that depends on a rich awareness of materiality, including and exceeding individual (human) bodies. Techne is a productive craft knowledge that is fueled by the embodied situatedness of mêtis and kairos. Importantly, however, both mêtis and kairos have deep associations with craft, specifically weaving. These largely unexplored ties are worth unearthing, given that craft—as both a metaphor and a practice—is so uniquely suited to feature the rich, co-constitutive materiality that is essential to rhetoric. Fueled by mêtis and kairos, the craft knowledge of techne positions rhetoric as an inherently material and contingent unfurling that is generated through intra-actions and that carries significant political and ethical weight. Together, then, these terms cement rhetoric's craftiness, and, as a result, provide the foundation for craft agency.

Beginning as early as the Sophists, rhetoric has been understood as a techne, which is most generally translated as *art, skill,* or *craft.* No precise English translation exists, however: techne is a relentlessly complex concept. On the most basic level, though, techne denotes not merely knowing, but doing: As "a process of making, . . . of producing or bringing-forth" (Pender 2011, 4), techne depends on both "an abstract knowledge" as well as a "procedural knowledge" (Porter 2009, 210). Because techne hinges on this distinction between "knowledge as production, not product" (Atwill 1998, 2), it is an inherently inventional practice. This generative capacity, coupled with its classical origins among "gods and goddesses who are identified with invention, craft production, and the disruption of lines of power" (Atwill 1998, 49), has resulted in techne's recurrent associations with cunning or trickery—not unlike craft's adjectival form, "crafty," or even rhetoric itself. Techne, then, might be described as *craft knowledge* that is contingent upon immediate situational and material constraints but is always attentive to potential outcomes.

Because techne has long been a central concept for Western rhetorical theory, it has accordingly garnered a great deal of scholarly attention. Many of these readings have centered around understanding techne as a heuristic, or "explicit strategies for effective guessing" (Young 1980, 345). In this view techne is simply "an object to be possessed by subjects" (Hawk 2004, 372), the means by which a skilled rhetor can exert some level of control over unpredictable, continually shifting rhetorical situations.[6] Yet, scholars have started to trouble this instrumentalist view of techne, particularly as our entanglements with technology become increasingly difficult to ignore. Byron Hawk (2004), for instance, has argued that the posthumanist perspective necessitated by digital writing technologies demands a move "away from a reductive, generic, a-contextual conception of [techne] toward a sense that operates through human bodies in relation to all other bodies (animate and inanimate) in larger, more complex contexts" (372). Hawk terms this sense of techne "post-techne," which he characterizes as "the use of techniques for situating bodies within ecological contexts in ways that reveal models for enacting that open up the potential for invention, especially the invention of new techniques" (384). From his perspective, techne is not mere theoretical and practical mastery, but is instead fluid and unpredictable, emerging from the intra-actions between bodies and their environments.

Hawk's post-techne is a productive starting point for understanding how invention, agency, and rhetoric itself emerge from complex material relationships. Here, though, I want to enrich this understanding of techne by juxtaposing it against the interconnected concepts of mêtis and kairos, which highlight not only how rhetoric and rhetorical agents emerge from complex intra-actions, but how those intra-actions are ultimately *crafty*. Techne, as a material, embodied, craft knowledge depends on mêtis and kairos, two concepts that are rich with craft associations, particularly in terms of weaving. Articulating the craft origins of mêtis and kairos further defines a new materialist techne as a craft knowledge that attributes rhetorical action to the co-mingling of (human and nonhuman) bodies in material assemblages and thus recognizes the political and ethical weight of the intra-actions that bind those bodies. An understanding of techne that is grounded in mêtis and kairos, then, centers craft's place in rhetorical history.

Only relatively recently have rhetorical scholars initiated thorough investigations of mêtis, the "bodily intelligence" (Hawhee 2004, 46) that makes techne possible. The work of Debra Hawhee, Jay Dolmage, and Marcel Detienne and Jean-Pierre Vernant in particular has been instrumental in demonstrating the prominence of mêtis in Greek thought. Mêtis denotes the craftiness that emerges from emplaced, specific bodies: it is variously described as "wise and wily intelligence" (Dolmage 2009, 5); "bodily intelligence and cunning" (Metta 2015, sec. 1, para. 8); "wisdom that is cunning" (Pomykala 2017, 266); and "a form of practical, cunning, or skillful intelligence" (Cocker 2017, 139). Mêtis has its roots in the story of the Greek goddess of the same name who was "equipped with an attunement to contingencies, an inherent preparation for unexpected situations" (Hawhee 2004, 49). Metis was "known as a shapeshifter," literally becoming one with other bodies (Hawhee 2004, 49). Metis's transformative abilities are perhaps best illustrated by the myth in which Zeus swallows her after she becomes pregnant with their child, whom Zeus fears will eventually overpower him. Metis's powers were not fully subsumed within Zeus, however: their child, Athena, emerged fully formed from his head.

It is no surprise, then, that Athena became associated with *mêtic* craftiness in her own right, not just in terms of the cunning befitting her role as the goddess of war. Athena was also recognized as the goddess of handicrafts, especially weaving (Detienne and Vernant 1991; Håland 2004) and was thus "as skilled at weaving cloth as she is at weaving subtle thoughts" (Detienne and Vernant 1991, 239). Weaving in this case serves as the perfect expression of Athena's shrewd nature. Metis and Athena are not the only Greek figures who signal mêtis' ties to craft, however; Dolmage's (2006) rereading of the myth of Hephaestus, the Greek god of fire, metallurgy, masonry, and sculpture—that is, of craftwork—further demonstrates how mêtis emerges from bodies working in concert with their shifting surroundings. While Hephaestus was typically portrayed with a physical disability in his feet or legs, he is also often shown seated in a self-made wheelchair of sorts, described by Dolmage as a "winged chariot" (120). Through "both his bodily difference and his craftsmanship," argues Dolmage, Hephaestus exemplified mêtis, relying on embodied knowledge to successfully navigate his dynamic environment (122).

Mêtis' relationship with craft goes well beyond the figures of Metis, Athena, and Hephaestus, as it is frequently connected to weaving, especially in Greek thought. Throughout their important book, *Cunning Intelligence and Greek Thought*, Detienne and Vernant (1991) demonstrate how often Greek myths employ weaving "as a model of intelligent activity," as woven goods such as nets, traps, veils, and baskets repeatedly symbolize *mêtis* (138). Such a close association with weaving, a sign of feminine craft and cunning, thus feminizes mêtis, as does its linguistic identity: Detienne and Vernant note that "the common noun mêtis was, for the Greeks, a feminine one" (134). This suggests that mêtic intelligence specifically emerges from marginalized or disadvantaged groups—such as women or people with disabilities—as it is frequently understood as a means of reversing power inequities. Indeed, claims Erin Brock Carlson (2020), mêtis "focuses on moments in which marginalized actors utilize resources in unanticipated ways" (4). Likewise, Jennifer Lin LeMesurier (2019) argues that mêtis "is not just a neutral form of cunning (144)" but is instead "formed at the margins . . . [by] vulnerable populations" (152). Mêtis, that is, "constitutes a threat to any established order . . . [and] operates in the realm of what is shifting and unexpected in order the better to reverse situations and overturn hierarchies which appear unassailable" (Detienne and Vernant 1991, 108). Mêtis thus not only represents subversive power—the potential to undo or upend even the most entrenched power differentials—but, importantly, it also locates that power specifically within embodied difference.

Mêtis' insistence "that bodily difference fires rhetorical power" has thus rendered it "subject to derogation" throughout rhetorical history, argues Dolmage (2009, 8; 5). For Dolmage, mêtis' inherently embodied nature presents a problem to a rhetorical canon that has figured "the body [as] a distraction or, worse, a deterrence to clear thought" (3). What's more, mêtis' traces can be difficult to locate, argues LeMesurier (2019), because it "requires looking for forms of bodily labor that are often ignored . . . [or that disappear] into the background" (147). As a result, rhetorical history has favored a view of techne that obscures its ties to the body as articulated by mêtis. However, it is mêtis' embodied, radical potential that makes it ultimately inventive, and thus situates it firmly in the realm of techne as craft knowledge. Mêtis highlights how rhetoric, as a techne, is always material, embodied, and unsettled, ready for disruption. What's more, mêtis insists that emplaced, material, diverse bodies are not just generative but perhaps even a prerequisite for enacting techne. Indeed, suggests Janet Atwill (1998), "the significance of techne often lies in the power of transformation that mêtis enables" (56). The craft knowledge of techne—fueled by the embodied intelligence of mêtis—is thus material, emergent, and values the body, or even "assemblages of multiple bodies," as a source of rhetorical power (Carlson 2020, 4). Techne, as enacted in part through mêtis, is not "[located] strictly within the mind or consciousness" (Hawhee 2004, 48) but in the intra-actions between human bodies and their surrounding material circumstances.

Mêtis emphasizes "the indeterminacy of both subjects and objects" (Atwill 1998, 56), locating inventive potentials within the continual shapeshifting that characterizes its namesake goddess. Mêtis' blurring of boundaries indicates that the craft knowledge of techne does not depend on (and even refuses) the stable subject and instead values the fluid agency of new materialism. In fact, William C. Trapani and Chandra A. Maldonado specifically point to mêtis as a productive concept for theorizing new materialist agency. "Occurring in the middle space between actor and environment," they note, "metistic rhetorics are pragmatic, situational, and strategic just as they are partial, reflexive, and generative of subjects entangled in and emergent through their circumstance" (Trapani and Maldonado 2018, 282). Mêtis, in other words, takes new materialist subjectivity and agency as a starting point, recognizing how various actors in a given assemblage work to create each other, refusing the strict boundaries that would separate them in more traditional accounts of agency. The ever-shifting identity of metistic intelligence is not employed for the sake of idle trickery, however (although that may well be an outcome of mêtis' cunning). Instead, mêtis demonstrates how rhetoric meant to disrupt power inequities must be agile, responsive, and, most importantly, emergent from mutually constitutive material agents.

Through this logic, mêtis fuels the inventional capacities of techne as a craft knowledge, locating rhetorical action not in individual actors but in agential intra-actions. The craft knowledge of techne is made possible by mêtis' extraordinary ability to recognize transformative potential in the everyday entanglements of various (human and nonhuman) actors. Mêtis' attunement to these intra-actions is what prompts design scholar Benedict Singleton (2014) to identify mêtis as an especially fitting term to describe the "dynamic relationship between what is designed and the person designing it, responsive to the vicissitudes of material, and therefore necessarily improvised, at least in part" (107). Mêtis, he suggests, perfectly highlights the overlaps between craft and craftiness, as it is able to "[elicit] *improbable effects from unpromising materials*" (108; emphasis original). Mêtis, then, not only articulates rhetoric's inherent craftiness, but it also positions that craftiness as situated, embodied, and subversive.

Because *techne*, as a craft knowledge, results from the unpredictability of these contextual, material relationships, it is therefore also inevitably kairotic. As deCerteau (2011) notes, "Mêtis counts and plays on the right point in time (kairos): it is a temporal practice" (82). Without attention to kairos, rhetoric as a materially enmeshed techne is impossible. Like techne and mêtis, kairos is an intricate concept, and its many nuances make it difficult to define or translate precisely. Consider, for example, the many connotations Philip Sipiora (2002) attributes to kairos. He lists symmetry, propriety, occasion, due measure, fitness, tact, decorum, convenience, fruit, and profit as some of its possible meanings (1). Despite this complexity, kairos eventually morphed into a means of indicating the *when* of rhetoric, specifying "the right or opportune time to do something, or right measure in doing something" (Kinneavy 2002, 58). Most discussions of kairos position it specifically in opposition to another Greek conceptualization of time, *chronos*, which is more suited to descriptions of static, linear time (Hawhee 2004; Sipiora 2002). Kairos, in contrast, "marks the quality of time rather than its quantity" (Hawhee 2004, 66), connoting dynamism, fluidity, and an element of chaos or volatility.

Kairos was central to Sophistic rhetoric, which is likely why its rediscovery within the field of rhetoric coincided with renewed interest in Sophistic rhetoric throughout the 1980s and 1990s. James Kinneavy is especially credited with kairos' resurgence. His work productively highlighted how kairos might inform rhetors as they seek to adapt to various rhetorical situations. Another important perspective on kairos is found in the work of James S. Baumlin, who saw in kairos a way for rhetors to exert control, essentially creating their own rhetorical situations. While these models were influential in recovering kairos for contemporary rhetoricians, Hawhee (2004) claims that both are ultimately limited. She argues that in each approach, kairos "exists for the most part outside the rhetor, and as such supports a version of rhetoric grounded primarily in rationality and reasoned principles wherein the rhetor/subject analyzes or produces rhetoric as a situation/object" (68). Much like the instrumentalist conceptions of techne described above, then, these understandings of kairos failed to fully account for its complexity, rendering it as external to self-possessed subjects who must either harness or invent it as a way of navigating rhetorical situations.

Yet, more recent readings of Sophistic kairos recognize it not as something external to or wielded by individual rhetors but as the dynamic result of the co-mingling of actors within a rhetorical situation. Rickert (2013), for example, positions kairos as "a moment placed not as something between a subject and exterior situation but as mutually involved and evolving vectors of material and discursive force" (90). Similarly, Hawk (2007) argues that recognizing how kairos "requires the rhetor's ability to participate in the co-adaptive development of a situation . . . updates the traditional concept of kairos—both the situation's ability to seize a rhetor at an opportune moment and the rhetor's ability to recognize the right timing and discourse for a given situation" (183–184). Kairos, that is, is not an external force that governs rhetorical situations, nor is it a simple tool that rhetors can generate internally to control rhetorical situations. Kairos refuses these boundaries altogether and is neither inside nor outside individual rhetors. Rather, as actors within dynamic assemblages produce each other, they also produce kairotic moments. Like mêtis, then, kairos emphasizes the co-constitutive nature of agents and thus serves to further elucidate new materialist subjectivity and agency. As Rickert argues, because kairos recognizes "subjectivity not as something individual, strictly speaking, but rather as something fundamentally dispersed and connected to various aspects of the external environment" (77), it is uniquely suited to theorize the complex models of rhetorical agency favored by new materialist rhetorics.

This renewed understanding of kairos—one perhaps most clearly articulated by Hawk and Rickert—thus centers around relationships, both in terms of their inventive potential as well as their ethical dimensions. What's more, given the specificity and situatedness of kairos, materiality is key on both accounts. Rickert argues that recognizing how kairos is mutually precipitated through the intra-actions that form a rhetorical assemblage is ultimately generative, not constraining, "[suggesting] kinds of invention attuned less to seeking advantage over or success against an audience than to working with what an audience and a material situation bring forth" (91). For Hawk, kairos' emphasis on material encounters forces actors to consider the ethical implications of their location within a rhetorical assemblage, and how that location in turn produces rhetorical agency and identity. "The subject is not simply the political position or identity someone chooses," he writes, "but the relationships established through those identities and the effects of those relationships on bodies" (189). As a result, ethical rhetorical practice is a matter of how a "body sets itself into relations or compositions with other bodies" (189). Understanding kairos in this way recognizes the contingent, relational nature of rhetoric, suggesting the importance of intra-actions both in terms of their inventional and ethical capacities.

These readings clarify how kairos positions material entanglements as the condition for rhetoric, but it is within classical Greek thought that the full depth of kairos' embodied dimensions emerges. Rickert (2013) traces its early Greek usages to argue that kairos "is grounded in a sense of place, particularly the body" (78). Indeed, writes Sipioria (2002), kairos' first known usage was in the *Iliad*, "where it denotes a vital or lethal place in the body, one that is particularly susceptible to injury" (2). Hawhee (2004) notes that the rhetorical sense of kairos draws from yet another Greek mythological figure, the god of the same name, Kairos, who is depicted with "the bodily form of an athlete," ready to move at any moment (72). Accordingly, she suggests, rhetorical kairos "becomes figured as . . . a bodily capacity for instantaneous response" (75). Kairos thus emphasizes the importance of the body specifically as a location both of potential power and of vulnerability, an interface through which kairotic possibilities unfold.

The body, however, is not the only material location of kairotic opportunity. Notably, kairos—like mêtis—has long been associated with weaving, both in its ancient and contemporary manifestations (Cocker 2017; Gelang 2013; Hawhee 2004; Rickert 2013; White 1987). Hawhee (2004) demonstrates just how consequential this relationship is, noting, "kairos indicates, variously, the place where threads attach to the loom; the act of fastening these threads (*kairoō*); a web so fastened (*kairōma*); and the root was even used to indicate a woman who weaves (*kairōstis* and *kairōstris*). The related *kairoseōn* is used to describe that which is tightly woven" (67). Weaving is in fact an apt metaphor for kairos, argues Marie Gelang (2013), as the act of weaving depends upon "the moment in weaving when the odd and even threads are separated so that the weft threads can be passed through the warp. The instant when the warp opens exemplifies kairos as an opportune moment, the right instant, the right opportunity, because the opening in the weave only lasts a short time" (91). Successful weaving depends on the precise, timely orchestration of the weaver's body as well as physical objects like the loom and the thread. In the act of weaving, then, we can see how kairos does not exist independent of the material actors that together constitute any rhetorical assemblage; rather, it both produces and is produced through those actors' varied intra-actions.

The historical ties between kairos and weaving thus demonstrate the rich sense of materiality that informs kairos: Just as the weaver responds to and is altered by physical things—which in turn will respond to and be altered by the weaver—kairos connotes the myriad interdependencies that make it possible. The fact that this relationship is so often expressed through the metaphor of the loom is fitting, I suggest, given that the craft knowledge of techne depends so heavily on the inventive capacities of kairos. As Trapani and Maldonado (2018) argue, kairos' value lies precisely in its generative potentials: "Kairos gathers and gives possibility to the subjects, bodies, and circumstances it renders available" (285). Kairos informs the craft knowledge of techne as it emerges through the tangle of bodies, technologies, and tools that constitute rhetoric.

Together, mêtis and kairos call attention to rhetoric's material, relational nature as enacted through the craft knowledge of techne, and thus offer robust theoretical grounding for new materialist approaches to agency and rhetorical action. As their historical relationships with women, bodies, and weaving make clear, both mêtis and kairos recognize how actors create one another, and how rhetoric is the product of those intra-actions. The craft knowledge of techne relies on metic craftiness and kairotic unfurling, both of which result from highly situated material encounters. Agential intra-actions, then, are key to theorizing how the material, craft knowledge of techne unfolds: as Cooper (2019) notes, techne is "a correspondence . . . an ongoing entanglement involving not only makers and materials but also things and forces" (11–12). Through their intra-actions with each other and their environments, human and nonhuman actors together constitute not just each other, but the rhetorical situations they inhabit. While the history of mêtis and kairos suggests that new materialists' attention to materiality is well-founded, it also emphasizes that because materiality both produces and is subject to power relationships, participation in rhetorical assemblages is, at base, a question of ethics. Kairos' insistence on the mutually constitutive nature of actors demands that actors consider the ethical implications of their position(s) within a rhetorical assemblage, as that position results in rhetorical possibilities as well as rhetorical impossibilities. Similarly, mêtis' transformative nature hinges on the co-constitutive nature of actors, seeing in their intra-actions not just power inequities, but the conditions for their reversal. Together, these terms inform the craft knowledge of techne as an ethical, embedded practice,

highlighting the ways in which materiality both produces and is produced by power relations.

Techne—as a craft that depends on both embodied mêtis and situational kairos—thus holds significant promise for articulating the political
and ethical consequences of new materialist rhetorics. Techne highlights
the ethics of our intra-actions, recognizing how they are simultaneously
the location from which power hierarchies can be built as well as the location of their undoing. Because techne's inventional nature carries "the
potential . . . to disrupt lines of power [that challenge] existing orders
at many levels" (Atwill 1998, 108), it is particularly well-suited to inventing new ways of being and new relations—relations that have the capacity to dismantle power inequities. Rather than seeing techne as merely
instrumental, then, it might better be imagined as "a disruptive—even
subversive—kind of tactical knowledge, capable of dealing with contingent situations and fully harnessing their capricious force" (Cocker 2017,
140). Techne, especially when grounded in mêtis and kairos, becomes a
matter of creating productive, inventive, ethical assemblages that challenge power hierarchies, a means of recognizing what the varied intra-
actions within an assemblage make possible and what they preclude.
Techne considered in these terms is thus essential for craft agency.

LOCATING CRAFT AGENCY

Craft and rhetoric share much more than a bad reputation: Craft, like
rhetoric, rejects fixed subject/object boundaries, and finds in the dissolution of those boundaries the conditions for agency. As a result,
both rhetoric and craft are process-oriented, wherein making is a continual process of collective becoming. Despite rhetoric's inability to
contend with its craft heritage, then, fully embracing the material turn
means acknowledging rhetoric's *craftiness*: Emerging from intra-actions
between human and nonhuman bodies, environments, and technologies, rhetoric, like craft, is embedded, relational, and potentially subversive. Importantly, however, craft also centers the ethical implications
of making-with. That is, craft not only recognizes how agency can only
emerge from assemblages of human and nonhuman agents, but it also
understands that those assemblages are inherently political. Yet, because
rhetoric has so far failed to recognize itself in craft, it is unable to fully
define the implications—both ethical and political—of its newly articulated material contours.

Understanding rhetoric as a techne can help achieve this admittedly
lofty goal. The craft knowledge of techne is undergirded by both mêtis

and kairos, both of which emphasize the reflexive material complexities of rhetorical assemblages. Notably, though, mêtis and kairos have historically represented this reflexivity through craft. Through their close associations with weaving specifically, both mêtis and kairos demonstrate how the process of making-with alternately shapes and is shaped by power relations. Figuring rhetoric as a techne, infused with the craft ethics of mêtis and kairos, thus requires a deep examination of how we situate ourselves and others "within particular contexts with any and all objects—a building, a text, a human body, a rock" (Hawk 2004, 379). This ethics is not just responsive to our immediate contexts; it is also fundamentally forward-looking. Because the craft knowledge of techne takes materiality broadly conceived as a starting point for ethical, political action and intervention, it recognizes how material intra-actions are the location from which power hierarchies can be challenged and even undone altogether.

Techne, then, usefully bridges new materialist rhetorics and craft ethics, and provides a position to understand how the intra-actions that produce rhetorical agency are always inherently political. Craft agency, as a concept and as a practice, captures this dynamic, recognizing that just as rhetorical agency emerges through encounters between human and nonhuman agents alike, it is also always responsive to materiality and the power relations that govern it. Craft agency may thus usefully inform new materialist rhetorics' embrace of an increasingly sophisticated understanding of agency and subjectivity by working to shed light on the practices of making that create the conditions for rhetorical agency—both in terms of their political potential as well as our ethical obligations to the co-agents who make us, and making itself, possible.

3
CRAFTIVISM AND THE MATERIAL
SPECIFICITY OF RHETORICAL ACTION

A World War II combat tank sits in the streets of Copenhagen, adorned with a shockingly pink knit and crocheted cozy, complete with pom-poms hanging from its gun. Knit uteruses arrive by the dozens to the offices of (male) members of US Congress. Meanwhile, a handmade stuffed mouse, toting a sign reading "No More Fat Cats!" stands along-side activists at the Occupy protests in London. These varied instances of protest—objecting to the Iraq War, restrictions on women's repro-ductive rights, and the economic injustices spotlighted by the Occupy movement—might be dismissed as isolated novelties, or even as empty kitsch, but they are in fact emblematic of a larger, more cohesive move-ment. Craftivism, a relatively new term that highlights the old practice of merging craft practices with activist goals, is becoming more prominent as a growing number of crafters recognize and exploit the inherently subversive potential of craft.

Craft is not just an important figure in rhetorical history; it is a con-tinuing location for critical rhetorical engagement, modeling a new materialist approach to rhetoric that recognizes intra-actions as the location for political change and ethical practices. Craftivism makes this dynamic particularly visible: through the deliberate cultivation of embodied, emplaced encounters with specific composing tools and technologies, craftivists demonstrate how to embrace the new material-ist argument that rhetorical action is a product of complex intra-actions between a network of human and nonhuman actors while also maintain-ing an explicitly activist agenda.

In this chapter, I begin my case studies of craft agency at work with an examination of craftivism, an enactment of craft agency that values the unique material specificity of human and nonhuman actors alike and sees in that materiality the possibility for ethical entanglements as well as political transformation. I first review the history of craftivism, which highlights craft's capacity to orchestrate human and nonhu-man intra-actions for specific political goals. I then turn to an analysis

https://doi.org/10.7330/9781646422555.c003

of contemporary craftivism, studying how specific craftivist acts—as both product and process—might (re)theorize new materialist rhetorics as a means of restructuring power in productive and ethical ways. I close by considering how my discussion of craftivism helps clarify craft agency, particularly in terms of how its embrace of an ethics of entanglement—an ethics grounded in the recognition of the material specificity of rhetorical action—fuels a coalitional politics that values the agential intra-actions of new materialism.

UNDERSTANDING CRAFTIVISM

While the convergence of craft and activism is by no means a new phenomenon, the term *craftivism*, which was coined in the early 2000s, is.[1] There is not one static definition of craftivism, although craftivists and academics agree that the term, as its root words suggest, is meant to represent the relationship between craft and activism. Craftivists variously describe their work as "the practice of engaged creativity, especially regarding political or social causes" (Greer 2007); "craft that challenges, provokes" (Greer 2014b); "making something that made a difference, even a very small difference" (O'Farrell 2014); and a movement that "engage[s] people . . . in a transformative and respectful way" (Corbett, in TEDx Talks 2013). Even across these wide-ranging definitions, it is apparent that craftivism aims to reframe the connotations of both craft and activism, positioning craft as a political act, and activism as a means of building relationships.

With such varied understandings of craftivism, it is perhaps best characterized not as a singular, well-defined movement but rather a diverse array of materials, practices, and participants. While craftivism often addresses large-scale, global issues, such as economic inequality, women's health, food insecurity, AIDS, and war, many also see craftivism as a means to create local alliances among individuals or communities. Craftivism generally manifests in public spaces, targeting broad audiences, but it can also appeal to more specific, local audiences. Whatever the audience or purpose, however, craftivism always makes visible how power circulates—and can be challenged—through the material. In craftivism, materiality matters, as bodies, tools, spaces, and objects work together to intervene in political struggles and inequitable relationships, with the ultimate goal of remaking a more ethical, just world.

Although the specific term "craftivism" may be relatively new, the practices it represents have been around, arguably, as long as craft itself (Niedderer and Townsend 2018; Robertson 2011). Indeed, historical examples of craftivism abound, as it has for centuries represented a method of direct protest as well as a means of more covert resistance. Consider, for instance, the prominent role craftivism played in the women's suffrage movements in both the United States and Britain. Suffragists fashioned mixed-media banners, sashes, and floats adorned with messages like "Votes for Women," "All This Is The Natural Consequence of Teaching Girls to Read," and "More Ballots, Less Bullets" (Borda 2002; Parker 1984). A conspicuous feature of suffragist parades, these handmade items created a "spectacle of stunning visual display," cementing the goals of the movement in the minds of audience members (Borda 2002, 35). Craftivism also helped mark the private struggle of many suffragists. Imprisoned suffragists commonly embroidered handkerchiefs with their signatures to memorialize their suffering (sometimes including forced feedings in response to hunger strikes) and to declare their status as political prisoners, a distinction that jailers often refused to acknowledge (Goggin 2009; Parker 1984). Craftivism, in the eyes of suffragists, performed the work of the common suffrage slogan "deeds not words," as the act of making became a means of embracing and enacting "active protest over passive acceptance" (Goggin 2009, 22).

Countless other movements across history have made use of craft as a mode of direct protest, both to create visibility as well as to invite participation and action. To protest nuclear armament, the Women's Peace Movement of the 1970s and '80s made "large, brightly colored embroidered and appliquéd banners" as they camped and marched at Greenham Common Air Base in England (Parker 1984, 210). The use of craft in this case was a particularly effective mode of activism, argues Kirsty Robertson (2011), because the feminized nature of craft highlighted "the brutality of (masculine) police oppression and the wider politics that had brought the threat of nuclear war" (185), thus drawing attention to the goals of the protestors. Craftivism can also foster wider involvement with a specific cause, as the instance of the AIDS Memorial Quilt demonstrates (figure 3.1). Beginning as a local outlet for remembrance, the quilt has since become a national memorial honoring the lives of those who have died of AIDS. At its inaugural display in 1987 at the National Mall in Washington, DC, the quilt attracted half a million visitors, and it has only continued to grow as it travels across the country ("History of the Quilt" n.d.). The quilt's striking visual representation of the scope of the AIDS crisis not only raises awareness, but its literal patchwork elicits additional contributions, as any member of the public is welcome to create a square in remembrance of a loved one.

Figure 3.1. AIDS Quilt in Front of White House, *photograph by Scott Chacon, 2004.*
(CC BY 2.0)

Historical manifestations of craftivism can be less overt as well, particularly in precarious circumstances. During his captivity as a Nazi prisoner of war, British officer Alexis Casdagli created a cross-stitch sampler that bore the relatively innocuous message, "This work was done by Major A. T. Casdagli, No. 3311, while in captivity at Dossal-Warburg Germany, December 1941." The Nazis, however, apparently failed to recognize the sampler's hidden messages: Casdagli had stitched "God Save the King" and "Fuck Hitler" in Morse code disguised as a decorative border. Casdagli's subversive cross stitch was displayed throughout his imprisonment at four different German camps. This small but potent act of resistance offered Casdagli a sense of agency and even pleasure despite his captivity, reports his son (Barkham 2011). Similarly, Chilean women subverted the use of everyday craft to resist violence and injustice. During the reign of dictator Augusto Pinochet, many women turned to the traditional textile craft of *arpillera,* the decorative "colorful embroidered tapestries" that typically feature bucolic scenes (Strycharz 2014). Through arpillera, women were able to evade government censorship and "record the loss of their loved one, the brutal violence of the military, and the daily oppression they faced," ultimately creating "the unpublished history of the dictatorship of Chile" (Strycharz 2014). Craftivism was thus often a matter of life and death. This is perhaps most evident in the craft of enslaved people in the American South who created quilts with "literal maps" that guided the path to freedom (Banks

2006, 124). Taking advantage of the everyday nature of craft, these quilts would surreptitiously act "as maps of lands surrounding plantations, charting routes and distances to safe houses, including the distances between them, and advice on how to navigate those routes," writes Adam Banks (2006, 125). In these cases, craft's banal, everyday nature made it an ideal location for covert political action.

Indeed, it is likely that craft's historic devaluation is precisely why it became such a frequent site for activism and resistance. Because craft was so often used to enforce normative expectations of feminine propriety across racial and class boundaries, it became a critical yet relatively safe location for the political expressions of groups who were frequently denied access to more traditional outlets for protest. What's more, craft's many communal dimensions make it an ideal space for forging political alliances. Knitting circles, for example, often served as important origin points for political action. Despite its solitary connotations, knitting served an important function in the social lives of women, who would gather in knitting circles "to swap stories, skills, knowledge, and strategies and generally speak about the more oppressive aspects of the social home" (Bratich and Brush 2011, 240). Together, "like-minded people and communities" could join around the shared craft of knitting, and in the process "[recognize] the power of group work, discussion and activism" (Turney 2009, 175, 203). Paradoxically, then, craft was both a mechanism of control as well as a venue for resistance, as it brought together groups of people who were then able to recognize and capitalize on craft's normative connotations.

Contemporary craftivism continues to exploit this dynamic, taking advantage of craft's gendered history in particular to subvert stereotypes about both craft and activism. The modern craftivist movement emerged alongside the wider third-wave feminist efforts of the 1990s and early 2000s to rehabilitate craft and domesticity discussed in chapter 2 (Goggin 2015; Groeneveld 2010; Krugh 2014; Pentney 2008). Like the broader reclamation of craft from which it sprang, present-day craftivism is explicitly political and casts craft's perceived feminized domesticity as an advantage rather than a liability. For example, in her book *Knitting for Good!*, craftivist Betsy Greer (2008) argues that one of craftivism's many potential merits is a renewed appreciation of women's labor: "By making the domestic a source of pride and strength, we have the opportunity to culturally redefine 'woman's work' as an act of progress instead of regression" (19). From this perspective, domestic crafts like knitting enable women—and other groups who have been historically controlled through craft—to use craft subversively, challenging stereotypes about craft while simultaneously challenging limiting notions about identity categories like gender, race, and class. Jamie Chalmers (2014), a cross-stitcher who is perhaps better known as "Mr. X-Stitch," capitalizes on these connotations in his work. For him, craft's feminized connotations only "adds to the success of cross-stitch as a political medium; one cannot help but feel kindness toward cross-stitched pieces, as though they had been created by a senior matriarch." Chalmers, in other words, argues that craft not only self-consciously calls attention to the processes of its making, but also who has made it—and because craft is often assumed to have been made at home, by a loving maternal figure, it has a great deal of political value. It is this paradoxical disruptive potential that has led feminists in particular to value craft as a vehicle for activism.

Craftivism reframes the denigration of craft, and crafters, as a political stance that values the labor and knowledge of historically oppressed peoples. Central to this process are the collaborative partnerships and social ties that are typical of crafting practices. Craftivism, that is, sees its project of reclaiming and transforming the negative stereotypes around craft, femininity, and domesticity as a specifically communal one, and understands the social spaces that craft fosters as generative and politically valuable. Craftivism thus self-consciously engages with craft practices of the past, invoking nostalgic or even idealized connotations of craft's history that are then "transformed and reworked into the creative powers at establishing a public, active community of like-minded people" (Myzelev 2009, 153). The political value of craftivism, in short, is often located specifically in its ability to bring marginalized or otherwise disempowered people together around the generative processes of *making*.

Part of the reason that contemporary craftivism has been so successful in building transformative communities is because it has taken full advantage of the affordances offered by internet technologies. Indeed, some craftivists and scholars explicitly attribute the recent resurgence of craftivism to its lively digital presence, noting how craft's social dimensions make it particularly well-suited for online spaces that can facilitate relationships through the sharing of knowledge and interests (Black and Burisch 2011; Bratich 2010; Turney 2009). In fact, claims Jack Bratich (2010), these technologies in many ways reproduce the kinds of durable, reciprocal connections long valued by craft communities (307 n. 4). Many craftivists rely on these tools for "organization, coordination, and communication," and, as a result, contemporary craftivism is often "a hybrid space where physical space is overlaid with digital information," destabilizing material and digital distinctions altogether (Wallace

2012). Alongside social media platforms, websites like Greer's craftivism .com and Sarah Corbett's craftivist-collective.com help mobilize existing craftivists and inform crafters and activists alike about new causes and methods. Without these digital tools, it is unlikely that contemporary craftivism could become the worldwide phenomenon it is today.

Even as craftivism has begun to surface as a coherent movement, however, it has faced criticism. Some have suggested that craftivism simply isn't radical enough, especially in its less conspicuous manifestations. While some craftivists insist that even the simple choice "to make, rather than buy" is an activist position that "reject[s] the dominant ideology and . . . [reacts] against consumerism" (Turney 2009; 178), others say this position reproduces an overly simplistic binary separating craft and mass production (Campbell 2005, 25). These kinds of craftivists aren't eschewing capitalist economies, says Colin Campbell (2005); rather, they simply "[take] any number of mass-produced products and [employ] these as the 'raw materials' for the creation of a new 'product'" (27–8). As a result, critics argue that craftivism functions much like contemporary craft more broadly, relying too heavily on individual consumption rather than presenting a serious challenge to capitalist economies (Krugh 2014, 296).

What's more is that even in its more patently radical forms, craftivism is often dismissed as a "safe form of activism" (Robertson 2011, 188–189), akin to digital "slacktivism" that requires no real sacrifice or commitment on behalf of protesters. Especially because it so frequently invokes a feminized ethos, craftivism remains vulnerable to charges that it is an empty pursuit that is ultimately "so nonconfrontational as to be completely ineffective" (Robertson 2011, 188). More pointedly, critics suggest that craftivism is a fundamentally normative mode of reproducing "the provincial sensibilities of Western, middle class whiteness" (Hahner and Varda 2014, 302). That is, because craftivism both participates in systems of capitalist consumption and fails to engage seriously with the questions of race and class that face the craft world more broadly, it can never be truly transformative.

Indeed, the vast majority of criticism surrounding craftivism stems from concerns that it simply reproduces the same exclusionary class and racial structures that have marked craft more widely, rendering it a practice of privileged white women who have the time and resources to engage in the slow and often expensive work of craft (Close 2018; Feliz 2017; Groeneveld 2010; Hahner and Varda 2014; Portwood-Stacer 2013). Specifically, claims Julia Feliz (2017), "The craftivist movement is one that takes pride in some of the most nonsensical white feminist privileged stances that actually works to silence people of color, like

Figure 3.2. Yarn Bombed Bike Racks, *photograph by Paul Krueger, 2011. (CC BY 2.0)*

myself, instead of actually doing the work to create real change" (para. 3) The result, she writes, is a movement that "fails to recognize its privilege and uses it to take actions that don't truly accomplish anything" (para. 8). The common craftivist practice of yarn bombing[2] and/or knit graffiti (figure 3.2)—in which a public object is clothed in a knit or crocheted covering—is a good example of craftivism's reluctance to critically examine its own privilege. Here, craftivists have appropriated the terms "bombing" and/or "graffiti"—terms that typically signify often-criminalized street art—and cloaked them in "an invisible aesthetic of whiteness" (Close 2018, 880). Leslie Hahner and Scott J. Varda criticize especially the language of "graffiti," arguing that "while many forms of street art struggle to gain legitimacy—with unsanctioned works often treated as vandalism—yarn bombing's incredible popularity affords it exceptional treatment" (Hahner and Varda 2014, 301). These concerns are further compounded by the tendency of white craftivists to appropriate language that is most often associated with communities of color: the "first yarn graffiti crew," Knitta (Moore and Prain 2009), for example, marked their craftivist pieces with signs reading "knitta, please!" or "whaddup knitta?" (Plocek 2005). As a result of this kind of cultural appropriation, many critics fear that craftivism undermines its political potentials, relying on or even perpetuating a regressive, essentialist, and exclusionary model of feminist activism.

Some craftivists have directly grappled with these criticisms, recognizing the dangers that unexamined privilege can pose to the movement. In a series on craft and privilege on her blog, Greer (2015b) argues that until craftivists contend with their relative privilege, the "movement will not be seen as helpful and exciting and freeing . . . [but] will be seen as privileged and boring and perfectly milquetoast" (para. 5). Greer (2015a) suggests that craftivists reframe craft itself to account for activities that "cost nothing and take up no extra time" (para. 9). Such an approach not only combats privilege within the craftivist movement, but ultimately supports the larger craftivist goal of refiguring craft not as a domestic leisure activity but as an inherently political and subversive practice. However, there is little doubt that many craftivists (and the crafting world more broadly) have yet to fully explore the privilege that marks their community, and without doing so, craftivism risks simply reifying the structures of power it claims to seek to undo.

Despite the fact that whiteness remains one of craftivism's most visible features, it is important to note that contemporary craftivism is by no means practiced solely by white women. Black and Indigenous craftivist groups in particular are producing compelling craftivist work that can help push more mainstream craftivism in more progressive directions. Consider the Million Artist Movement (n.d.), "a collective of Black-Brown-and-Radical Artist Revolutionaries and Activities" that "believes in the role of Art in the campaign to dismantle oppressive racist systems against Black, Brown, Indigenous, and disenfranchised people." They have worked with community members to create the Power Tree Quilt, which is comprised of an ever-growing array of individually crafted panels that "represent the diverse contributions of individuals and groups to the struggle for liberation" (Million Artist Movement 2015, 13). Another notable Black craftivist organization is The Yarn Mission, a "knitting collective that is purposefully Pro-Black, Pro-Rebellion, and Pro-Community for the achievement of Black Liberation" (Yarn Mission, n.d.). They provide knitting support and instruction in addition to selling knitting supplies and goods from Black fiber artists. While neither of these groups specifically invoke the term "craftivism" to describe their work, they clearly share the belief that craft can lead to political change. The Million Artist Movement's (n.d.) claim that they "stand at the nexus of art and politics, using art as an agent to coalesce people, art, and power into change" perhaps illustrates this shared commitment most directly.

Craftivism is also an important political tool across various Indigenous rights movements. Artist and activist Cannupa Hanska Luger's Missing and Murdered Indigenous Women, Girls, Queer, and Trans People Bead Project is one notable example. Created with "4000 individual handmade clay beads created by hundreds of communities," the finished project combined the beads to form a pixelated image of a woman (taken by Indigenous photographer Kali Spitzer). According to Luger, who is of Mandan, Hidatsa, Arikara, and Lakota heritage, each bead is meant to represent "an individual from our Indigenous communities we have lost" (MMIWGQT Bead Project n.d.).[3] Consider too the many instances of craftivism that emerged as part of and in response to the #NoDAPL movement, a coordinated effort that resisted the Dakota Access Pipeline on the grounds that it would endanger the water quality as well as disturb sacred burial sites on the Standing Rock Indian Reservation. In addition to the countless protest signs and banners, other potent acts of craftivism stand out, such as the barbed wire dreamcatchers created by Pueblo protesters who set up camp at Standing Rock. Made with the same "barbed wire that was previously used against water protectors" (Dupere 2017), the dreamcatchers were then sold to fund the continued protest efforts. The practices highlighted here—practices that clearly imagine making as resistance—certainly suggest some kind of productive overlap with more mainstream craftivism, even if most Indigenous craftivists (like their Black counterparts) eschew the explicit "craftivist" label, a choice that is most likely a deliberate one meant to dissociate their work from the more stereotypical, ineffectual white woman craftivism that still serves as the face of the movement. However, even without the formal "craftivist" label, these examples suggest that there is already diversity within the craftivism world, even if it is rarely acknowledged as such.

The practices of these groups can also help address the criticism that craftivism as a whole is simply not radical or aggressive enough to be effective. Generally speaking, one of craftivism's central goals is to redefine what activism itself looks like, even if it is not always entirely successful. Just as craftivists challenge reductive conceptions that figure craft as apolitical kitsch, they also resist the idea that activism is always aggressive, violent, or preachy. Craftivism instead intentionally blurs the distinctions between these terms, creating something altogether new: craft becomes "a neat political tool to fuck with the fuckers' minds" (Craft Cartel, quoted in Greer 2014b) while activism is a "quiet and happy and joyful" (Greer 2008, 76) means of "provoking conversation" (Corbett, in TEDx Talks 2013). This redefinition allows craftivism to be simultaneously radical and familiar, collaborative and confrontational, or what craftivists describe as "slow," "gentle," or "quiet" activism (Corbett, in TEDx Talks 2013).

Craftivists, in fact, see the rhetorical value in this juxtaposition. Craft Cartel argues that "The combination of craft and activism is still considered unusual and quirky enough that it grabs people's attention, catches them off-guard, and affords a moment of communication with people who normally wouldn't have you on their radar" (quoted in Greer 2014b). For them, the unexpected pairing of craft and activism afforded by craftivism not only demands attention but also, and just as importantly, creates a dialogue. Indeed, craftivists credit this ability to create affinities—between people, objects, and spaces—as the source of craftivism's political potentials. As Catherine West (2014) explains, craftivism's value lies in its ability to evoke "the silent conversation, the shared ideas between a maker or a collective of makers and a recipient or viewer . . . the reflection and communication inspired by craftivism may create more connection and real change than thousands of names on a petition." Likewise, Greer (2014a) notes that "there is a back-and-forth in craftivism" that ultimately can "foment dialogue." Dialogue may seem an altogether toothless aim, but craftivists believe that the discussion craft makes possible can lead to more concrete outcomes, especially when paired with existing social justice movements. In a blog post titled "On why knitting can be part of the struggle for Black Liberation," for example, Yarn Mission member CheyOnna (2017) explains that although "[craft] will not prevent the loss of life and liberty . . . it can be a tool used in the struggle," especially because of its ability to "promote engagement, community education/building/strengthening, and inclusion." Craftivism, in other words, calls attention to the varied intra-actions that bind humans and nonhumans and acknowledges that those intra-actions are the condition for political change.

Craftivism, like any living political movement, is full of contradictions and conflict. However, what remains consistent throughout almost all accounts of craftivism is the insistence that it offers the possibility of (re)making equitable material alliances, even if those possibilities are not always realized. From a rhetorical perspective, that is, craftivism focuses on the creation and/or manipulation of assemblages—of bodies, digital and physical locations, and objects—and sees the ethical significance and political importance of this work. The combination of craft and activism that comprises craftivism is fundamentally a claim on materiality's capacity to do rhetorical work. Craftivism productively extends current conceptions of new materialist rhetorics by focusing on the political function of materiality. In the next section, then, I analyze contemporary craftivist acts to explore how they enact craft agency. By remaining attentive to materiality (especially the materiality of bodies) and recognizing that objects have important rhetorical functions, craftivism demonstrates a politically focused new materialist rhetoric that offers a productive model for craft agency.

CRAFTIVISM'S CAPACIOUS MATERIALITY

Craftivism is, in many ways, a succinct demonstration of new materialist agency: In the material assemblages that make craftivism possible, it is clear how agency results from intra-actions between humans and nonhumans. However, I argue, craftivism can productively highlight the political consequentiality of new materialist rhetorical agency. Craftivism, in other words, illustrates craft agency at work. While it encourages the creation of intentional entanglements between varied human and nonhuman actors, craftivism is also able to maintain an intense focus on political outcomes that is steeped in an ethic of relationality. Craftivism's dependence on the mutual recognition of the material specificity of all actors, I suggest, is in part responsible for its capacity to articulate the ethical consequences of (re)making material assemblages. In this section, then, I analyze instances of craftivism in order to demonstrate how craftivism creates alliances between craft(ed) objects, public space, and human bodies. Through this rich materiality, craftivism aims to create assemblages, and sees those assemblages as the necessary condition for political action.

Craftivism, like new materialist rhetorics, begins from an acknowledgment of the agentic capacity of nonhumans, including inorganic things and the places they inhabit. Craftivism would be impossible without this understanding that craft objects are rhetorical, and as such, they respond to and reshape the world around them. Craftivist Collective (2013), for example, describes craft's ability to "encourage [and] engage," while Faythe Levine (2014) explicitly acknowledges the rhetorical nature of craft objects, arguing that they can present "a point of view that's designed to persuade us." Craftivists also draw a connection between the specificity of craft materiality and its rhetorical possibilities. As Maria Molten argues, because craft inevitably "takes time and thought," it "is difficult to ignore, dislike, or contest" (quoted in Greer 2014c). Craftivists recognize that craft's materiality—both the conditions of its making and its final form—make it a potent political actor.

Because craftivists recognize the important rhetorical role of materiality, they are especially attentive to the materials they use to create craftivist objects. Craftivist processes are marked by a thoughtful consideration of the affordances of specific tools, techniques, and materials.

Craftivists recognize these choices as having material, and thus rhetorical, consequences. In yarn bombing, for example, the durability of yarn matters. Edie of the Ladies Fancywork Society (quoted in Moore and Prain 2009) explains: "Almost all of us agree about using the crappiest acrylic yarns that we can. They stay brighter longer" (47). Knitting collaborative Artyarn (quoted in Moore and Prain 2009) agrees, noting "Color is important to us; the brighter the better" (47). Because yarn bombing typically is meant to stay in place as long as possible, calling attention to itself in contrast to its often dull or banal surroundings, colorful, acrylic yarns are preferred over fussier and less durable natural fibers. Likewise, in the directions for contributing panels to their Power Tree Quilt, the Million Artist Movement (2015) offer suggestions focused specifically on longevity, such as, "Do not rely on glue—it won't last" (27). In craftivism, then, the materiality of the item constitutes its rhetorical efficacy.

Craftivism's interest in the materiality of craft objects is thus not limited to the finished object itself; rather, it includes the materials and process used to create those objects. The agency of nonhuman things, that is, is intimately tied to their making, which is perhaps why so many craftivists are interested in calling attention to the conditions that produce nonhuman objects. Mexican American artist Margarita Cabrera, for example, crafts fabric versions of household goods like cleaning products and appliances in order to provoke awareness of who tends to make and use such tools, as well as to highlight the labor involved in the creation of the craft objects themselves ("Solo Work," n.d.). Likewise, craftivist duo Varvara Guljajeva and Mar Canet create projects that critically examine industrial labor practices, such as the full-sized knitted VW Kombi they created after its 78-year production came to an end in Brazil. Not only did they hope to call attention to the reality that "thanks to VW's lobbying efforts, [Brazil] has networks of roads, rather than an extensive railway," but also to the limits of industrial manufacturing, particularly in terms of it changing how humans relate to nonhuman objects (quoted in Greer 2014e). Even as some craftivist practices may ultimately only reify capitalist structures, criticisms of modern capitalism are still common within craftivism, argues Robertson, who suggests that many craftivist projects demonstrate "a sophisticated understanding that the making of any textile is connected to the capitalist system (no matter how tangentially)" (2011, 198). The desire to highlight the complexities of global capitalist systems of production is rooted in the recognition that the making of objects is just as critical as the use of objects, especially when it comes to recognizing their agential capacities.

Craftivism, then, enacts the new materialist argument that materiality not only informs but often defines how all actors—human and nonhuman alike—function as rhetorical agents. Importantly, however, craftivism sees this materiality as a means of subverting and resisting power dynamics. Craft Cartel's Cunt Fling-Ups project highlights how craftivism understands the inherently political nature of materiality. Described on Craft Cartel's website as "Crafted female genitalia attached to shoes & flung over power lines" ("Cunt Fling-Ups!" 2013) Cunt Fling-Ups take a crafted representation of cis female bodies—which are often positioned as objects themselves—as serious actors in their own right. The genitalia they signify is political, but so is the material that comprise the Cunt Fling-Ups: as Craft Cartel founders Rayna Fahey and Casey Jenkins note, the "Cunt Fling-Ups are brightly colored and soft and sparkly. You have to work pretty hard to find them threatening" (quoted in Greer 2014b). In other words, Fahey and Jenkins reshape negative perceptions of female bodies through the (pleasant) materiality of the Cunt Fling-Ups. The materiality of these craft objects—which are not just representational of but also crafted by (mostly) cis female bodies—thus directly dictates their rhetorical functions.

Craft(ed) objects hold a critical place in any craftivist assemblage, which recognizes their ability to make arguments about new ways of being as well as their role in creating new rhetorical possibilities. These are not the only nonhuman agents that craftivism recognizes; however, craftivism's privileging of the material is also reflected in its tendency to insist on the rhetoricity of place, which it understands as a product of power relations. As Jacqueline Wallace (2012) explains, "Craftivists are constantly negotiating the geography and social relations of public space to practice their resistance and to counter the hegemonic structures embedded within public space." Accordingly, craftivism might be understood as a matter of place-making, as it works to relocate craft from private, domestic spaces into public space.

Craftivism participates in the long-standing feminist project of undoing the strict public/private boundaries that can marginalize women and other groups. From this perspective, even the seemingly apolitical act of knitting in public can become an activist performance, argues Turney (2009): "Knitting in public becomes a performative activity. . . . This can be understood as the merging or infiltration of the private into the public, and as women reclaiming public spaces for themselves" (144). Bratich and Brush (2011) agree, noting that crafting in public spaces can draw attention to the binaries that have rendered craft, and the women who practice it, as exclusively domestic. "Knitting in public is *out of place*," they write, because "knitting in public turns the interiority of the domestic outward, exposing that which exists within enclosures, through invisibility and through unpaid labor: the production of home life" (237; emphasis original). Many craftivists push this logic further, however, displaying completed products in public spaces. The practice of yarn bombing, for example, is intimately tied to public spaces, as craftivists will use the juxtaposition of domestic materials like yarn against hard, urban objects like parking meters or street signs to "[disrupt] the domestic use of yarn and the public use of space" (Goggin 2015, 151). As a result, argues Wallace (2012), "the spatialities of social life are upset by craftivist interventions, which force a new contemplation of everyday patterns of movement embedded within public, urban space." By bringing craft into the public, yarn bombing forces critical questions about the production of public space, particularly as it relates to gendered (and raced and classed) power relations.

Yarn bombing, and craftivism more generally, thus seeks to blur boundaries between public and private spaces. Specifically, craftivism undermines divisions between feminized domestic spaces and exclusionary public ones and understands this muddling as a radical act in its own right. Greer (2008), for instance, claims that craftivism can have the potential to make public spaces more domestic, as it "individualize[s] and soften[s] the streets we traverse . . . [to] expand the notion of 'home'" (62), while Mandy Moore and Leanne Prain argue that craftivism can shift connotations of craft from a private to a public practice, changing "what can be a very solitary medium to become a very public one" (Moore and Prain 2009, 29). By bringing ostensibly feminine, domestic craft practices into public spaces, craftivism makes an argument about who—and what—belongs in and has the power to construct public places.

It is easy to see how this attitude informs the Cunt Fling-Ups project: Just as it recognizes the rhetorical agency of craft objects (in this case, handcrafted fabric vulvas), it also serves as an argument about how women's bodies are defined in—and often excluded from—public spaces. Fahey and Jenkins explain: "Just because a handful of rich dudes have put their erections all over the city doesn't mean they own the public space. The streets belong to ALL genders & our bodies only to ourselves. We're taking it all back, one fling at a time" ("Cunt Fling-Ups!" 2013). By displaying crafted representations of cis female genitalia in public, Cunt Fling-Ups demonstrate how physical spaces reflect power relationships and suggests that acknowledging the material actors (including physical spaces) that construct those relationships can create the conditions for their reversal.

Another vivid example of craftivism undermining public and private distinctions can be found in the Clothesline Project. Started in 1990 as a way to commemorate survivors and victims of domestic violence, the Clothesline Project has become a well-known international craftivist display ("History of the Clothesline" n.d.). Participants design a T-shirt to mark their (or a loved one's) experience with domestic violence, which is then displayed among others on a clothesline in a public place such as a college campus or city park. The goal is to make the assumed private experience of domestic violence public, creating "alternatives to traditional, mainstream and institutionalized public forums such as legislative bodies which have historically been reluctant to address the issue of violence against women and its cultural bases" (Gregory et al. 2002, 437). The collective craft experience of designing a T-Shirt with materials ranging from markers, paint, embroidery thread and more "presents a challenge to the commonly held opposition of public and private writing, and the position that private, personal texts cannot or do not function to communicate publicly" (Julier 1994, 251). What's more, the physical objects themselves—the shirts, the clothesline, along with the public space they occupy—create "a collective actor," through which "collective political action [is] made possible" (Gregory et al. 2002, 442). Clothesline Project displays, then, use craft objects alongside physical spaces to change conceptions of gendered experiences like domestic labor, intimate partner violence, and textile design from hidden, private affairs to visibly public matters of common concern.

While craftivism offers a clear demonstration of how material objects and physical spaces exert rhetorical agency through their intra-actions with one another, it also productively expands new materialist definitions of "the material" to include the human body. That is, craftivism makes visible the ways in which bodies are themselves material, and how that materiality is marked by power that constrains or enables their agential capacities, often through raced and gendered embodied identities. While craftivism affords agential capacities to nonhuman objects—and, indeed, insists that political action depends on recognizing nonhumans as rhetorical actors—it also recognizes how human agency is mediated through bodies that are marked, politicized, and constrained. Just as the materiality of nonhuman objects shapes their rhetorical capacities, craftivism recognizes how the materiality of human bodies is essential to their position as rhetorical agents. Indeed, it is this valuation of the material specificity of all actors—including humans—that offers craftivism both its ethical framework as well as its political possibilities. For craftivism, bodies matter because bodies are matter.

The political power of bodies is at the center of the Cunt Fling-Ups and Clothesline Project efforts, both of which use the materiality of objects and spaces to make (female) bodies and their ostensibly private experiences public. Similarly, the 5.4 Million Project calls attention to the politicization of gendered bodies, making use of the materiality of gendered bodies as well as the materiality of craft objects. The 5.4 Million Project was organized in response to the US Supreme Court case *Whole Women's Health v. Hellerstedt*, which ruled on the legality of Texas' strict abortion regulations (often called TRAP laws)[4] that resulted in the closure of nearly all the state's abortion clinics and restricted the reproductive rights of "5.4 million women of reproductive age in Texas" (5.4 Million n.d.). Led by artist Chi Nguyen, supporters from around the country embroidered ten-inch fabric squares with tallies meant to represent all 5.4 million Texans affected by the law. These squares were stitched into a larger quilt that participants displayed in front of the Supreme Court during the *Whole Women's Health v. Hellerstedt* hearing on March 2, 2016, and again when the court decided in favor of Whole Women's Health, striking down the restrictive law, on June 27, 2016 (Textile Arts Center 2016.).

The 5.4 Million Project's quilt called attention to gendered bodies—and the laws that govern them—in a number of ways. First, the tallies on each square, together numbering 5.4 million, offered a stark visual representation of all the Texans with uteruses who would potentially be affected by the outcome of the case. The handmade nature of the quilt also called attention to bodies: each tally was stitched by hand, which required substantial bodily labor. Finally, when the quilt was displayed in front of the Supreme Court, both during the case's hearing as well as when the decision came down, it was accompanied by pro-choice activists from both the 5.4 Million project and the National Center for Reproductive Rights (which supported the project, in part). The overall rhetorical effect is one that is deeply attentive to bodies: 5.4 million hand-stitched tallies representing all the people whose reproductive health may be at stake, the embodied labor that produced the quilt, and the bodies holding the quilt all demonstrate how central the (gendered) body is, especially as a location where power centers and is exercised.

In all these examples—Cunt Fling-Ups, the Clothesline Project, and the 5.4 Million Project—women's bodies are refigured as appropriate public actors. This claim on the agential capacities of female bodies is significant, given that legislation, cultural convention, and history too often figure women as passive objects. In this way, craftivism radically extends the new materialist position that nonhuman objects exert rhetorical agency, as it not only highlights the ways in which human bodies can be objectified but also resists that objectification through its claims on the inherent agential capacities of those bodies. For craftivism, human bodies—like any material actor—are political, and like any other material actor, human bodies are both subject to and able to resist normative power relations.

It is through this claim on the rhetorical and political potential of all material actors—objects, locations, and human bodies—that craftivism foregrounds relationality. For craftivism, it is not enough to merely acknowledge the agential capacities of the material (however broadly it is defined); rather, craftivism insists on recognizing the intra-actions that make that agential capacity possible and sees in those intra-actions the possibility for amplifying (or constraining) the power of particular assemblages. Indeed, craftivism rejects the notion that these various agents are separate entities at all and strives to make our mutual co-constituency apparent. This is why craftivists often describe their goal as associative; for them, craftivism is "a catalyst for discussion," a vehicle for "connection with others" (Greer 2008, 101), a means to "build a respectful relationship" (Craftivist Collective 2013) that recognizes that "there is no *us* and *them*" (Greer 2011, emphasis original).

Craftivism's relationality is, in part, due to its intensely process-oriented nature, which strives to shed light on the practices, labor, and power relations that make the assemblages that result in rhetorical action. As a reflection of "an epistemic and an ontological perspective that values *making* over *made*, production over consumerism, and process over product" (Goggin 2015, 155; emphasis original), craftivism asks its participants and its audiences to reflect on how rhetorical assemblages are made, and how those rhetorical assemblages might be made differently. The Boston-based NCAA (New Craft Artists in Action) Net Works project, for example, invites crafters to create hand-knit nets for neglected neighborhood basketball hoops in order to "build proactive relationships between artists, athletes, and neighbors" (quoted in Greer 2014c). Similarly, London-based organization Significant Seams' E17 Neighborhood Quilt project strove to create community relationships through a patchwork map of the Walthamstow neighborhood. Local residents, some of whom donated material for the quilt, marked their homes with a fingerprint in gold paint (Significant Seams 2012). These projects both see the creation of physical things—a quilt or a basketball net—as a means of creating assemblages that share the ultimate goal of bettering the experience of all community members, human and otherwise. Craftivism encourages a consideration of how these intra-actions—between neighbors, locations, and the nonhuman things that populate communities—unfolded in the past, and how they might unfold differently in the future.

Consider one final example of craftivism at work: the hand-embroidered handkerchief that Corbett, founder of Craftivist Collective, created and delivered, in person, to her Member of Parliament (MP). Adorned with the phrase "Don't Blow It!" Corbett explains that her handkerchief was meant to remind her MP "to use her influence to support the vulnerable in society, to help people fulfill their potential, and not to blow her chance of making a positive difference in the world." Corbett credits the handkerchief with creating a relationship between her, her MP, and other constituents, noting that the handkerchief "opened up a respectful conversation between the two of us. Now . . . the hanky is permanently on her constituency office desk to encourage her as an MP" (quoted in Greer 2014d). Corbett's hanky does not advocate for a specific cause; rather, its function is to remind Corbett's MP of her obligation to use her political power wisely and with an eye toward improving lives, both locally and globally. The hanky, then, is an agent in its own right, not just articulating a symbolic message but serving as a material bond between Corbett, her MP, other constituents, and the world they all inhabit.

Craftivism, then, invites reciprocal entanglements between human bodies, nonhuman objects, and the spaces they occupy, and positions these entanglements as the means through which craftivism "transforms the world we live in" (quoted in Greer 2014b). Craftivism goes well "beyond a method of campaigning," argues West (2014), and instead "transforms people, places, and ways of co-existing." While it enacts the new materialist claim that rhetorical action results from the intra-actions between human and nonhuman agents, craftivism's interest in the ethics of these intra-actions, as well as their political significance, is what makes it such a potent illustration of craft agency at work.

CRAFTIVISM'S ETHICS OF ENTANGLEMENT AND COALITIONAL POLITICS

Just as the human body serves as a material interface from which we act with the world, the materiality of the nonhuman actors we act alongside shapes their intra-actions with us and each other. Craftivism recognizes how materiality mediates our entanglements with others (either human or not), and thus insists on materiality's capacities to simultaneously create connections as well as vulnerabilities. That is, craftivism stresses that the process of relating to others is always located within the material specificity of actors and understands that process as both generative and fraught with uncertainty. Because it insists on locating power in materiality, craftivism sees the process of making rhetorical assemblages as an ethical act that carries great political significance.

Craftivism thus adopts an ethics of entanglement that recognizes how the specificity of every actor's materiality shapes their positioning, their values, and their allegiances, which in turn shapes what kind of intra-actions are possible within any given assemblage. As Barad (2007) explains, "The specificity of entanglements is everything" (74); as a result, "any proposal for a new political collective must take account of not merely the practices that produce distinctions between the human and the nonhuman but *the practices through which their differential constitution is produced*" (59; emphasis original). That is, political outcomes are impossible without first adopting an ethics of entanglement that demands that all actors work to understand how the material positioning of their co-actors (and as themselves) guides their needs, goals, and obligations. Agential responsibility, from this perspective, is about recognizing the unique material locations of our mutual intra-actions.

Seeing ourselves as responsively attuned to others this way might be most easily described as *empathy*, which is a familiar concept to many writing studies scholars.[5] Much of this work highlights how empathy necessarily "relies upon some recognition of a self-other overlap for the possibility of understanding another" (Leake 2016, sec. 2, para. 4). Empathy, that is, demands at least some acknowledgment of the degree to which agents construct one another. Importantly, empathy also recognizes the limitations of our embodied, material specificity and is thus "always at best an approximation of understanding" (Leake 2016, sec. 5, para 1). Most discussions of empathy in writing studies, however, frame it as a practice between human actors. Craftivism, however, locates its ethics of entanglement between all agents in a given assemblage, human or not. This ethics—one that is not exclusive to human actors—is very much in line with what Richard Marback (2008) describes as "opening and extending the hand of embodied rhetoric" (59). He proposes that we build upon our understandings of (human) embodiment and the empathy it signals to "[give] the object its due" (59). This reconfiguration, he argues, "requires of us that we embrace mutual vulnerability and forego the claim to agency we make when we project our sovereignty over objects. Substituting our willingness for willfulness. Here the concern is less with the agency of a subject and the forces that subjectify and more with being subject to acting and being acted on"

(59). Marback's argument highlights how an ethics of entanglement requires both a sophisticated understanding of agency (as the result of intra-actions between humans and nonhumans) and an acceptance of the vulnerability that follows the admittance of a lack of total rhetorical sovereignty. Craftivism's ethics of entanglement, then, arises from a willingness to acknowledge both the co-constituency of rhetorical agents as well as an understanding that the particularity of materiality grants only a limited and partial scope of intra-actional possibilities.

Craftivism is in many ways characterized by its desire to create responsivity and openness through people's embodied encounters with craft objects. It is no coincidence, I suggest, that so many craftivists locate craft's political potential in its "non-threatening" reputation (Hamilton 2014). While "traditional forms of activism can be overwhelming" (Hamilton 2014) or "polarizing" (Greer 2014a), craftivists argue that craft's air of "gentility and familiarity" (Hamilton 2014) make craftivism approachable and therefore capable of inviting the kind of openness and attendant vulnerability that are essential to an ethics of entanglement. This understanding of craftivism as an invitational practice[6] is why so many craftivists rely on feminized language to describe their work, labeling it as "gentle" ("What Exactly" n.d.), "quiet" (Greer 2014a) or "nurturing" (Hamilton 2014) activism. While there are, of course, limits to this kind of protest, and such language may perpetuate a regressive, feminized understanding of craft, I suggest that these characterizations also indicate craftivism's potential to create reciprocal, equitable, and ethical entanglements among all actors that constitute a craftivist assemblage.

This ethics of entanglement—one that invites receptivity through its recognition of the co-constructive nature of actors—is what enables craftivism's political possibilities. As the examples above suggest, the goal for craftivism is often less focused toward specific policy outcomes (although that can certainly be a desired result) but to create a *coalition*, an assemblage of actors from which political outcomes might arise. This is a politics that depends upon what Karma R. Chávez (2011) calls "coalitional subjectivity," which, like an ethics of entanglement, "moves away from seeing one's self in singular terms" and, accordingly, moves "toward a complicated intersectional political approach that refuses to view politics and identity as anything other than always and already coalitional" (3). By rejecting the idea that agents are isolated actors and instead insisting on the agential overlaps and co-constituencies that make rhetoric—and political action—possible, craftivism thus understands that politics is a matter of building and sustaining coalitions through material entanglements.

Such an ethics can also ensure that craftivism remains vigilant to the possibility that it may merely perpetuate the power structures it seeks to dismantle. Attunement to co-actors in a craftivist assemblage means acknowledging those agents with less power and reacting accordingly. Craftivism, then, models exactly the kind of transformative, equitable politics that new materialism can foster. Byron Hawk, Chris Lindgren, and Andrew Mara explain that this is a politics that "bring[s] together things, people, and issues to express the material conditions that make politics possible" (Hawk, Lindgren, and Mara 2015, 197). It is, in short, a politics based upon the (re)assemblage of material actors and their intra-actions. Unlike most new materialist approaches, however, craftivism makes the generation of this coalitional politics the goal of all agential entanglements, most notably through its insistence on recognizing not just the material specificity of all agents but also the power relations that produce that specificity.

Through its ethics of entanglement and its coalitional approach to politics, craftivism performs craft agency. It both embraces a new materialist approach to rhetorical agency and values rhetoric as an ethical practice with political consequentiality. Despite the uncritical tendencies of some craftivist iterations to simply recreate exclusionary racist and/or classist power structures, it is still worth examining craftivism's capacities to illuminate the relationship between power and materiality that new materialist rhetorics leave largely unexamined. Craftivism invites awareness of the degree to which all actors are mutually embedded in and constitutive of material circumstances and maintains that political change can only be achieved through recognizing this mutual material entanglement. By locating power in materiality, craftivism is able to acknowledge how varied agents might all meaningfully work together to reshape a more just and equitable world.

4

MANIFESTING MATERIAL RELATIONSHIPS ONLINE THROUGH RAVELRY

Craft, as I've argued, holds many meanings and can, accordingly, serve many functions. Despite this richness, however, one connotation that craft rarely seems to evoke is any relationship to the digital. Even considering its role as inspiration to Lovelace or the vibrant online world of craftivism, craft still seems to be firmly rooted in the physical, not the digital, world. As intensely material phenomena, craft and craft agency rely on and call attention to the way in which physical things (broadly defined to include human bodies, nonhuman objects, and locations) interact and make rhetorical agency possible. Where, then, does the digital fit in this understanding of craft? How does the materiality foregrounded by craft and craft agency manifest itself online? And how does thinking about the materiality of digital spaces change how we study, use, and understand them?

While this book has thus far focused largely on tangible, physical manifestations of craft and craft agency, in this chapter and the next, I expand my framing of the materiality that fuels craft to explore how the digital and material intersect and inform one another. Just as we are not autonomous actors free from the influence of other agents, the digital and material intra-act with each other in significant ways. Understanding this complex relationship can thus highlight "the fundamentally multimodal aspects of *all* communicative practice," as Shipka (2011) notes (13; emphasis original). However, our conceptions of digital too often rely on (and thus perpetuate) a false dichotomy that positions *digital* as wholly separate from and unrelated to *material*, and, as a result, we fail to fully acknowledge their interdependent nature. This chapter begins the task of accounting for this complex relationship, outlining how digital spaces reflect and are reflected in "real" (offline) life. By making the materiality of all online intra-actions visible, I argue that we can better account for the power relations that inform rhetorical agency both online and off.

https://doi.org/10.7330/9781646422555.c004

Here, then, I explore how craft agency functions online through a detailed exploration of Ravelry, a site that connects knitters, crocheters, and other fiber artists to each other and to an impressive database of patterns, yarns, designers, and retailers. Ravelry boasts nearly nine million users—the majority of whom are women—from more than one hundred countries (Ravelry 2020).[1] What makes Ravelry so notable, however, is how it is able to embrace and enact craft agency, even within the confines of its digital interface. On Ravelry, the material assemblages formed by bodies, objects, and locations are not only highly visible, but those assemblages are always figured as the location rhetorical agency. This radical digital materiality, I argue, models how craft agency need not be confined solely to the physical but can be performed even in digital spaces that might otherwise appear to erase or obscure traces of materiality. While Ravelry is afflicted by many of the same privileges that mark craftivism (users are overwhelming white, for example), the kind of intra-actions that emerge on Ravelry not only serve as a starting point for understanding how craft agency operates online but also challenges the perceived separation of the digital and physical.

In this chapter, I draw on interviews with and surveys of Ravelry users ("Ravelers") as well as analysis of the site's interface to explore how craft agency unfolds in this digital community. After a brief review of the knitting literacies and traditions Ravelry emerges from, I provide an overview of the site's functions, users, and interface. I then present a more detailed exploration of Ravelry's digital materiality. Through my research with Ravelers and analysis of the site itself, I demonstrate how Ravelry not only evokes the materiality of objects, locations, and human bodies, but also highlights the intra-actions of these material actors. The craft agency enacted on Ravelry, like craftivism, figures the material specificity of rhetorical agents as a permeable interface where their co-constitutive nature is rendered visible. On Ravelry, however, this interface extends to digital spaces as well. Ravelry thus serves as an example of craft agency's ethics of entanglement. Specifically, I argue that Ravelry's emphasis on reciprocity among humans and nonhumans alike might model how to practice the kind of ethical entanglements that craft agency depends upon.

KNITTING A COMMUNITY: RAVELRY'S CRAFT CULTURE

All digital technologies build upon and reshape older literacy traditions, media, and technologies. Ravelry is no exception, as it emerges largely from the practice of knitting, which—like other domestic crafts—has had multiple, often conflicting, functions in the lives of those who practiced it. While the practice of knitting itself dates back to at least ancient Egypt (Hamilton-Brown 2017; Van Strydonk, De Moore, and Benazeth 2004),[2] most scholarly accounts of knitting and its history are rooted in the West and whiteness specifically. As Black knitter and scholar Lorna Hamilton-Brown (2017) explains, the truth is that "most books on the history of knitting are written by white people," and, as a result, the history of Black knitters in particular still tends to be overlooked (22). While there is no question that knitting was an important practice across many cultures, most analyses of knitting's history focus on its role in the production and maintenance of Western womanhood from the early modern period onward. Like other feminized crafts, knitting in this context was often understood as an important aspect of young women's education, both in formal and informal settings. Not only was it a critical household skill, it was also taught "as a means of instilling discipline and obedience" (Turney 2009, 13) among women of all races and income levels. As the arrival of the industrial revolution and its advances in textile manufacturing "lessened the importance of exclusive home production of necessities" created by women, knitting evolved into a leisure activity that signified white, middle-class feminine domesticity (MacDonald 1988, 175).

Despite its domestic or even restrictive connotations, knitting also provided women an outlet for creative expression and community-making. Anne MacDonald (1988) claims that for women, knitting together transformed a tedious task into an enjoyable one, and knitting eventually became an integral part of many women's social lives: "With cloth manufacture such an indispensable home function, sharing the more arduous tasks with neighbors substituted conviviality for solitary spinning, sewing, carding, dyeing, knitting, and turned the cooperative social activity, or 'bee,' into a highly anticipated affair" (13–14). That is, despite its connotations as a solitary activity, knitting can also be understood "as a collective activity, undertaken by individuals working toward a common aim" (Turney 2009, 175). This collaborative ethos is how many knitting circles and bees became locations for overt political action (as described in more detail in the previous chapter). Thus, even as knitting remained "synonymous with home and motherhood" (MacDonald 1988, 322) well into the twentieth century, it also held political value—even when not channeled directly into activist causes—because of its ability to create and maintain communities of practice, especially among women.

Despite its revolutionary potential, knitting's fundamentally social character is still deeply tied to the domestic sphere. Turney (2009) describes knitting as "both familial and familiar" (5), arguing that the act of knitting "[creates] bonds and relationships between female relatives" (12). Passing down knitting patterns and tools as well as the embodied practice of knitting itself over time allows knitting to act "as a communicative tool, expressing histories that had hitherto been hidden, marginalized or ignored" (Turney 2009, 203). While all knitters make use of established techniques like the cable cast-on or the kitchener stitch, each time they use one of these techniques, its history is rewritten and passed on anew. Suzanne Kesler Rumsey (2009) names this process of handing down communicative, literate practices over time *heritage literacy*, which "describes how literacies and technology uses are accumulated across generations through a decision-making process" (576). While her study of heritage literacy is grounded in the literacy practices of Amish quilters, this term is also well-suited to describe the ways in which knitting—its practices, its products, its cultural associations—has evolved over time. Like Rumsey's Amish quilters, the work of knitting "shows interdependence between generations as the new generation depends on the old for their intellectual inheritances, and the old depends on the new for innovations and adaptations, as well as adoptions of literacy traditions" (490). Knitting, then, may signal deep familial or cultural traditions, but is also fundamentally dynamic, as it changes to suit the needs of different practitioners, purposes, and contexts. Ravelry takes advantage of this fluid quality, building from knitting's social domestic traditions while also repurposing it for contemporary crafters in the digital spaces of the internet.

Although Ravelry was certainly not the first website to address knitters' desire to communicate and create together, it is, according to most Ravelers, the most successful. Spouses Cassidy and Jessica Forbes founded Ravelry in 2007 as a place for knitters, crocheters, and other fiber artists to come together and share patterns and expertise. Ravelry's design encourages making user-created content: its interface emphasizes both the creation of knitted and/or crocheted goods as well as the creation of social connections. As its "About Us" page explains, "The content here is all user-driven; we as a community make the site what it is." (Ravelry n.d.). A reliance on user-created content perhaps explains why a staff of just six can manage a site with over eight million members. Together, Ravelry's users have helped build site content like forums, yarn and pattern search, a help wiki, and a database of millions of completed projects.

Ravelry's unique interactive features are what attracted me to Ravelry, first as a user and then later as a researcher. As a relatively new knitter, both the depth of technical, knitting-related resources and the community's welcoming, supportive spirit impressed me, and it didn't take long for me to become a regular Ravelry user. While I only belong to a few groups and rarely participate in the forums, I use the yarn and pattern search databases often and occasionally post my finished projects. I am certainly not the most active Ravelry user, but my use of the site afforded me a familiarity with its community and interface, which undoubtedly guided my investigation from the dual position of both outsider researcher and community insider. While perhaps more methodologically complex, embracing this position enabled me to undo the strict subject/object (or self/other) dichotomies that can plague research and instead enact the reciprocity that characterizes the site more broadly.

My status as a fellow knitter and Ravelry user thus shaped the research relationships I developed throughout my research on and with the community. From this unique vantage point, I created a study that relied on a variety of data: rhetorical analysis of the site's interface, design, and language, secondary research on and about Ravelry, and person-based research (specifically, survey and interview data).[3] Because I posted all recruitment requests through my personal Ravelry account, potential participants could click through to view my profile and site activity, confirming my position as someone who knew and participated in the community. Throughout this chapter, I incorporate results from this study, which includes survey responses from sixty-one participants as well as interviews with three Ravelry users: Audrey, an academic woman in her thirties; Lynn, a woman in her fifties who works in a yarn store; and Helen, who describes herself as a "middle-aged, middle class woman."[4]

While it's difficult to get a precise sense of just who is using Ravelry—in part because Ravelry itself doesn't track such information[5]—my participants suggest that Ravelry users are, by and large, a relatively privileged group of women. My survey data, while by no means a representative sample, indicated that most Ravelers have social, racial, and economic advantages not typical of women around the globe. Most (75%) respondents indicated that they lived in North America, most (73%) are married, most (78%) have obtained an undergraduate or graduate degree, and, perhaps most notably, an overwhelming majority (92%) noted their race as some variant of "white" or "Caucasian." Although I do not claim that this data represents all Ravelry users, it does suggest that Ravelers—specifically those whose experiences I analyze throughout this chapter—are well-educated, financially secure, and racially privileged.

There are likely many reasons why Ravelers represent a generally privileged group of women. One may be the practice of knitting itself.

Figure 4.1. #diversknitty search on Instagram (screenshot by author).

Although there are certainly those who knit out of financial necessity, contemporary knitting is, in many respects, a leisure activity that
requires both time and money, especially in Western nations. As a result,
knitting is vulnerable to many of the same criticisms that plague craftivism or craft more generally: namely, that as the province of economically privileged white women, knitting is inherently conservative. It is
important to emphasize that knitters and fiber crafters of all races and
ethnicities exist, despite the overall whiteness of the knitting world. Just
browse the Instagram hashtag #diversknitty (figure 4.1) or consult the
directory of designers, dyers, artists, and organizations on the website

BIPOC in Fiber for evidence that knitters are not and never have been exclusively white. Yet, these efforts at visibility are relatively recent: as Black knitter Jeanette Sloan (2018) writes, "I grew up in the 1970's in a household where my mother was a crafter but I don't remember ever seeing one picture of a black person knitting or crocheting in any textbook or painting" (para. 8). More pointedly, Hamilton-Brown (2017) recalls being told by a white academic, "Black people don't knit." Stories like these only underscore just how central whiteness has been to the knitting world as a whole.

These concerns about representation and privilege in the knitting community have recently become more visible than ever. In early 2019, a white knitter blogged on a different site about a trip to India she had planned; many, however, read this post as not merely culturally insensitive but fully imperialistic. This incident incited a flurry of discussions about racism in the knitting world. As Jaya Saxena (2019) wrote in Vox, "Hundreds of people of color have shared stories of being ignored in knitting stores, having white knitters assume they were poor or complete amateurs, or flat-out saying they didn't think black or Asian people knit" (sec. 2, para. 4). These experiences suggest that the knitting community continues to perpetuate harmful and exclusionary practices and narratives that position it as not merely homogeneous but completely regressive.

The fact that so many knitters of color feel unwelcome in the larger knitting world likely informs the demographics of Ravelry. Because knitting is so strongly raced and classed, it follows that those who do not fit within the conventional image of knitters (middle- or upper-class white women) may not choose to knit or may not seek to join a community of knitters that so strongly embodies the stereotypical knitter identity. Issues of internet access also inevitably intersect with Ravelry's demographics: knitters who cannot reliably or regularly access the internet obviously have a much lower likelihood of joining the site. Ravelry's userbase thus strongly mirrors the privileged identity categories that characterize the knitting world more generally.

For its part, Ravelry seems aware of the privilege endemic to the knitting world and is taking steps to make its community more inclusive—even if some critics argue those steps are not effective enough. Ravelry and its users have always skewed a bit to the left and small gestures of inclusion have been common from the site's founding: the small rainbow flag at the bottom of each Ravelry page, for example, is a simple signal of support for the LGBTQ + community. Recently, however, Ravelry has become more aggressive in making sure its community is welcoming for users who deviate from the stereotypical knitting norm. In June 2019, Ravelry announced it would no longer allow users to post support of Donald Trump or his administration. As the policy explains, "We cannot provide a space that is inclusive of all and also allow support for open white supremacy. Support of the Trump administration is undeniably support for white supremacy" (Ravelry 2019). While the response to this new policy was generally positive (Clark 2019), some knitters did express doubts about its efficacy. Unfinished Object, a collective for crafters of color, explained in a blog post that they were unsure if this policy would matter in the long term. After all, they reasoned, "Banning Trump supporters does not address white supremacy in its all-pervasive form" (Sukrita 2019).[6] No matter the outcome of the policy, however, it is clear that Ravelry still has much work to do to diversify its user base.

With such a privileged group of users, Ravelry is likely a rather exclusionary community. At least one of my interview participants seemed to share this sentiment. Audrey told me that her experiences in the community suggested that Ravelers were "privileged" and "hugely white." However, most participants did not seem particularly attuned to or even aware of this possibility, as the vast majority of Ravelers I surveyed or interviewed described the community as "friendly," "kind," and "welcoming." Ravelers, in other words, largely don't see racism or exclusion as a problem on the site and, in fact, value Ravelry most for the community and social interactions it provides. Of those surveyed, 86 percent said that they use the site to talk to other knitters. These users said that Ravelry offers them "some sense of belonging to a community" and opportunities "to connect with others." While it is likely that Ravelry's racial homogeneity contributes to the sense of community so valued by participants, it is clear that Ravelers have strongly positive feelings about the site as a whole. Overall, participants offered a great deal of praise for Ravelry, calling it a "wonderful site," a "very effective and efficient space," and "a well-designed, intuitive site [that is] easy and enjoyable to use." Indeed, when I asked survey participants about their *least* favorite part of Ravelry, fifteen of the forty-nine participants who responded said that there was either nothing difficult about the site at all, or that Ravelry is "so exciting you forget to knit."

Even mainstream media outlets have noted Ravelry's remarkable ability to attract near-obsessive devotion from its users. Farhad Manjoo (2011) at *Slate* suggests that "what makes Ravelry work so well is that, in addition to being a place to catch up with friends, it is also a boon to its users' favorite hobby—it helps people catalog their yarn, their favorite patterns, and the stuff they've made or plan on making. In other words, there is something to *do* there" (para. 2; emphasis original). Communication scholar Maria Hellstrom (2013) agrees, writing that although "Ravelry's social network requires a lot of labour, . . . this is to a great extent work knitters themselves have determined to be important and meaningful" (7). Users are, in fact, doing a lot of work on Ravelry: Together, they've knit up over five billion kilometers of yarn, adding seven thousand new projects every day (Ravelry 2014). Almost 90 percent of users who responded to my survey say they visit the site daily—even though just 69 percent said they knit daily. Clearly, Ravelry is doing more than just helping users knit.

How exactly does Ravelry manage to draw together so many users, and what exactly are they *doing*, if not knitting? Ravelry is a highly interactive site that expects its users to contribute. And contribute they do: Ravelry currently houses over seven-hundred thousand knit and crochet patterns (some free, others for sale),[7] a database of more than one-hundred thousand distinct yarns, as well as thousands of groups and forums focused on content as varied as knitting techniques, local yarn stores, yarn swaps, politics, and even specific television shows. The user contributions that keep Ravelry functioning are the result of both a community and an interface that encourages users to see themselves first and foremost as active contributors, not passive consumers. Together, then, users, along with the interface that guides their interactions, enact a craft agency focused on the creation of assemblages in both digital and physical locations.

Users' contributions, like any activity on Ravelry, are mediated by the site's interface, which relies heavily on fill-in-the-blank-style templates for user productions within the site. These templates are easy to use and create uniformity among entries, making them easily searchable. However, there are significant limitations to this kind of interface, which Kristin Arola (2010) has criticized for their tendency to "render form standardized and invisible" (4). Users are also left with "little control over a large part of [their] representation," obscuring "the ways in which design functions to make meaning and produce selves" (Arola 2010, 7). Ravelry, in some respects, falls victim to this content-form split. User profiles (figure 4.2) are fairly limited, including only basic information such as first name, profile picture (alongside more irreverent questions like "fave curse word"), as well as the option to include additional textual or visual "about me" information via a WYSIWYG (What-You-See-Is-What-You-Get) editor.

Even with these limitations, however, Ravelry's fill-in-the-blank-style profiles highlight how specific identities emerge from the intra-actions

smartypants989

edit profile	First name	Leigh
	My pronouns are	she/her
	Raveler since	February 10, 2012
	Online?	🟢 yes
	Website or blog	
	Location	🏴 Opelika, Alabama
I'm in 7 groups	Pets? Kids?	A corgi and a kitty.
	Favorite colors	
ANTHROPOLOGIE	Fave curse word	Fuck. It's syntactically flexible and satisfying to say.
	About me	

Figure 4.2. My Ravelry user profile (screenshot by author).

of various human and nonhuman actors. The data fields provided indicate that users are defined through their entanglements with others, both online and off: profiles ask users to share if they have children or pets and automatically display any groups the user belongs to. The equal valuation of digital and physical presence is further reinforced by the default displaying of the users' physical and digital location, noting both the city/nation that the user resides in as well as if they are currently logged in to Ravelry or not. Importantly, however, user profiles are just one of many locations in which intra-active identities are crafted on Ravelry. Site activity like group affiliations, individual projects, and friendships with other users all emphasize users' positions within the larger assemblages they inhabit, situating identity, and making itself, as an intra-active process.

Perhaps the location that is most significant in terms of assembling Ravelers' identities is the project page, where users display their knitted work, both completed and in-progress. In many ways, the project page digitizes and publicizes the traditional genre of a knitting journal. Ravelers can include notes on the project, which can vary from tracking progress, reasons for knitting the projects, and any modifications made to the pattern, as well as photos of the project (either finished or in-progress). All three interview participants said that they use the project page: Lynn explained that she keeps notes on projects to remind herself of "the reason why I made it at the time," calling her notes "more of an internal dialogue," and Helen similarly views it as a way of keeping a record of her knitting. Audrey was even more explicit, pointing to the project page as one of the primary locations from which she assembles her identity on Ravelry: "When it comes to who I am on Ravelry," she told me, "I can make this mythical cohesive identity [through my projects]. . . . And I think it also kind of shows my evolution in knitting." Importantly, the project page also offers significant connective capacities: Users can link their projects through Ravelry's database to specify what pattern and yarn they used, and even link to the store where the yarn was purchased, thus foregrounding the various people, tools, and locations that made the making of a specific assemblage possible.

Thus, while the interfaces that govern user-created content like the project page are fairly limited, they do emphasize Ravelry's self-consciously collaborative, intra-active approach to identity production and rhetorical action, and, on a practical level, makes organizing the vast quantities of information on Ravelry much easier. Indeed, participants cited Ravelry's cross-listed databases of yarns, patterns, tools, vendors, and projects as one of the site's most useful functions. Ninety-eight percent of Ravelers who took my survey said that they use the site to locate patterns and/or yarn, and many spoke enthusiastically about this feature. When I asked survey participants to identify the most valuable aspects of Ravelry, 63 percent of open responses specifically praised these databases. One survey participant, for example, explained that "Ravelry has some really great search features that also make it easier to find and compare specific kinds of patterns." Ravelry's fill-in-the-blank-style templates are what enable the cross-listed search functions that users value, and, just as importantly, they emphasize the intra-actions—online and off, among humans and nonhumans—that produce Ravelry's rhetorical capacities.

Given its multiple functions, it is perhaps unsurprising that participants spoke highly of Ravelry's interface. All three of the women I interviewed praised it. Audrey called the site "very accessible," and Helen described the interface as "extremely well thought-out and extremely well designed." Lynn, who says she's "not the most techno-savvy," believes Ravelry was intentionally designed to be easy to use: "I think whatever [Ravelry co-founder Cassidy] has done, [she's] done an amazing job. . . . I mean, [she's] really set it up for non-technical people. And I think we go on there not because we're techno but because we're trying to find patterns." In a podcast interview, Ravelry co-founder Jessica Forbes confirmed Lynn's suspicion that the site was designed for "non-technical people," explaining that she and her spouse always make design decisions with special concern for ease and intuitiveness: "We want it to be really accessible for people to come on and know what it is, like 'oh, okay this is where you add your projects, or this is where you can talk to people about this subject.' So we do want to make it as simple and concise as possible" (Wade 2011). Cassidy Forbes explains that this accessibility is important, as it encourages Ravelers to "[use] the organizational tools" and "contribute to the yarn and pattern directory" (Bray 2009). The simplicity of Ravelry's interface thus offers specific affordances as well as corresponding constraints: While it may limit how Ravelers use the site, it also encourages them to use it in particular ways that emphasize the intra-active, ecological nature of digital and physical making.

Together, then, both Ravelry's users as well as its interface make the materiality of rhetoric visible, even online. In the next section, I present a detailed analysis that examines exactly how Ravelry foregrounds the material. By valuing the entanglements that bind material actors, Ravelry enacts a reciprocity that predicates ethical action and political outcomes on the dismantling of the boundaries that separate self and other as well as human and nonhuman. The radical reciprocity at work on Ravelry is not just a potent illustration of how craft agency's ethics of entanglement function online but also works to undermine the distinctions that separate physical and digital altogether.

MAKING THE MATERIAL VISIBLE ONLINE

Ravelry is able to enact craft agency in the ostensibly ephemeral digital world because of its ability to make the material—tools, physical objects, locations, and, of course, human bodies—visible. In fact, these material actors are the center of the Ravelry community, as most of the site's functions revolve around them in some way. On Ravelry, online activity and "real life" experiences are not mutually exclusive; they complement and enrich one another. Whether in photos of completed patterns, local yarn shop pages, or through the users' offline knitting labor, "reminders of the offline, material world are always present on Ravelry" (Hellstrom 2013, 19). Hellstrom argues that a Raveler's offline work (or, more precisely, the digital representation of that offline work) helps to strengthen digital ties: "Ravelers have found a way of translating manual labour offline into an affective reality within their online social space, and through this translation they reap positive benefits in the form of community-building and social capital" (55). In other words, while Ravelry's interface enables users to represent or even create local alliances and texts, the community itself helps to reinforce the sense that online and offline worlds are inseparable. With these reminders, Ravelry demonstrates how important materiality is to making, even in digital spaces.

It may seem counterintuitive to locate a community so invested in the production of material goods—knitted and crocheted items—online. After all, users cannot touch yarn for sale, or physically examine a completed object to determine its fit, weight, and texture. Instead, they must rely on the details provided and mediated by Ravelry's interface, which does a remarkable job of centering materiality in a number of ways, from its interest in material things such as knitted objects or tools, to its focus on embodied experiences, as well as its attentiveness to physical locations. Ravelry recognizes how all these material actors play a role in making, and thus works to center them—as well as the intra-actions that construct them—throughout its digital landscape.

Perhaps the most obvious indicator of Ravelry's emphasis on materiality is found in its relentless encouragement to *make*. For example, the "Welcome to Ravelry!" video tour begins by showing users how to *create* on Ravelry. Before showing users how to browse data on patterns and yarns, it first explains how to create a profile and how to update the project notebook. This video, meant to introduce new users to Ravelry and its features, privileges production (of material projects) over consumption (of digital information on patterns, yarns, and stores) in Ravelers' use of the site. This dynamic is only reinforced by the design of the site itself. The "my notebook" tab, located on the top right of the page, contains all of a user's work on Ravelry, including the project notebook, a queue (of projects to knit), a digital "stash" listing the physical yarn a user has accumulated at home, and an inventory of tools like knitting needles and crochet hooks. Even when browsing patterns or yarns, users are encouraged to interact—digitally and physically—with the content, with options to "save to favorites," "add to queue," or even "cast on project" (the technical term for "start knitting"). By making the physical tools, processes, and results of knitting so central to the site's functions, Ravelry encourages users to see themselves first and foremost as active makers.

Several participants spoke about how Ravelry's interface can motivate them to craft objects. The searchable databases, for example, offer rich visual representations of any particular yarn or pattern, which can in turn help users develop new projects. For Audrey, the yarn search feature helps her imagine new uses for materials she already has: "Sometimes I look through the yarn that I already have at home and then I'll start with the yarn . . . all this stuff is cross listed. So, it's like, 'ok I have this stuff, what can I make with it?'" Even if a user logs on to Ravelry without a specific goal in mind, its production-oriented design can prompt users to make (mostly material) things, as Lynn explains. "I knitted this pair of daffodil [baby] booties because I saw it listed in one of the forums. Now, do I have any babies in my life? No. Did it make my husband a little nervous? Yes. . . . I had to make them because they were adorable! You know, so would I have ever seen that anywhere else? No. So . . . do I knit things that maybe I would have never knitted? Yeah." Because Ravelry's interface puts so much emphasis on making (and often provides the means for that making, in terms of patterns, information about yarn, notes from other users, etc.), Ravelers are encouraged to physically produce what Ravelry's interface digitally represents.

Photographs are especially important in terms of achieving this digital materiality: They provide an indication of what finished objects look like, and how specific patterns or tools might function in actual use. Photographs of knitted goods abound on Ravelry, from the front-page blog to the pattern search functions, or even in the forums.[8] These images are particularly valuable for users planning new projects. Because users can link an individual project to its source pattern (as archived in Ravelry's pattern database), users can see multiple versions of the same pattern knit by different Ravelers. Some patterns have hundreds of versions, knit by different individuals using different yarns, colors, techniques, and sizing. Survey participants appreciate how this feature helps them to "see what a pattern looks like with a substituted yarn," and noted that "seeing how other knitters complete a pattern [helps] me plan my own project." All three interview participants agreed that photographs, particularly within the pattern search, play a crucial role in their Ravelry usage. Photographs are "really important" for Audrey, and Lynn insisted that she "will not knit a pattern that doesn't have a picture on it." Helen said that when she's searching for patterns, she "go[es] a lot by the visuals. The pictures are probably the most important thing, and if [she] like[s] the way a finished object looks, then [she'll] consider it." For these Ravelers, digital traces of materiality (that is, photographs) are essential to the site's functionality.

Just as Ravelry's photo-heavy interface draws attention to material objects and tools, representations of physical knitted labor also work to foreground the material body: after all, a hand-knit sweater requires a pair of hands. Even though the body is implicitly present in the many photos of knitted goods that populate Ravelry, photographs of actual bodies are also visible all over Ravelry, from users' avatars to project photos where users model their finished products. Photos of bodies wearing completed projects are especially valued by the community, because it helps users imagine, as one survey participant put it, "what patterns look like when actually knit up and [worn] on other human bodies."

Audrey explained that she likes to "look at people's different versions of [a project] to see [how] actual knitters who aren't the designers style the photos, what their actual projects actually look like, what it looks like on a body. My dream is to find a knitter who's better than me and has the same measurements as me and I can just knit everything they do after them." Helen also appreciates when users model the projects they have completed because it helps her judge sizing: "For example, with mittens, I have very small hands. If somebody says that they knit the size small and I see that it looks kind of gigantic on theirs I'll know it's not a pattern for me. My husband, on the other hand, has pretty large hands so if somebody knits a large size glove, and they look tight, then I know I'll either have to find another pattern or do the math and size it up." Seeing others' bodies, especially in relation to completed projects, helps users make design choices in their own work, and, as a result, bodies are never far from view on Ravelry.

Even in Ravelry's more text-heavy locations, users' bodies—and their embodied experiences—are never entirely obscured. Indeed, these embodied experiences can provide social capital within the Ravelry community, especially in the forums, where knitting expertise is highly valued. Survey participants pointed to the forums as an important means of accessing the knowledge of fellow Ravelers, describing them as "a crowd-sourced education." For these Ravelers, the forums—and, specifically, the experienced knitters who populate them—are "a really valuable resource for all kinds of knitting" that can "help me out of a sticky spot or give me a different perspective on how to solve a problem or learn something new." Because the forums offer a "wealth of knowledge" that can ultimately "improve knitting skills," they are an essential part of the site's functionality, particularly for the 74 percent of survey participants who indicated that they use Ravelry to learn more about knitting. On Ravelry, though, the expertise found in the forums is located specifically in embodied experiences, as participants said that they value how the site offers them access to "real" knitters and appreciate "seeing what stuff looks like after [being] finished by real people rather than the experts." By positioning expertise as the result of embodied experiences—rather than something to be found in less tangible sources like instructional books—Ravelry thus figures the material body as an important actor that deserves appropriate recognition both online and off.

Many participants also noted that they get more than just knitting-related assistance on Ravelry. Several described Ravelry as an important social space where they can discuss "anything and everything." "We share parts of our everyday lives," one Raveler explained, noting that their communications with other users are "a lot like chatting with good friends." Survey participants overwhelmingly described the community in positive terms, characterizing their fellow Ravelers as "respectful, thoughtful, considerate," "very supportive," and "kind and helpful."[9] Many explained that the Ravelry community provides "social connection," and functions much like "a large family." Some participants even claimed that Ravelry acts as their primary location for social interaction. One wrote, "as a single, work-at-home parent . . . I don't get out much. [Ravelry] groups make up the bulk of my 'social life,'" while another noted, "I am a widow and this is a window into the world. . . . With Ravelry I am alone but not alone." The social ties built on Ravelry are for these users just as real and fulfilling as any face-to-face connection, as they see their interactions on Ravelry not as disembodied text but as a means of building alliances with other humans.

These alliances can take on crucial support functions for some users. Helen told me that she joined a cancer support group on Ravelry while both her parents were battling cancer. Lynn also noted that she often turns to Ravelry for encouragement and comfort: "If it hadn't been for Ravelry . . . it's helped me through a divorce, you know, just having support. It helped me through the death of my mom [and] moving. . . . It's like a female support group. I see it a lot of times like an old-fashioned quilting bee, where you go out and you all get together and chatter and talk. . . . And I find that very supportive that way." Notably, five separate survey participants described Ravelry as a "safe" space in an open response. One of these participants specifically attributed this sense of safety to the lack of men on Ravelry. She wrote that she "feel[s] more free to speak there [Ravelry] than many other places. . . . The lack of 'mansplaining' is wonderful for a change!" For at least two participants, then, the perceived—and actual—lack of men in the community creates a sense of safety and support. While it's also likely that the racial homogeneity of Ravelry's community might also result in this sense of safety, it is notable how at least some shared embodied performances (such as gender) or experiences (like dealing with a loved one's cancer diagnosis) can create the condition for intra-actions on Ravelry.

While its emphasis on objects and bodies are perhaps the most obvious manifestation of Ravelry's robust materiality, its persistent attention to physical location also demonstrates Ravelry's continual commitment to making the material visible. Many participants reported using the site to connect with local communities, either by strengthening existing local ties or fostering new ones. In part, this is because Ravelry's features make it easy: Clicking on the groups tab, for example, will bring up "browse groups by location" as the first search parameter. Group forums are in fact one of the primary means by which users connect to local knitters. Audrey called the forums "very place-based besides being online," explaining that "when [she] moved . . . [she] tried to join all the local groups [she] could find." Others use forums for "sharing local information," or to organize meetups. Lynn told me that she uses group forums to locate other Ravelers when she travels. "I've contacted groups that I'm going to be in the area. . . . I did that when we went to England, that was really cool. . . . I went to a group there, it was wonderful." Users can even search for nearby yarn spinners and dyers in the yarn database, which offers a location search parameter for those who wish to buy materials from local producers.

In addition to these search features, Ravelry also connects users to local communities by offering brick-and-mortar local, independent yarn stores the ability to create a page. These pages show information about the store, its staff, its yarn, and its patrons. Ravelry cofounder Jessica Forbes says that she and her staff try to make these local yarn stores visible on Ravelry because they are key to sustaining any knitting community. "We do try to think about our local stores as much as we can. It's so important that they're around, and healthy and happy," she explained on the *Fiber Beat* podcast (Wade 2011). Ravelry even enables users to link back to the local yarn store from which they bought the materials used for a specific project (figure 4.3). Audrey told me that she uses this feature often because "part of my Ravelry persona is showing that I support local yarn shops, and when we travel, I try to buy yarn for specific projects and then tag the store when I make it." Audrey is making a rhetorical choice—one enabled by Ravelry's interface—to demonstrate support for local communities and economies. Ravelry tries to make this kind of local shopping as easy as possible, even offering a "road trip planner" tool that will list all local yarn shops located along a given route. Rather than existing in a separate, isolated online space, then, Ravelry is uniquely enmeshed in users' local, lived experiences and values local entanglements both online and off.

Ravelry's interest in foregrounding physical location does not simply revolve around individual users, however. The site takes care to highlight the geographic diversity of all Ravelers. A national flag denoting a user's home country appears as part of their avatar, and while the vast majority of site content is in English, it is common to come across a pattern written in several languages (some translations are even provided courtesy of multilingual users).[10] The Ravelers I

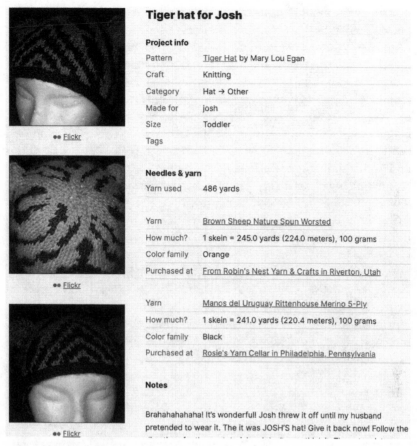

Tiger hat for Josh

Project info

Pattern	Tiger Hat by Mary Lou Egan
Craft	Knitting
Category	Hat → Other
Made for	josh
Size	Toddler
Tags	

Needles & yarn

Yarn used	486 yards

Yarn	Brown Sheep Nature Spun Worsted
How much?	1 skein = 245.0 yards (224.0 meters), 100 grams
Color family	Orange
Purchased at	From Robin's Nest Yarn & Crafts in Riverton, Utah

Yarn	Manos del Uruguay Rittenhouse Merino 5-Ply
How much?	1 skein = 241.0 yards (220.4 meters), 100 grams
Color family	Black
Purchased at	Rosie's Yarn Cellar in Philadelphia, Pennsylvania

Notes

Brahahahahaha! It's wonderful! Josh threw it off until my husband pretended to wear it. The it was JOSH'S hat! Give it back now! Follow the

Figure 4.3. Lynn's "Tiger Hat for Josh" project, with materials linked to local yarn stores (screenshot by author).

spoke to value this geographic diversity (and the varied knitting expertise and traditions it brings). Lynn told me during our interview that seeing patterns and techniques from all over the world has made her a more "international knitter," and survey participants noted that they appreciate how "knitters all over the world" populate Ravelry, which affords them access to "a worldwide community . . . [that provides] knowledge about cultures and shared similarities/differences between communities in different geographical areas." Others simply "like reading about other people's lives in different parts of the world." On Ravelry, then, physical space is not secondary to digital space; rather, the materiality of location is never far from view and, in fact, informs many of the intra-actions on the site.

Ravelry is unique not just in its ability to make materiality so visible, but because it is able to define materiality so robustly, even within the confines of a digital community. On Ravelry, materiality—in the form of digital texts like images, alphabetic texts, and videos as well as physical things like knitting tools, bodies, and places—guides the site's function and the community's behavior. While the digital and material are always intertwined in any online community, Ravelry is notable because it makes this relationship so conspicuous, as users are constantly reminded of the material actors that surround them and make their work (both on Ravelry and off) possible. This affordance likely has much to do with the materiality of the knitted object itself: Regardless of its source, knitters often value an object's visual appearance (and all that it connotes such as personal style or functionality) when choosing a new project. But Ravelry is able to translate this offline materiality into the condition for action online, thus redefining the material itself to include both physical *and* digital elements. Through Ravelry's insistence on acknowledging and actively valuing the material intra-actions between actors that enable and inform rhetorical action, it not merely demonstrates how craft agency can function just as effectively online as it does in more overtly physical modes, but it refuses the distinctions between the two altogether.

Consider, for, example, Ravelry's Ravellenic Games, held in concert with the Summer and Winter Olympics.[11] An expanded form of a knit/crochet-along (where various users will work on the same pattern at the same time), the Ravellenic Games highlights the craft agency that is at the heart of Ravelry. Either individually or in teams (teams are sometimes based on location, sometimes based on other affinities), users participate in various events of their choosing, with the goal to complete at least one project during the Olympics. The most recent Ravellenics, held during the 2018 Winter Olympics in Pyeongchang, featured events such as "bag biathlon" and "sweater skeleton," and inspired more than 11,000 separate projects among 4,660 users. Completed projects receive medals (in the form of badges users can add to their profiles or personal blogs), and various techniques such as cabling, weaving, and felting also receive special recognition. Events like the Ravellenic Games or other knit/crochet-alongs gather both human users and nonhuman things (such as Ravelry message boards and knitting tools) around the making of specific objects and make clear just how vital the intra-actions that bind these material actors are to the process of making. Without a pattern to work by, or the code that creates badges that motivate knitters, or the athletic bodies that Ravelers watch during the Ravellenic Games, the projects that resulted from this event would not exist, at least not in their current iterations. Making, in this case and all others on Ravelry, results from entanglements between humans and nonhumans, online and off.

RAVELRY'S RADICAL RECIPROCITY

While Ravelry may be notable as an innovative and successful social media platform, it is the site's digital materiality that makes it most significant from a new materialist point of view. Ravelry is not only able to foreground materiality (in terms of physical objects, human bodies, and locations) in digital spaces, but to position rhetorical action—even online—as the result of the intra-actions of these material actors. Ravelry, like craftivism, thus models the ethics of entanglement necessary for craft agency. However, it also invites us to think more critically about the practices of reciprocity that mark this ethics of entanglement; specifically, Ravelry demonstrates that reciprocity is not limited to humans alone but instead can also guide nonhuman intra-action as well. In doing so, Ravelry highlights the mutually constitutive, interdependent relationship between the digital and material.

Reciprocity is perhaps most readily associated with feminist scholarship, even if it is typically confined within discussions of feminist research methodologies where it is invoked to describe how researchers deliberately construct their relationships with participants (Cushman 1996; Kirsch 1999; Powell and Takayoshi 2003). Cushman (1996), for example, describes reciprocity as "an open and conscious negotiation of the power structures reproduced during the give-and-take interactions of the people involved on both side of [a research] relationship" (16). Reciprocity, in other words, is rooted in respect for the agency of those we enter into research relationships with, even if those others have historically been defined as exclusively human.

Reciprocity also figures prominently in Indigenous knowledge traditions. However, given that Indigenous thinking has also always acknowledged the agency of nonhumans, reciprocity is seen as similarly expansive. As Grant (2017) explains, "For many indigenous people, the nonhuman beings of the world . . . have agency because they have always had agency; reciprocity with them is a given" (80). In Indigenous frameworks, then, reciprocity is an ethical practice that both acknowledges the agential capacities of nonhumans while also seeing that agency as limited, partial, and co-constitutive: "An ethic of reciprocity is a practice of attending to the way our existence is interdependent with networks of relations of other humans and non-humans. It is a practice of considering the consequences of our actions," writes Rosiek, Snyder, and Scott L. Pratt (Rosiek, Snyder, and Pratt 2020, 340). Reciprocity, from this perspective, emerges from an awareness that we are always the result of our intra-actions with others—others which are not always or even primarily human.

An understanding of reciprocity focused on the intra-actions that bind all actors, human and nonhuman, within a new materialist assemblage, is thus essential for the ethics of entanglement I am arguing for. Reciprocity, in this formation, emerges from the entanglements of actors who recognize that even if other actors in a given assemblage do not necessarily share the same point of view or obligations, the agential capacities that arise from their intra-actions necessitate careful reflection and deliberation about how to relate to one another. An ethics of entanglement, rooted in this sense of reciprocity, thus asks how the intra-actions between humans and nonhumans alike may perpetuate or dismantle power inequities, and what kind of coalitions might result from those intra-actions. Reciprocity, then, positions the dismantling of subject/object boundaries as an ethical act, and sees the formation of the assemblages that result as politically powerful.

The kind of reciprocity at work on Ravelry is useful for understanding the relationship between the physical and the digital more generally. Physical things—knitting needles, local yarn stores, or human bodies—are not self-contained units demarcating individual actors but rather a point of convergence where the intra-actions that produce us become visible. Figuring these material actors as permeable works to undermine tidy distinctions between self and other, as agents bleed into each other such that they become co-constitutive. The physical, in other words, does not disappear online. Importantly, however, Ravelry also suggests how the digital is likewise inseparable from the physical: On Ravelry, physical things both construct and are constructed by digital actors. Thus, rather than thinking of the digital and the physical as separate entities, Boyle, James J. Brown, and Steph Ceraso argue that "*the digital* is no longer conditional on particular devices but has become a multisensory, embodied condition through which most of our basic processes operate" (Boyle, Brown, and Ceraso 2018, 252; emphasis original). The digital, that is, is not somehow apart from the body or physicality more generally; rather, it is "everywhere and nowhere, everything and nothing, invisible and ever present" (Boyle, Brown, and Ceraso 2018, 258). The craft agency at work on Ravelry thrives in this blurry middle ground, emerging from reciprocal entanglements between nonhuman and human, digital and physical, actors.

It is no accident that such a robust understanding of the ethics of entanglement are found on a website devoted to craft. Ravelry is rooted in craft practices that understand the co-constituency of all actors and models practices of reciprocity that respect the mutual entanglements that are critical for making. As she knits, the body of the Raveler becomes one with the yarn, the needles, the digital patterns she references, and the world that surrounds them. Together, they make something altogether new as they make each other. Knitting—like all craft—is only possible through this entanglement, which embraces subject and object as one and the same. As the Raveler rejects the rigid binaries that position self and other, human and nonhuman, digital and material as wholly separate, she finds the grounds for solidarity and political action. A potent depiction of how craft agency emerges online, Ravelry serves as a model for the kind of ethically engaged, politically potent new materialist rhetorics we require.

5

THE WOMEN'S MARCH, DIGITAL-
MATERIAL ASSEMBLAGES, AND
EMBODIED DIFFERENCE

On a cloudy Saturday in January 2017, the day after the inauguration of Donald Trump as the forty-fifth president of the United States, roughly half a million people took to the streets of Washington, DC. Across the country, another 3.6 to 4.6 million more people joined them in sister marches (Wortham 2017). All told, political scientists estimated more than 1 in 100 Americans marched that day (Franke-Ruta 2017), along with hundreds of thousands more in at least 261 other countries (Chenoweth and Pressman 2017). Together, these protesters joined forces to participate in the Women's March, a massive and inevitably contentious movement that aimed to, as its organizers claimed, "affirm our shared humanity and pronounce our bold message of resistance and self-determination" (Women's March 2017).

Born on Facebook, the Women's March relied heavily on digital tools like social media platforms and mobile devices. Indeed, it is difficult to imagine the Women's March (or any other modern protest movement, for that matter) achieving such a massive scale, both in terms of sheer numbers of protesters and media attention, without such technologies. Digital artifacts like live streams, photos, and text messages helped protesters communicate with each other and with the broader world and were undoubtedly central to the successes of the Women's March. Perhaps the most recognizable symbols of the march, however, were the copious physical (and often hand-crafted) objects that saturated the crowds of marchers. Many protesters wore pink knit hats with cat ears—dubbed "Pussyhats"—while others carried signs advocating causes ranging from women's rights, racial justice, health care, religious freedom, general anti-Trump sentiment, and much more. Together, these artifacts signal how craft agency collapses boundaries between the digital and the physical, building ethically attuned assemblages of human and nonhuman agents. Like Ravelry, the 2017 Women's March illustrates the rhetorical value of a capacious understanding of materiality—one

https://doi.org/10.7330/9781646422555.c005

that values both physical and digital, as well as human and nonhuman agents. However, the Women's March used this radically redefined materiality in service of explicitly political, self-described feminist goals.

Even as these digital-material hybrids might suggest a coherent, unified movement, the Women's March still received its fair share of criticism, much of it echoing the concerns that have dogged the mainstream feminism movement in the West since the nineteenth century. Chief among these objections was the charge that the Women's March was simply a shallow, feel-good action that lacked an intersectional understanding of power or the organizational durability to advocate for change; it was, in short, just another manifestation of empty, middle-class, white feminism. Many women of color, for example, argued that the march failed to listen to and include their voices and thus reproduced an exclusionary vision of feminist activism that ignores embodied racial difference, while trans women objected to the widespread embrace of pussyhats and other symbols that seemed to equate womanhood with specific genitalia.

In this chapter, then, I argue that both the successes and failures of the Women's March signal the significance of materiality in a politics of craft agency. While the Women's March demonstrates the promise of a richly conceived materiality that values both digital and physical artifacts (and the overlaps that constitute both), it also serves as a warning. Specifically, by not creating enough space for the embodied differences of protesters, the Women's March reproduced the manifestly problematic understanding that the normative feminist body is a highly privileged one, usually white, middle- or upper-class, cisgender, heterosexual, and able-bodied. Without accounting for the embodied specificity of all actors, craft agency—and the ethics of entanglement and coalitional politics it aims for—are impossible. Craft agency's metic sensibilities, however, make it well-suited to perform the difficult task of creating capacious coalitions that simultaneously value embodied differences as well as the interdependencies that co-construct all agency.

I begin by offering a short history of the 2017 Women's March, tracing both its origins as well as the many criticisms it faced, particularly in terms of its lack of intersectional awareness. I then situate this march within protest movements more generally, noting especially how protests have always been a robustly material affair, even more contemporary movements that increasingly rely on digital spaces and technologies. This tradition of protest-as-materiality, I argue, is essential for understanding both the promises and the weaknesses of the 2017 Women's March, which embraced a wide expanse of material actors while also ignoring the real, embodied differences that exist between those material actors. Through an analysis of artifacts from both the national Women's March on Washington and my own experience as a participant at a local sister march, the Women's March Alabama, I argue that the Women's March demonstrates the necessity of simultaneously valuing agentic co-constituency while also acknowledging material difference. Failure to do so, I contend, will endanger any attempt at political action and the relational ethics of entanglement that craft agency is grounded in.

INTERSECTIONALITY AND FEMINIST PROTEST AT THE 2017 WOMEN'S MARCH

Born in the immediate wake of Donald Trump's election as US president on November 8, 2016, the initial iteration of the Women's March was the idea of a retired lawyer in Hawaii named Teresa Shook and New York fashion designer Bob Bland. Independently, both women took to Facebook to propose that women march on Washington, and RSVPs began rolling in for a Facebook event in calling itself the "Million Woman March." This event, however, neglected to consider that Black women activists had already organized a Million Woman March twenty years earlier in Philadelphia. That this new event—created in response to the calls of two white women—coopted the name of a protest organized and attended by Black women only "crystallized the idea that the nascent movement was being run by a handful of white women with no organizing history" (Hess 2017). Many saw parallels with other instances of feminist protest in the United States, which have historically centered the voices and concerns of the most privileged middle- or upper-class white women (consider, for example, how arguments for women's suffrage in the nineteenth century almost always focused exclusively on *white* women's enfranchisement).

Despite these rather significant oversights, support for *some* kind of march kept growing. That's when Vanessa Wrumble, "a white producer and co-founder of the media company OkayAfrica," stepped in, offering not just a new name for the march but the support of a much more experienced and diverse activist network, including future board members Tamika Mallory, Carmen Perez, and Linda Sarsour (Hess 2017). With the support of these women, along with other knowledgeable organizers, the Women's March on Washington[1]—as it had by then been renamed—articulated a policy platform, secured the required permits, and booked guest speakers. On January 21, 2017, the day after

Trump's inauguration, more than half a million protesters turned up in Washington, DC, alone, while sister marches in other cities across the nation attracted another 4 million protesters (Wortham 2017). These numbers, along with "media coverage, organization, and visibility," meant that the Women's March was largely considered a success (Mosthof 2017), with news outlets calling it "historic" (Mason 2017) and celebrating it as a "peaceful" (Chira and Alcindor 2017) and "positive" (McCausland 2017) beginning to a larger "movement that's about to dig in" (Gade 2017).

Even with these positive reactions, the Women's March also attracted a good deal of criticism, mostly concentrated around its "centering [of] cisgender, heteronormative, able-bodied white women in its execution" (Mosthof 2017). Black women in particular were vocal about the March's "lack of cross-racial unity" (Brewer and Dundes 2018, 50), seeing it as just another manifestation of white feminism's "continued neglect, dismissal and disregard of the issues affecting black women and other women of color" (Holloway 2018, para. 20). In their investigation of Black women's reactions to the Women's March, Sierra Brewer and Lauren Dundes found that many saw the march as non-inclusive, merely "a means to protest the election rather than a way to address social injustice disproportionately affecting the lower social classes and people of color" (Brewer and Dundes 2018, 54). As writer Jamilah Lemieux (2017) explained, "Many of the White women who will attend the march are committed activists, sure. But for those new-to-it White women who just decided that they care about social issues? I'm not invested in sharing space with them at this point in history." As a result of these and other criticisms (Gökariksel and Smith 2017; Rose-Redwood and Rose-Redwood 2017; Solis 2017), many feminists came to see the march as an instance of a reductive and superficial feminism that merely "[reproduced] hegemonic notions of the feminine body" (Boothroyd et al. 2017, 711–712) rather than creating a truly inclusive and radical coalition.

These criticisms, in essence, all centered on the march's lack of intersectional engagement on the part of organizers as well as the majority of participants. This is especially critical given the weight that the term *intersectionality* has come to carry in contemporary feminist theory and activism. While the term itself wasn't introduced until legal scholar Kimberlé Crenshaw coined it in 1989, the work it signifies has long characterized the thought of feminists of color (see, for example, Gloria Anzaldua, bell hooks, Audre Lorde, and Cherrie Moraga). In her initial articulation, Crenshaw (1989) introduces the metaphor of streets intersecting to describe how Black women's experiences are not simply additive (that is, racism + sexism) but instead are "greater than the sum of racism and sexism" (140), something wholly different and unique. A means of theorizing difference, intersectionality has become a means of undermining "the centrality of white female experiences" (144) to feminist thought and "helps reveal how power works in diffuse and differentiated ways through the creation and deployment of over-lapping identity categories" (Cho, Crenshaw, and McCall 2013, 797). In the decades since Crenshaw first introduced the term, intersectionality has been widely adopted as a robust theoretical tool for understanding how power is written on and expressed through marginalized bodies and it is widely invoked as a shorthand acknowledgment that feminism should work for *all* women rather than the privileged (white, middle-class, straight, cisgender, able-bodied) women that have historically dominated feminist thought.

Although intersectionality has become something of a foundational concept for contemporary feminism, some have expressed concern that it does not offer a method, either for analysis or for the address-ing of social inequities (McCall 2005), while others fear its emphasis on categorizing difference only reifies the problematic categories it purports to resist (Martinez Dy, Martin, and Marlow 2014). For these reasons, some feminists worry that intersectionality has lost its critical promise and is increasingly less of a potent means of contending with difference within feminist movements and more of an empty gesture to some vague sense of diversity. Jasbir Puar (2012), for example, criticizes white feminists for their empty appeals to intersectionality: "Much like the language of diversity," she writes, "the language of intersectionality, its very invocation, it seems, largely substitutes for intersectional analysis itself" (53). These concerns are legitimate and worth reckoning with, especially because it is clear that intersectionality remains an influential concept for many feminist theorists and activists. Consider, for instance, Women's March co-founder Bland's admission that she "didn't know the term 'intersectionality' when we started" (quoted in Hess 2017). Bland seems to acknowledge her ignorance almost shamefully. It is not surprising that this formulation of feminism—one that was both central to the origins of the march and one that also seemed completely blind to the contributions and experiences of women of color—would be understood as privileged and exclusionary.

The tensions that characterized the Women's March from its incep-tion to its execution and discussions following it may represent the difficulties of feminist activism more broadly, but they also speak to the difficulties of large-scale social movements as a whole. Protests have long struggled with the challenge of creating solidarity along the lines of difference necessary to build broad, durable coalitions. In most cases, that difference is inscribed through the materiality of various agents: the bodies of protesters, for example, or the places they can safely inhabit. Successful protest movements thus depend on recognizing and making space for the material specificity of all actors—a formidable task, given the many actors (both physical and digital) that are increasingly central to contemporary protest. In short, the challenge of protests, including the Women's March, is to embrace a capacious sense of materiality, one that values the physical and the digital, while simultaneously accommodating the material particularities that both connect and differentiate agents.

THE ROBUST MATERIALITY OF PROTEST ACTORS

The outcome of any protest, like all rhetorical assemblages, depends on the intra-actions between material actors such as texts, bodies, places, and technologies. From the material constraints of texts (including digital ones but also more low-tech kinds like paper flyers or cardboard protest signs), to the physical occupation of specific places, to the embodied presence and experiences of protesters, all protests depend on material agents—broadly defined to include and exceed the digital as well as the physical—for success. Like Ravelry, then, protests productively expand our sense of material to include the digital. However, successful protest actions go further than just recognizing the mutual, material co-constituency of agents; they also force us to examine the material differences among agents as well. Thus, a truly transformative protest will not just recognize the agentic capacities of a broad range of material agents but also acknowledge the degree to which these agents overlap and the degree to which they differ.

Well before the development of digital technologies, robust material networks of texts—composed and circulated by various authors—supported protest work. Consider the textual ecologies at work in the 1955–1956 Montgomery Bus Boycott. Nathaniel A. Rivers and Ryan P. Weber's analysis of these networks highlights the role of more mundane texts like fliers, resolutions composed by organizers to clarify the boycott's goals, newsletters, "literature about nonviolent protest" (Rivers and Weber 2011, 199), "handwritten signs placed at bus stops" (200), lists for carpooling—not to mention oral texts like speeches, sermons, and word-of-mouth. The specific material features of each of these texts was central to their function in the boycott. Zeynep Tufekci's 2017 description of the work of Alabama State College professor Jo Ann Robinson highlights the various material resources at work in the crucial period of the boycott's earliest days. Robinson first "typed up an announcement of the boycott. . . . [Keeping] the description short . . . meant that three copies fit on a single page, minimizing the number of pages that needed to be printed. She then spent the night in the duplicating room and, with the help of two students who were enrolled in her 8 a.m. class, mimeographed fifty-two thousand leaflets" (63). Delivery was the next challenge: relying on the "sixty-eight African American organizations in Montgomery" (63), organizers were able to deliver the leaflets to "practically every African American home" in just one day's time (64). These material resources—paper, mimeograph machines, volunteers, and pre-existing community networks—helped create, deliver, and circulate important messages about the boycott. Indeed, it is hard to imagine how such a large-scale movement could be coordinated without the existence of these material networks of texts.

Even with the benefit of digital technologies to create and circulate important protest-related information, contemporary protesters still rely on physical texts to create unity within the movement as well as to address broader audiences. The signs carried by protesters are one example of how texts function as important material actors in social movements. "Due to their relatively low cost, ease of production, broad visibility, and ability to quickly convey a message," signs remain an important material resource for protesters, explain Susan Wildermuth and coauthors (2014, 16). They note that the materiality of protest signs shapes their rhetorical functions: "[Signs] are limited in space and, in order to remain inexpensive to produce, they are limited in color and in quality. They are often viewed as 'ephemeral' in that they don't last long, and yet, great effort sometimes goes into making them. They can be made with what is 'on hand' and can even be created moments before use, so they may be rushed, sloppy or of poor quality" (19). Because of these material features, protest signs commonly employ short enthymematic messages or symbolic images such as the peace sign or the Black power fist. Protest signs can thus become "indexes of a shared identity, unity and solidarity" (Lou and Jaworski 2016, 638) and can come to represent the movement as a whole, either among protesters or among external audiences.

Physical texts are undoubtedly central to the work of protest, but materiality also matters in terms of the protesters' bodies. Indeed, physical protests depend on the presence of human bodies, which can serve as a shorthand indicator of the strength or degree of support behind the movement. As early as 1969, Edward Corbett (1969), relying on the bodily metaphors of the "open hand" and "closed fist," argued that protests enact "body rhetoric . . . simply by massed physical presence" (291). Other scholars have since followed Corbett's lead, investigating how bodies in protest "become not merely flags to attract attention for the argument but the site and substance of the argument itself" (DeLuca 1999, 10). Through analyses of nude protest (Alaimo 2010), protests involving human blood splashing (Adsanatham 2018), or the bodily tactics of environmental protesters (DeLuca 1999), scholars have asserted "the significance of human bodies as sites of protest" (Sasson-Levy and Rapoport 2003, 382). The body, that is, holds particular rhetorical power as a means of protest because of its specific *material* features.

This is especially the case for bodies that do not fit within the categories that might define the normative public, political body (that is, white and male). For this reason, (female) bodies have historically carried a particular potency for feminist activism (Betlemidze 2015; Dubisar 2015; Parkins 2000; Sasson-Levy and Rapoport 2003). Because female bodies have so often been consigned to private spaces, barred from the active public participation that protest often demands, the simple existence of the protesting, political gendered body in public space can be a rhetorical claim in its own right. Wendy Parkins (2000) points to nineteenth-century suffragists as a case study on this point: Through physical demonstrations in the street, along with more private but equally physical acts like prison hunger strikes, these women "understood their bodies as a powerful means of dissent" (70). Suffragists, then, recognized their gendered bodies "not as a limitation but as a means by which the parameters of the political domain could be contested" (73). Through the positioning of their bodies—in particular public places or in the midst of acts like marching the streets or hunger strikes—suffragists were able to use their culturally meaningful female bodies to make a claim about what is appropriate for women (in this case, inhabiting the position of full citizens with equal voting rights). Even today, the body continues to be a significant rhetorical resource for feminist protest in particular since the body remains such a potent location for the inscription of power and identity.

Together, texts and human bodies often function as important material actors in any protest. However, it is also worth noting how the materiality of place can function in protest, even as many contemporary protests are increasingly organized or even located either partially or wholly online. Bodies, texts, and the other material actors that comprise any protest—digital or otherwise—are all firmly rooted *in place*. While rhetoricians have been comparatively slow to acknowledge the agency of place, the field has recently begun to explore how the spatial functions not as a passive backdrop onto which rhetoric unfolds but instead as a productive agent that makes rhetoric possible through "the collision of multiple material trajectories coming into arrangement in relation to one another" (Ewalt 2016, 138). For protests in particular, place often carries a great deal of rhetorical weight, as Danielle Endres and Samantha Senda-Cook note (2011). Protests, they write, regularly exploit the product of "the confluence of physical structures, bodies, and symbols" (276) that is place, either by "*[building] on a pre-existing meaning of a place* to help make their point . . . [or by] *temporarily [reconstructing] the meaning* (and [challenging] the dominant meaning) of a particular place" (259; emphasis original). Place, in other words, is just as meaningful of a material actor in protest as the bodies, technologies, texts, and structures that occupy it.

Consider, for instance, the rhetorical deployment of space in the Occupy Wall Street protests: By literally occupying the symbolic home of the "one percent" (that is, in Manhattan's Zuccotti Park, located in the financial district), protesters made a claim on the location of economic opportunity and privilege they had been otherwise excluded from. In the process, they both built on the prior meanings of their protest place while also re-creating those meanings. Similarly, place was essential to the protest efforts of the #NoDAPL movement, as protesters literally situated their bodies between industry and police forces and the sacred land they sought to protect. The agency of place is especially notable in this instance, given how Indigenous knowledge traditions have long figured place and environment as vibrant agents in their own right (Anderson 2018; Rosiek, Snyder, and Pratt 2020; Todd 2016).

While more conventional kinds of materiality—in varied forms including texts, bodies, and places—remain central to contemporary protest movements, there is no doubt that the materiality of digital technologies is also an increasingly critical consideration for many protests. These technologies can complicate how we understand what counts as material—or how, for that matter, we even define materiality—but there is no denying that digital technologies, particularly social media, have played a significant role in contemporary protest movements, especially as they become ever more entangled with the physical actors that make protest possible.

One widely discussed example of protest and digital technology is the Occupy movement's use of Twitter. As a worldwide movement that quickly spread beyond its physical origins in New York City, the Occupy protesters relied on Twitter to communicate with both internal and external audiences. In their study of the Occupy movement's use of Twitter, Joel Penney and Caroline Dadas found that this specific social media platform served a number of (often overlapping) purposes such as "facilitating face-to-face protests via advertisements and donation solicitations; live reporting from face-to-face protests; forwarding news via links and retweets; expressing personal opinions regarding the movement; engaging in discussion about the movement; making personal connections with fellow activists; and facilitating online-based actions" (Penney and Dadas 2014, 79). In the end, they argue, Twitter was a valuable tool that helped to build physical turnout and participation in the Occupy movement. Sky Croeser and Tim Highfield's research on the Occupy Oakland protest echoes these findings, noting how integral Twitter was to the function of the "real world" physical work of protests. While the physical place of protest is significant, particularly for the Occupy protests, Twitter and other social media platforms enable activists to "'step outside' the limitations of place in order to organize and . . . retain cohesion for the movement" (Croeser and Highfield 2014, sec. 1, para. 2).

This research highlights Twitter's essential role in the Occupy protests, but perhaps more important, it also points to the difficulties of separating the material and the digital in evaluating contemporary protest. Indeed, argues Manuel Castells (2012), most successful protest movements today rely on a "hybrid space" (169) that "links cyberspace and urban space" (177). That is, write Croeser and Highfield (2014), movements like Occupy depend on the hybridity afforded by digital and physical places, as "the physical and digital are not distinct aspects of the movement, occurring in isolation, but are interlinked" (sec. 2, para. 4), indicating "a deeply intertwined relationship between online and off–line spaces, in which online and off–line actions rely heavily on one another" (sec. 4, para. 7). What's more, I argue, this hybridity extends beyond place to other material actors in protests: the physical bodies of protesters, for example, undoubtedly perform important rhetorical work, but they are often motivated and/or represented through digital means. Texts like posters and signs may appear in physical form, but they are often also created on or circulated through digital tools. In short, it is far too reductive to characterize protest movements as either digital or material; rather, contemporary protest typically enacts a craft agency wherein digital and material actors are intertwined and construct one another.

While this digital/material hybridity might present challenges in terms of accounting for the agential assemblages that constitute protest, it also offers significant benefits to protesters, who can make use of the affordances all these varied actors carry. Although some continue to express fear about online "slacktivism"—that is, online engagement with protest movements that has little measurable "real-life" outcome—the reality, writes Henrik Serup Christensen (2011), is that "most evidence in recent years points to the Internet having a positive effect on off–line mobilization" (sec. 5, para. 11). Studies of the 2011 Egyptian revolution, for instance, consistently highlight the symbiotic digital/material relationship that is so common to modern protest. Tufekci and Christopher Wilson found that social media use in this specific case greatly increased the likelihood that someone might join the physical protest, centered in Cairo's Tahrir Square (Tufekci and Wilson 2012). As Castells (2012) explains, "The Internet provided the safe space where networks of outrage and hope connected. Networks formed in cyberspace extended their reach to urban space" (81). Likewise, in their study of the Black Lives Matter (BLM) movement, Deen Freelon, Charlton McIlwain, and Meredith Clark argue that protesters can "attract elite attention via social media as their concerns are broadcast through news outlets" (Freelon, McIlwain, and Clark 2018, 1005). That is, protesters can leverage the power of social media to gain more media coverage and, ideally, elicit more support such as additional protesters or monetary contributions.

Despite the considerable affordances that this digital/material hybridity can offer to protests, there are drawbacks, particularly when it comes to the use of social media. Most notable perhaps is its vulnerability to surveillance, both by governmental forces as well as other detractors. Occupy protesters worried that their use of Twitter rendered them visible to police (Croeser and Highfield 2014; Penney and Dadas 2014), as did the Tahrir Square protesters (Castells 2012; Tufekci 2017). Christina Neumayer and Gitte Stald note that the ever more widespread use of mobile technology (such as phones, tablets, and wearable devices) can make protesters even more susceptible to such surveillance (Neumayer and Stald 2014, 119). Additionally, while increased visibility within specific platforms can result in increased material support, online prominence can make movements in general as well as specific activists targets of harassment and trolling (Croeser and Highfield 2014; Tufekci 2017). This kind of digital attention can drive protesters away from otherwise valuable public spaces (be they digital or physical), or even inspire fake protest accounts that provide false information or make outrageous claims meant to create controversy within and beyond the movement.

Movements that depend on social media platforms are also bound by the structures of the platforms themselves. That is, while protesters can and do take advantage of affordances (like Twitter's easily searchable hashtags or the capacity to create events on Facebook), they are likewise at the mercy of the algorithms and design features that govern specific platforms. As a result, social movements rely on a "digital communications gatekeeping ecosystem [that] has been reduced to a very few but very powerful choke points" (Tufekci 2017, 135). In her discussion of the relationship between digital social movements and the platforms that alternately constrain and enable them, Tufekci (2017) analyzes how Facebook's algorithms responded to the initial posts from Ferguson, Missouri, that followed the shooting of Michael Brown. Because of its design—an unclear process that relies on user engagement such as "likes" or clicking through links—many posts from and about Ferguson did not feature prominently in users' news feeds, thus potentially limiting the circulation of what would become a major protest event. Today, social movements are in many ways dependent on social media, but the "proprietary, opaque, and personalized nature of algorithmic control" that governs most of these platforms "makes it difficult even to understand what drives visibility on platforms, what is seen by how many people, and how and why they see it" (160). Protest movements that rely on social media platforms are thus in many ways subject to the whims of the private companies that own these spaces, and risk their message being obscured altogether by those companies and their technologies. The materiality of power—as expressed through access to public spaces (be they physical or digital)—is thus not separate from but is instead woven robustly throughout digital spaces such as the social media platforms that are increasingly essential to contemporary protest.

Even with the risks that digital technologies can present, it is clear that most contemporary protests do rely, at least in part, on digital agents, and that these agents frequently overlap with the material agents that also constitute any protest movement. Materiality, then, might be better understood not merely as a physical, tangible quality, but in a more capacious sense that acknowledges the increasingly prominent digital/physical hybrids that constitute not just protest movements but other agential assemblages. Successful protests will thus recognize how digital and material agents construct one another. Importantly, however, protests must also be sure to understand that the co-constitutive nature of agency does not come at the expense of agents' material particularities. In other words, successful protests embrace craft agency, which recognizes how the material specificity of all actors shape their agential capacities while also acknowledging how agents—both physical and digital—bleed into and shape one another.

The Women's March provides a productive case study of this dynamic: its dependence on digital-material assemblages demonstrates how a robust understanding of materiality—one that recognizes it as both digital and physical—can promote solidarity and lead to concrete political outcomes. However, the general failure of the Women's March to provide an intersectional and inclusive platform suggests that protest must also simultaneously accommodate the material specificity of all its participants. To further explore how exactly these successes and failures manifested in practice, I center the analysis that follows around both the national Women's March on Washington as a whole and as one specific local corollary to the national Women's March on Washington, the Women's March Alabama (WMAL), a much smaller sister march held in a politically conservative state. Both marches embraced the capacious sense of materiality that characterizes craft agency and were, thus, in many ways successful. Yet, both the national march as well as WMAL failed to fully engage with material difference, thus diluting and undermining their political capacities.

THE CAPACIOUS MATERIALITY OF THE WOMEN'S MARCH

As one of more than six hundred sister marches held across the nation on the day following President Trump's inauguration (Chenoweth and Pressman 2017), WMAL was held in Birmingham, Alabama and was organized by local activists through Facebook. This was how I learned about the march: Some colleagues shared the event and eventually invited me to join a carpool they'd organized to drive the one hundred miles to Birmingham. Like the larger Women's March movement, WMAL made use of digital technologies to organize, mobilize, and strategize. WMAL had a Facebook event page, a Twitter account, and a website where protesters could learn more about the march and share information before, during, and after the physical event. Yet more traditional material agents were critical to the march's success as well. It is clear that both the larger Women's March movement as well as the WMAL specifically embraced a rich understanding of materiality that recognized the material/digital hybrids that are increasingly essential to contemporary protest work.

One of the most conventional material agents that mark a protest, the protest sign, was an important and frequent agent at the Women's March. While some protestors carried professionally printed signs

Figure 5.1. Signs at WMAL (photograph by author).

from organizations like the National Organization for Women (NOW), Everytown for Gun Safety, and Planned Parenthood, the vast majority of signs were hand-crafted from materials like poster board, markers, paint, and glitter. Given the broad political goals of the march, it followed that these physical signs spoke to a wide range of issues. Signs from the crowd at WMAL, for example, highlighted issues as varied as gun violence, women's rights, LGBTQ+ rights, education, environmental justice, healthcare, racial equality, immigrant rights, breastfeeding in public, workers' rights, religious freedom, science, disability rights, and general anti-Trump sentiment (figure 5.1). Many signs made use of visual elements like rainbow colors and the woman-power symbol (a clenched fist in a Venus sign), and signs with cat imagery—a clear reference to and repudiation of Trump's infamous "grab 'em by the pussy" comments—were widespread. Marchers generally kept the textual elements on signs short and simple, with statements like "Strength in Diversity," "My Body My Choice," and "Love Trumps Hate." These signs—and the many issues they supported—were consistent with the other protest signs featured at Women's Marches around the world.

Signs were not the only notable physical texts at work at the Women's March, however. Hand-knit pink Pussyhats became in many ways emblematic of the march. Friends Jayna Zweiman and Krista Suh first imagined what would become the Pussyhat Project as they considered how to create both "a visual signal of solidarity" at the march that would also "allow people who could not participate themselves . . . a visible way to demonstrate their support for women's rights" (Pussyhat Project n.d.).

Those who could not attend would still be able to participate by creating the hats, which would in turn create a powerful visual symbol that centered bodies, both in terms of the bodies wearing the hats as well as the bodies who made them. Indeed, explains LeMesuirer (2019), Pussyhat knitters were "explicit about the exigency of responding to the physical effort of Trump supporters with an equal measure of bodily labor" (149). Los Angeles knitting store owner Kat Coyle designed the now-iconic pattern that was simple enough for even inexperienced knitters to complete. Nearly always knit (or crocheted) in bright pink yarn, the hat features two pointed "ears" on either side of the crown and is meant to fit snugly over the wearer's head. Like other examples of craft protest, the Pussyhat Project turns a traditionally feminized, passive practice into a means of resistance and transformation, offering a mode of "activism that is at once accessible and multi-scalar, functioning at the personal (i.e., making and/or wearing hats), community (i.e., the exchanging of hats), national (i.e., wearing and making hats at the Women's March), and international (i.e., the making and wearing of Pussyhats at various marches throughout the world) levels" (Black 2017, 702).

As a material agent, the Pussyhat not only provided the symbolic benefit of offering "a feminized alternative to a masculinist Trumpism" (Larabee 2017, 216), but also presented the functional affordance of cohesive visual message, as the bright pink hats "[were made] to attract the camera with a seemingly simple message of mass protest" (Larabee 2017, 215). As a result, the Pussyhat succeeded in performing "a strategic denaturalizing of common markers of vulnerability and remaking them as collective proclamations of strength" (LeMesuirer 2019, 151). The results on the day of the march were unquestionably striking: Photos of the Washington, DC, march—where temperatures that day averaged 49°F—show a sea of Pussyhats despite the above-average temperatures (figure 5.2). Similarly, pink hats were visible throughout WMAL, even though the high temperature in Birmingham that day reached an unseasonably warm 68°F. Together, Pussyhats and signs alike worked to create a textual ecology for the March, one that valued the agency of these nonhuman actors.

These texts were especially meaningful when put in relation to the human bodies that carried them. Pussyhats are most effective not in isolation but when worn on a mass of protesting bodies. Additionally, many signs were designed to be read alongside specific human bodies. Consider, for example, the WMAL marcher who wore her baby in an infant chest carrier while also toting a sign that read "Tell My 8-Month-Old Who Weighs 25 Pounds that Breastfeeding is Disgusting,"

Figure 5.2. Women's March Washington, DC, *photograph by Ted Eytan, 2017. (CC BY-SA 2.0)*

or elder WMAL protester who bore a sign fixed above her wheelchair that read "I'm 97 years old and I say Women's Rights are Human Rights." Such texts gain additional rhetorical meaning when juxtaposed with specific bodies, suggesting that even in protest, material actors construct each other. Indeed, argues Corey Wrenn (2019), such textual/ embodied agential co-constructions are typical of feminist protest more generally: "Feminist protest," she writes, "frequently melds the symbolic with the corporeal" (5).

Perhaps the most notable feature of protesting bodies at the Women's March, however, was their sheer number. The millions of bodies that turned out to march in Washington took up a remarkable amount of space: Photos from the March show crowds spilling out of the National Mall for miles, while the Washington, DC, Metrorail reported its second-busiest day of ridership ever, only following Barack Obama's inauguration in 2009 (Wallace and Parlapiano 2017). Even at the much-smaller WMAL, the estimated five thousand protesters created a remarkable scene. Not only was this number much higher than anticipated—just a week before the march organizers told the local paper they'd be pleased if they could gather just two hundred protesters (Vollers 2017)—these bodies created a visible mass, filling the park that housed the march as well as the streets that surrounded it. What's more, these protesting bodies created an audible statement. During the WMAL rally, a speaker led the crowd in a series of protest songs like "Never Turning Back," and chants of "Love Trumps Hate" and "Si Se Puede"—a Spanish translation of Obama's well-known "Yes We Can" campaign slogan—roared through the streets as protesters marched. These chants resulted in not just a "a catharsis of shouting together" (Gökariksel and Smith 2017, 631) but also had the immediate rhetorical benefit of making the crowd's presence even more apparent to anyone who happened across the march.

Of course, the impact of these bodies was heightened by the way they interacted with the spaces they inhabited. Choosing to locate the Women's March on Washington adjacent to the National Mall, marching roughly from the Capitol to the White House, was no accident. Just a day earlier, this location housed Trump's inauguration. Holding the Women's March in this same location served as a deliberate refutation to his assumption of power. What's more, locating the march along the National Mall allowed for the protests to invoke the longer history of this place, which has historically served an important location for public protest, hosting events ranging from marches against the Vietnam War, the March for Women's Lives, the Million Man March, and, of course, the 1963 March on Washington, where Martin Luther King Jr. delivered his "I Have a Dream" speech. Even while many of these events have run counter to the goals of the Women's March on Washington—the National Mall hosted a KKK march in 1925, for example, and is still home to the annual anti-choice March for Life—it is clear that the National Mall holds a place in the national imagination as a place for citizens to publicly make their grievances known in the literal seat of federal governmental power, an especially significant location for the Women's March given its goal of contesting the traditional denial of women's public, political agency.

Place was profoundly important to WMAL as well. While Birmingham is not the state's capital, it is Alabama's largest city and also a painfully pivotal location for national civil rights struggles. WMAL began at Kelly Ingram Park, which is located across the street from the 16th Street Baptist Church, the site of a 1963 bombing by white supremacists that left four Black girls dead. The park is symbolic in its own right as the location of state exercise of white supremacy as memorialized by the famous photographs of fire hoses and dogs being unleashed on Black protesters. The decision to locate WMAL not just in Birmingham but in this specific park was meaningful, an acknowledgment of the march's indebtedness to the Civil Rights Movement and the Black protesters that made it possible. Even if protesters arrived to WMAL unaware of this history, the park and its surrounding streets are full of prominent, permanent signage and memorials that highlight how important this location was in the drive to secure civil rights. The weight of this particular place, then, signaled the intended intersectionality of the march as well as an acknowledgment of the fraught, racist history not just of the United States in general but of Alabama in particular.

The Women's March not only embraced the texts, bodies, and places that made it possible, but it also acknowledged the degree to which these material agents overlapped with and bled into digital agents, creating the physical/digital hybrids that are increasingly central to protest movements. Consider, for instance, the signs at the Women's March: despite their obvious material presence, many signs from the march also carried unmistakable digital traces. Numerous signs and/or slogans were born or circulated digitally, such as Shepard Fairey's "We the People" series, which made use of the iconic red, white, and blue color scheme of his Obama "Hope" poster to depict, alternatively, a Muslim, Latinx, and Black woman in posters that were made freely available for digital download and as full-page print supplements in national newspapers ahead of Trump's inauguration (Gelt 2017). Other (handmade) signs directly invoked digital campaigns: at WMAL, for example, protesters carried signs that featured hashtags like #BLM or #NoDAPL, which both demonstrated solidarity with these movements and also anticipated a digital audience beyond the physical one present at the march.

Indeed, it is likely that most marchers expected their signs to be photographed and/or filmed by traditional media outlets and shared informally through social media platforms like Twitter, Facebook, and Instagram. The digital circulation of these signs post-march only further cemented the coalition formed in person; many particularly humorous or evocative signs from the march were shared online, for example. This circulation, argue Inger-Lise Kalviknes Bore, Anne Graefer, and Allaina Kilby, can tap into a "collective affect" that is important for mobilizing and sustaining social movements (Bore, Graefer, and Kilby 2017, 538). The fluidity of signs at the Women's March—inhabiting both physical and digital spaces—indicates the difficulty of separating the two. Similarly, while Pussyhats were ostensibly physical artifacts, their rhetorical function depended heavily on digital networks. Prior to the march, protesters and supporters learned of the Pussyhat Project primarily through social media. The Women's March Facebook event page circulated information, but Ravelry, notably, was also an important catalyst for the Pussyhat Project's eventual success. Coyle's original pattern was the basis for more than 12,000 projects on Ravelry, and it still ranks as one of the most popular results in the "knitted hats" category. Like protest signs, then, Pussyhats were able to occupy both physical and digital realms.

Physical bodies and spaces, too, depended on digital environments throughout the Women's March. These technologies were essential to coordinating such a large mass of people in marches around the world on relatively short notice. As one Women's March organizer, Jenna Arnold, explained to *Wired*, "It would be hard to say that we would have had this kind of success without an existing platform like Facebook" (Laposky 2017). Such platforms would continue to be essential to solidifying the coalition formed at the march: the Women's March Facebook and Twitter pages became staging grounds for the movement that followed the march and are still regularly updated, both with hundreds of thousands of followers, more than three years after the 2017 march. The oscillation between physical and digital is clear, as bodies were initially mobilized online, then gathered together in the same physical space, and then reconvened online.

Mobile technologies were also essential to the orchestration of physical bodies in material spaces, allowing protesters to collect and share information among themselves as well as wider public audiences (Neumayer and Stald 2014). One tweet from the Women's March account, for instance, urged protesters to download an official day-of guide, complete with a map, list of services, tips for protesting safely, and emergency information, straight to their mobile devices (@womensmarch 2017). These devices also allowed protesters to document and circulate their experiences in real time. On Twitter alone, 11.5 million tweets tagged #WomensMarch were sent on the day of the march (@TwitterData 2017), and millions more posts were undoubtedly shared across other social media platforms as well. Digital technologies, then, enabled protesters to share their message with broader audiences in addition to those who were physically present at march locations. That ostensibly physical actors like protest signs, Pussyhats, and protesting bodies were in fact so richly embedded in digital environments suggests the difficulty of defining materiality in solely physical terms.

MATERIAL FAILURES AT THE WOMEN'S MARCH

While it's clear that the Women's March did successfully embrace a multitude of agents spanning digital and material worlds, it also failed to accommodate the embodied specificity of those agents, carelessly casting them as materially homogenous. While agents are undoubtedly co-constitutive of each other, that does not mean that all agents are constituted in exactly the same way—their intra-actions and locations within and between rhetorical assemblages are unique, specific, and consequential. The failure of the Women's March to attend to the material particularity of agency is perhaps most apparent in its repeated insistence on figuring its protesters as sharing an idealized feminine body: that is, a body that is uniformly cis and white. This elision of difference undermined the march's larger intersectional agenda, as it was unable to create space for the varied embodied identities that comprise the category of "woman."

One notable manifestation of this failure is the consistent, repeated presence of "pussy," both literally and symbolically. It is likely that this imagery was so extensive throughout the march (at least in part) because of Trump's aforementioned "grab 'em by the pussy" comments. The creators of the Pussyhat Project, for example, directly credit these remarks for the cat-eared design and explicit name of their hats. Their use of the word "pussy," they argue, is both an act of reclamation and an act of resistance, as it serves "as a protest against vulgar comments Donald Trump made about the freedom he felt to grab women's genitals, to de-stigmatize the word 'pussy' and transform it into one of empowerment, and to highlight the design of the hat's 'pussycat ears'" (Pussyhat Project n.d.). Likewise, many signs also invoked "pussy" as a direct refutation to Trump. One sign at WMAL, for example, proclaimed "Pussy Grabs Back," and was adorned with a hand-drawn cat whose claws were extended. Another insisted, "There will be no GRABBING of the PUSSIES," while yet another simply featured a cartoon-style cat with both paws shooting the middle finger.[2]

In the case of signs like these, "pussy," suggest Banu Gökarıksel and Sara Smith, is meant to "[embrace] and [celebrate] femininity while it simultaneously evokes a cheeky vulgarity through its multiple valences as a sexual symbol now proudly reclaimed against a violent record of masculine assault in which Trump unabashedly participates" (Gökarıksel and Smith 2017, 635). As such, cat imagery was widespread at the Women's March, with many signs employing feline symbolism as a shorthand for "pussy" (Wrenn 2019). This slippage between "cat" and "vagina" was easy to observe at WMAL, as marchers carried signs with slogans like "Keep your paws and your laws off my [hand-drawn cat]" and "My neck, my back, my pussy & my RIGHTS." Although the creators of these signs would likely argue that this imagery offers a playful way to reclaim a derogatory word that reduces womanhood to specific sex organs, to others, such reliance on cat symbolism only reproduces this conflation, defining "woman" as "those who possess pussies." Trans women like Katelyn Burns (2017), for example, expressed their frustration that the march's heavy use of these symbols "lays out a hierarchy based on genitals that is exclusionary and painful" (para. 14), ultimately "[letting] trans women know that their place isn't in your protest" (para. 13). Even signs that employed cat imagery to signal broader goals not explicitly identified with cis female bodies relied on this logic: At WMAL, a sign in the shape of a cat head, reading "equality hurts no one," and a sign featuring the outline of a Pussyhat perched atop a stylized rendering of the word "unity" both offered enthymematic arguments suggesting that pussies—both literal and figurative—are the only means to achieve feminist solidarity and justice.

The reductive but extensive presence of cat imagery at the Women's March was perhaps only matched by the sweeping sea of pink that seemed to characterize both the Women's March on Washington as well as smaller sister marches. Marchers wore pink clothing and carried pink signs, likely inspired by the popularity of the neon pink Pussyhat, which is depicted in the official pattern in a shocking pink color (notably, and unusually, for a knitting pattern, the pattern also explicitly calls for "any shade of PINK yarn") (Coyle 2016). Pink, in the case of the Pussyhat as well as its other manifestations at the Women's March, is invoked as a playful rebuttal of gendered stereotypes that figure the color as feminine and therefore frivolous or delicate. Consider, for example, how the official Pussyhat Project pattern describes what it calls the "Power of Pink": "Pink is considered a very female color representing caring, compassion, and love—all qualities that have been derided as weak but are actually STRONG. Wearing pink together is a powerful statement that we are unapologetically feminine and we unapologetically stand for women's rights" (Coyle 2016). Like the cat symbolism at the Women's March, however, the use of pink was seen by many as yet another instance of centering white women—or more specifically, the genitals of cis white women—at the march. Particularly when read in conjunction with the ubiquity of "Pussy" at the Women's March, the embrace of bright pink to symbolize the march suggested that the women the march was meant to uplift not only possessed pussies, but possessed the pink pussies more consistently identified with white women's labia (Shamus 2018).

Because of its reliance on cat imagery and its embrace of bright pink, the Pussyhat thus became in many ways symbolic of the Women's March's failures. It, along with other pussy imagery, resulted in a march that "[centered] an exclusionary and heroic embodied white femininity . . . both through the unconscious and uninterrogated 'pinkness' of the pussy hat, but also through the symbolism that highlights genitals define inclusion in the category women and deepen the reification of woman as category in ways that marginalize genderqueer and trans people" (Gökarıksel and Smith 2017, 636). That is, because the Pussyhat, in both its digital and material manifestations, figures womanhood in very limited and specific ways—equating it with a normalized white, cis female body—it fails to account for the varied embodied experiences that actually constitute womanhood, and, as a result, the Women's March fails to present a truly transformative politics.

This dynamic was succinctly captured in a photograph taken at the Women's March on Washington: Activist Angela Peoples holds a sign that reads "Don't forget: White Women Voted for TRUMP," while also wearing a hat that bears the message "STOP KILLING BLACK PEOPLE." Behind her, three white women—all sporting bright pink Pussyhats—are absorbed with their phones. One even takes a selfie with the Capitol behind her. These women, as CindyAnn Rose-Redwood and Reuben Rose-Redwood note, clearly "appear to be in a celebratory mood," while Peoples, in stark contrast, "doesn't appear to be celebrating anything at all" (Rose-Redwood and Rose-Redwood 2017, 647). This widely circulated photo highlights the "disillusionment with white feminism" that many Black women reported feeling in response to the march (Brewer and Dundes 2018, 52). While the three white women likely attended the march in order "to unify an opposition: love, not hate, unity, not divisiveness," their momentary performance of white feminism "cannot gloss over the ways that women and their allies are differently positioned in relation to the state and face different choices that hold different risks" (Gökarıksel and Smith 2017, 638). That is, the white women pictured here (and the Pussyhats they sport) are representative of the larger failure to substantively engage with—or even notice—the real, embodied differences that separated march participants.

These differences are not merely expressed or written through the physical body, but also impact the agential capacities of physical bodies. Consider, for example, the repeated criticisms from Black women regarding police presence at the march: While many white protesters celebrated the lack of police involvement as a sign of the march's success, Black women were quick to note the racialized elements of such a claim, as Black-centered protests routinely result in police intervention due to the perceived threat of Black bodies gathered in public protest. (Mosthof 2017; Ramanathan 2017; Tetreault 2019). As Gökarıksel and Smith (2017) note, choosing to march—to physically occupy specific material places—may indeed be "a necessary reaction," but is also one that "was always inadequate because of the haunting questions of who was there, who felt safe in that space, whose concerns were centered, and how" (631). This kind of exclusion was echoed in digital spaces: On the Facebook page for the Women's March Vancouver, for example, posts from Indigenous women and women of color criticizing the march's lack of intersectionality were repeatedly deleted. As a result, the digital agents of the Women's March "produce[d] and reproduce[d] specific understandings of feminine bodies" (Boothroyd et al. 2017, 717)—that is, white cisgender bodies—just as physical agents did.

Materiality, then, is key to understanding both the successes *and* the failures of the Women's March. The march did embrace a fairly capacious sense of materiality that not only acknowledged a wide variety of material agents such as texts, bodies, and space but also understood how those agents are but a smaller part of robust digital-material hybrids. This allowed for the creation of a resilient assemblage that could respond quickly and flexibly to the very real demands of on-the-ground protest work. Even so, the march failed to fully realize the promise of this broadly defined material assemblage because it was unable to reckon with the material specificity of all these embodied actors. That is, the march was unable to contend with the realities of how material difference can and regularly does shape the agential capacities of different actors. Without such an awareness of the relationship between materiality and agency, the Women's March was always doomed to fail to enact the true transformational politics of craft agency.

CONCLUSION: CRAFT AGENCY AND THE POLITICS OF FEMINIST PROTEST

Despite the many failures of the Women's March, it remains a potent and, so far, persistent location for contemporary feminist protest. Now a tax-exempt nonprofit organization, the Women's March organized follow-up marches across the country in 2018, 2019, and 2020. They also regularly partner with other activist groups to support progressive campaigns such as the #MeToo movement and the protests that took place in airports to challenge Trump's Muslim ban. The many successes of the Women's March—as an organization and as an event—can be traced to its embrace of the capacious sense of materiality that characterizes craft agency, valuing the rhetorical potentiality of all manner of physical and digital agents (and, in many cases, erasing the distinctions between the two). Yet, there is no doubt that the Women's March has failed in some critical ways as well. Even while its rhetorical approach was based on a broad understanding of materiality, it was unable to distinguish between and accommodate the many materiality-specific bodies that are required to form durable feminist coalitions. The Women's March, in short, demonstrates both the necessity and fragility of craft agency, which posits that an ethics of entanglement—and the political change it makes possible—depends on a reciprocity that recognizes bodies as simultaneously co-constitutive and materially specific.

To recognize the degree to which agents construct one another while also appreciating their material differences may initially seem to be a conceptual and practical impossibility: agents may either inhabit and act from self-contained bodies or their bodies are merely tenuous interfaces from which rhetorically and politically significant entanglements arise. Indeed, feminist thought—particularly white feminist thought—is in some ways responsible for perpetuating this dichotomy. Consider how feminist rhetorical history has theorized the body: while this scholarship arguably foregrounded the materiality of rhetorical practice well before new materialism's current popularity in rhetorical studies more widely, it is fair to say that this work has too long valorized the individual rhetor and her body at the expense of investigating the rhetorical assemblages that produce individual rhetors. As early as 1992, Barbara Biesecker (1992) expressed her concerns that feminist historiography efforts have not so much challenged the canon that excluded women rhetors in the first place but rather practiced what she calls "female tokenism" (141).[3] Biesecker suggests that feminist rhetorical scholarship too often celebrates the rhetorical acts of individual women, which only "resolidifies rather than undoes the ideology of individualism that is the condition of possibility for the emergence of the received history of Rhetoric" (144). More recently, Sarah Hallenbeck (2012) argues that the "tragic and heroic narratives of women's rhetorical action" that still characterize much feminist historiography have "tended to place the woman rhetor against her world rather than within it" (12). The result, she suggests, is a similar individualistic framework that prevents feminist rhetoric from adopting a new materialist approach to agency that would "capture the broadest possible range of rhetorical practices, including the embodied and material rhetorics emerging both from individual women and men and from the larger systems of power in which they are enmeshed" (14). Biesecker and Hallenbeck both highlight the risks of attributing feminist rhetorical action to isolated bodies rather than seeing those bodies as part of larger material assemblages. These dangers are not limited to feminist scholarship, though. As the Women's March illustrates, a feminist politics that only acknowledges the actions of individual bodies will only undermine any attempts at true transformational action.

Yet, completely disavowing the significance of agents' material locations and bodies is also problematic. There can be no doubt that power manifests itself through the materiality of specific bodies: While categories like gender and race may be social constructs, they are still rhetorically and politically significant, as they often delimit the kinds of intra-actions individuals may experience. Recent discussions of feminist intersectionality highlight this dynamic, recognizing the variable and relational nature of identity (and the structures that produce it). As Sumi Cho, Kimberlé Crenshaw, and Leslie McCall argue, identity categories are "fluid and changing, always in the process of creating and being created by dynamics of power" (Cho, Crenshaw, and McCall 2013, 795). Material markers of identity are thus both "exclusionary (i.e., they are constraining) *and* enabling (i.e., they allow for surprises). They are nothing but phenomenal interference patterns that are always on the move" (Geerts and Van der Tuin 2013, 176; emphasis original). Intersectional identities—that is, agents—are the product of specific power structures and intra-actions, and that specificity is in turn a product of the material embodiment of agents.

To not acknowledge those differences, writes Cooper (2019), is fundamentally unethical. Ethical rhetorical practice, she claims, "requires recognizing others not only as entities that act but also as individualizing entities, concrete others who have opinions and beliefs grounded in their own experiences and perceptions and meanings constructed in their bodies" (156). That is, while we can recognize the dissolution of boundaries between agents, the degree to which agents form each other and the world they inhabit, it is also essential that we do not erase difference—or our own role in constructing those differences—in the process. Barad (2007) explains how ethics is located within the processes of determining how difference is created; she argues that "accountability and responsibility must be thought of in terms of what matters and what is excluded from mattering" (394). As mutually entangled agents who both construct and are constructed by our intra-actions, we must be prepared to reflect on how our entanglements work to create, maintain, or contest difference. This is the work of an ethics on entanglement: to account for and honor the differences that arise from agents' material specificities, and to consider our role in the construction of those differences.

Craft agency highlights how the material body informs the kind of rhetorical actions—undertaken in concert with other materially specific agents—that are possible. This position builds on Elizabeth Grosz's (1994) contention that the body is akin to a Mobius strip, serving as "a point from which to rethink the opposition between the inside and outside, the private and public, the self and other, and all the other binary pairs associated with the mind/body opposition" (20–21). Grosz's understanding of the body helps articulate how feminist political action might balance the need to undermine orderly distinctions between self and other while also acknowledging the real material differences—particularly in terms of power—that exist between actors in any given assemblage. In craft agency, the body is materially significant because it determines how specific agents may construct one another and how they may refuse such constructions. The body, that is, is a location of power in that determines which kind of agential intra-actions—and political outcomes—are possible. Indeed, explains Barad (2007), "Any proposal for a new political collective must take account of not merely the practices that produce distinctions . . . but *the practices through which their differential constitution is produced*" (59; emphasis original). Any intra-action is bound to create difference, argues Boyle (2016), which is especially important to consider when rhetoric is framed as an ongoing practice (not a discrete event): "Practice is the repetitive production of difference," he writes, "even if that difference looks, to our conscious awareness, the same. . . . [This] difference is perceived and affirmed within an ecology, and relations within that ecology become activated in new ways" (547). From this perspective, it would be impossible to engage in political action *without* accounting for the particularity of individual bodies, or the processes that create that particularity. A politics of craft agency, then, depends on agents who are willing to form coalitions based not on the erasure of difference but on its thoughtful interrogation.

Without question, such work is difficult, but it is possible, especially when craft agency's mêtic sensibilities are foregrounded. Mêtis, as discussed in chapter 2, is "rooted in specificities of bodily vulnerability" (LeMesurier 2019, 145); it is the cunning reflexivity practiced by those whose embodied differences limit their agential capacities in some significant way. For mêtis, embodied difference is the prerequisite for rhetorical action, but to be successful, mêtic agents must remain actively attuned to the processes, structures, and intra-actions that produce those differences. This embodied, synergistic dexterity takes work: It is, in fact, better understood as "shared experiences of sustaining bodily labor," argues LeMesurier (152). Recognizing mêtis as a process of "coalitional labor," to use LeMesurier's framing (153), highlights how mêtis thrives within specific material intra-actions. Emerging from the malleable spaces of rhetorical assemblages, mêtis locates inventive capacities within "situations which are transient, shifting, disconcerting and ambiguous" (Detienne and Vernant 1991, 4). The mêtic practices at the heart of craft agency are inherently political, as they seek to reverse power inequities, but they also recognize that such reversals can only happen within the specific intra-actions that make rhetoric possible. Political change, in short, begins with the entanglements of co-constitutive, yet materially different, actors.

In the context of protest, adopting this mêtic sensibility means taking seriously Rose-Redwood and Rose-Redwood's reminder that when "bodies-in-alliance assemble in the streets . . . this collectivity does not represent a unified political subject. . . . Rather, it *embodies* a provisional assemblage of conflictual plurality which holds together so long as the threads that unite are stronger than the tensions that divide" (Rose-Redwood and Rose-Redwood 2017, 649; emphasis original). In other words, while successful protests may create the illusion of a unified agential body, they also depend upon assemblages of materially diverse agents—physical and digital, human and nonhuman. Such vibrant, reciprocal coalitions are necessary to create the kind of lasting political change feminist protest movements like the Women's March, and craft agency itself, seek.

6
RESCUING CRAFT FOR WRITING STUDIES

Throughout this book, I argue that craft can articulate rhetoric's material contours, and as such, helps to define the political implications and ethical weight of that materiality. Understanding rhetoric's inherent craftiness focuses our critical attention toward the intra-actions that produce materially bound agents and reframes rhetorical agency as the result of those intra-actions. Writing and writing pedagogies are no exception. Craft—as a material, intra-active unfolding—can and should inform how we understand and enact the rhetorical practices that are perhaps most readily associated with the field of writing studies. Yet, craft currently holds little purchase in the field, mostly because it remains an undertheorized concept that has devolved into shorthand for technical proficiency or mechanical expertise. Craft's relative absence from contemporary disciplinary conversations is particularly puzzling given that craft was once a widely used term within writing studies, most notably during the heyday of expressivist composition pedagogies of the 1970s, which valued craft's ability to highlight writing as an act of making-with. Why, then, has craft all but disappeared from our scholarship, and how might it continue to inform the intellectual and institutional work of the field?

This chapter grapples with each of these questions in turn, first tracing the decline of craft within writing studies and then arguing for its revival. Although craft was once an influential term for the field, one that signified or at least hinted at the material complexities of writing, because writing studies failed to explicitly reflect on or theorize craft, the term became associated with mechanical, skills-based understandings of writing—writing as technique, not *techne*—that undermined the field's claims to disciplinarity. Craft has thus come to hold a fraught position in the field: while its conceptual history suggests its ability to highlight the collective, material nature of writing and rhetoric, it has come to signal an unrhetorical understanding of writing, one that is often used to justify composition's institutional function as a manager or producer of neoliberal student subjects. Such a limited, skills-based

https://doi.org/10.7330/9781646422555.c006

understanding of craft poses an existential threat to the field, seriously limiting our disciplinary and intellectual possibilities. Yet, embracing the robust notion of craft that I argue for throughout this book can help mitigate this threat by reimagining the varied forms of intellectual labor that comprise the field. Craft, and craft agency, can not only help writing studies to articulate its value within an increasingly neoliberal, skills-focused university but also, and perhaps more important, can guide the practices of the field itself, productively informing our pedagogies, administrative work, and scholarly activities.

WHEN COMPOSITION WAS CRAFT

Craft once held prominence in the field of composition, most notably in the years in which the field began to define itself as a discipline. Yet, as the field began to mature into its contemporary form, it also began to neglect craft. The reasons for this abandonment are undoubtedly complex and multifold; here, though, I examine how the field's changing disciplinary identity informed its rejection of craft. Specifically, I argue that the contemporary field of writing studies has discarded craft because it has (mistakenly) been deemed an artifact of the allegedly unrhetorical, neoromantic pedagogies of the 1970s that have been widely criticized for their tendency to separate the "real" work of writing—the inventional capacities of the individual genius—from the more mundane but teachable work of craft (that is, writing techniques and skills). While craft is a formative concept—one whose rich rhetoricity I have detailed throughout this book—its meaning has, unfortunately, shifted over time to reflect a reductive view of writing as a mechanical, skills-based practice. This degradation of craft has come at a serious cost for the field: such a framing is not only at odds with the relational, material sense of craft I have worked to develop throughout this book, but it also undermines the complex intellectual and rhetorical work that defines the work of writing studies as a discipline.

To trace craft's downfall, it is first necessary to understand craft's once-significant position in the field, especially throughout the 1970s and early '80s, the period in which composition began to mature into a coherent discipline. During this time, craft was often invoked as a metaphor to describe the field's principal object of inquiry: writing. Consider, for example, a sampling of textbook titles from the period: William J. Brandt, Robert Beloof, Leonard Nathan, and Carroll E. Selph's *The Craft of Writing* (1969), Ray Kytle's *Concepts in Context: Aspects of the Writer's Craft* (1974), John Hersey's *The Writer's Craft* (1974), Thomas Elliot Berry's *The*

Craft of Writing (1974), William L. Rivers's *Writing: Craft and Art* (1975), and Frank O'Hare's *Sentencecraft* (1975). Based on these titles alone, it seems clear that the burgeoning field was eager to accept the notion that writing functions as a craft.

Textbooks like these—that is, textbooks that emphasized the writing-as-craft metaphor—were especially useful pedagogically, argues Carole Gottlieb Vopat in a 1976 *CCC* review, because of their ability to show students how writers are "primarily, craftspeople, painstaking workers, whose stories were made, as a necklace or a bridge is made, by people who worked hard over it" (Vopat 1976, 87). In other words, compositionists found the writing-as-craft metaphor valuable because it imagines writing as an act of making. Indeed, it seems that both student and professional writers also embraced such language, as they often invoked the writing-as-craft metaphor in their varied descriptions of the writing process. In the 1980s, Lad Tobin (1989) found that students tend to "think of writing in terms of cooking, building, or manipulating objects" (448), while Barbara Tomlinson's (1986, 1988) research on the metaphors professional writers most commonly use to explain their writing process points to the prominence of craft metaphors like cooking, gardening, and sewing.

The scholarship of the nascent discipline of composition likewise relied on craft, particularly within then-dominant discussions of process and expressivist pedagogies. In 1981, Donald Murray insisted that writing, and revision specifically, "is not an act of magic anymore [*sic*] than magic acts are; it is a matter of tuning an engine, kneading dough, sewing a dress, building a shelf" (Murray 1981, 34). Through an extended metaphor, Murray painstakingly positions revision as a "logical craft" (34): "Think of a workman who moves in close, measuring, making, sawing, fitting, standing back to examine the job, moving back in close to plane, chisel, mark and fit, standing back again to study the task, moving close to nail the piece in place, stepping back for another look, moving in close to set the nails, another step back, another look, then in close to hide the nail holes, to sand, stepping back to make sure the sanding is complete, then in close at last to apply the finish" (40). In his 1973 *Writing Without Teachers*, Peter Elbow similarly situates writing as a craft, devoting an entire chapter to exploring how the writing process is akin to cooking (Elbow 1973).[1] Sondra Perl is even more direct in a 1980 article, describing the writing process as both an epistemological and ontological craft: "In writing," she explains, "meaning is crafted and constructed. It involves us in a process of coming-into-being" (Perl 1980, 367).

Even across such varied contexts, these scholars see craft as a fruitful metaphor for the process of writing because it frames writing as *labor.* Whether undertaken by experts or novices, writing, like cooking or carpentry, is rarely a straightforward or simple process, and it always demands continual engagement with other actors, many of whom are nonhuman, and all of whom exist in specific material contexts. Writing-as-craft, in these instances, privileges process over product but does not ignore the material outcomes of the labor of writing, usually conceived of as "an effective piece of writing that [makes meaning] clear" (Murray 1981, 40) "so that it is intelligible to others" (Perl 1980, 368). While many contemporary compositionists would undoubtedly bristle at any approach to writing that demands amorphous and often racist and classist concepts like "clarity" or "intelligibility," what is most notable is how these usages of craft anticipate the creation of productive intra-actions (in this case, with readers) as a result of writing-as-craft. These uses of craft position writing as a process of *making-with*—a techne, in other words—that arises in inventional, embodied intra-actions between the writer and her surroundings.

Even as these early compositionists invoked craft in ways that implied its conceptual complexities, its use was frequently left uninterrogated or unexplained, which limited craft's theoretical potency. Because craft was "rarely if ever explicitly defined" (Mayers 2007, 65), let alone directly grounded in classical rhetorical theory, its meaning began to shift, or at least become less precise, rendering craft vulnerable to misuse or appropriation. Indeed, this is exactly what happened, argues Tim Mayers (2007), whose book *(Re)Writing Craft* traces how craft's "use has deteriorated . . . into a rather reductive definition" that signifies the "mechanical aspects of composition" (67). He attributes this shift primarily to the disciplinary discourses of creative writing, which were invested in the romantic desire to see "writers [as] born, not made" (67), and located the inventive capacities of writers within individual talent, genius, or inspiration, not within the craft practices of *making-with.* Craft thus became narrowed to "the one small aspect of creative composition —technique—that . . . [can] be taught" (67), problematically diminishing the complexities of writing to a series of learned techniques that individuals can study, practice, and master. As craft's meaning transformed to connote "the technical or mechanical aspects of composition completely severed from invention" (67), the writing-as-craft metaphor deteriorated to render writing merely instrumental.

Mayers's book helpfully outlines how such an overly-simplistic sense of craft-as-technique has come to dominate contemporary understandings of craft as it relates to writing. However, it is limited in that it attributes the atrophy of craft to creative writing discourses specifically, rather than examining the conditions within writing studies that resulted in the discipline's general abandonment of the term *craft* as an intentional descriptor of its activities. That craft's potency waned at the same time that the field sought disciplinary legitimacy is no coincidence, I argue. As craft became increasingly associated with a reductive view of writing that locates invention wholly within the individual genius rather than within the intra-actions between various actors, the field sought more complex accounts of writing that rendered it knowable and thus teachable. No wonder, then, that craft fell out of favor among writing studies scholars: As the field rejected romantic writing pedagogies that framed craft as technique rather than techne, craft became a threat to the fledgling discipline.

One of the clearest contemporaneous explanations of this disciplinary shift—and one of the only early explorations of the relationship between craft and techne—is found in Richard E. Young's 1980 article "Arts, Crafts, Gifts, and Knacks," which distinguished composition pedagogies between "new romantics" and "new classicists." In this account, new romantics equated craft with "skill in technique"—that is, mechanics and grammar—while art described the *real* work of composing, those "more mysterious powers" of invention, "which may be enhanced but which are, finally, unteachable" (Young 1980, 344). The new classicist position, on the other hand, tended to refuse this distinction, instead seeing art as "the knowledge necessary for producing preconceived results by conscious, directed action. As such, it contrasts not with craft but with knack, that is, a habit acquired through repeated experience" (344). For Young, a new classicist approach is the most pedagogically sound because it moves writing from an unintelligible, opaque process to one that can be understood and thus taught.

Young's account is important for understanding why craft fell out of favor in the field at the same time that the field sought disciplinary legitimacy: craft was increasingly identified with "new romantic" pedagogies that undermined the field's claim to writing expertise. This limited sense of craft was especially tied to expressivist pedagogies that were beginning to attract criticism for their tendency to privilege the role of "personal experience and voice" (Fishman and Parkinson McCarthy 1992, 647) in composing.[2] Because expressivism is commonly understood as a pedagogical "[heir] to romanticism" (Fishman and Parkinson McCarthy 1992, 648) in which writing, and invention, are "located within the individual subject" (Berlin 1988, 484), the field discarded craft as it moved toward more complex accounts of writing such as those identified by Young (new classicism) and James Berlin (social-epistemic).

In many ways, then, it makes sense that the field abandoned craft in its zeal to professionalize throughout the 1980s. When craft connoted such a reductive, limiting view of writing—one that diminishes it to mere technique and separates it from the inventional practices of the individual genius—it accordingly held little value for a discipline invested in theorizing and teaching writing as a generative, situated, social practice, especially as that discipline simultaneously sought to accumulate institutional power through endeavors such as the establishment of journals, conferences, graduate programs, and the growth of tenured/tenure-track positions for composition specialists. Craft's abandonment by writing studies is thus linked directly to the field's disciplinary evolution: it was deemed an artifact of romantic pedagogies that problematically framed writing as either the result of the interior processes of the individual genius (as in expressivism) or as simple mechanical skills (as in current-traditional pedagogies). The burgeoning field had no interest in understanding writing in these terms, as both positions render the complex, inventive work of writing as unteachable technique. Under these circumstances, then, it was perhaps inevitable that the maturing field of writing studies didn't demonstrate much interest in claiming craft, too often understood as technique, as its own.

Framing writing instead as a learnable techne held much more value for a field seeking to establish itself as legitimate academic discipline. Adopting Young's "new classicist approach" to techne, writing studies was able to both gesture to its ancient foundations and provide a justification for its continued existence. As Pender (2011) argues, when we frame writing as a techne, "we are claiming that we can know writing through rational explanations of causation and that these explanations can be used to create transferable strategies that will give writers more control over writing" (83). Positioning writing as a techne, that is, "provided the outlines of a research agenda that . . . could help substantiate rhetoric and composition's claim to disciplinarity" (40). Yet, this version of techne—one that saw writing as knowable "through rational explanations of causation and that . . . can be used to create transferable strategies that will give writers more control over writing" (83)—also presents a problem for the field. While techne helped to establish writing studies as a legitimate, knowable subject of inquiry, it (especially in its most simplistic renderings) also runs the risks of eliding the contingent, fluid nature of writing and rhetoric, thus again situating both as mere technique. Pender explains the dangers of this slippage between techne and technique, writing, "while techne did, in fact, help to establish the research agendas necessary for improving pedagogy in first-year courses and establishing graduate programs in English departments, it also circumscribed those agendas within clear parameters, namely that rhetoric was to be understood as an instrumental form of discourse" (6). Paradoxically, then, techne—at least its most reductive understandings—is responsible for the growth of the field at the same time that it limits its potential.

CRAFTING A DISCIPLINARY IDENTITY IN THE NEOLIBERAL UNIVERSITY

While approaches to techne that hew too closely to technique may have been useful in establishing legitimacy for writing studies, they also simultaneously restrict the growth of the field, confining it to its "service" status. This has real consequences for the future of the discipline, especially given how simplistic understandings of writing as mere technique persist throughout the university, where composition is still often framed as a skills-based gatekeeping course that students must master before moving on to the more serious intellectual work that awaits elsewhere in the English department (i.e., literature courses) or university. This history has haunted the field, says Robert Connors (1985), who notes that during "most of its history as a college subject, English composition has meant one thing to most people: the single-minded enforcement of standards of mechanical and grammatical correctness in writing" (61). As a result, argues Wendy Bishop (1990), composition courses have become devalued, especially in comparison to literature courses: "In many departments, literature courses, as 'content' bearing courses, are considered much more valuable than writing courses, which may be viewed as contentless craft courses, or worse, as therapeutic" (9). That is, even though the field has consistently resisted such an identity, composition has historically been understood (both within English departments and within the university more broadly) not as a site of meaningful intellectual inquiry but as mere craft in its most pejorative sense. Composition serves as a gatekeeper, reinforcing a view of writing as a mundane or even remedial practice that is somehow beneath but nevertheless essential to actual academic disciplines.

As a result of this institutional history, the field has adopted what Donna Strickland (2011) calls a "managerial unconscious," which can rely on and reproduce such flawed skills-based conceptions of writing to justify its existence within the university. That is, writing studies must often resort to framing writing as mere technique to external institutional audiences in order to ensure its survival. In doing so, some scholars claim that the field has made itself complicit in its own alienation from the rest of the university. Sharon Crowley (1998), for example, contends that the field has always been willing to position itself as the ideal location for the management or disciplining of student subjects in exchange for (limited) institutional power. She writes, "The required introductory composition course has always been justified, at bottom, in instrumental terms: this is the site wherein those who are new to the academy learn to write its prose" (250–251). As long as writing studies relies on arguments that, at base, frame writing as skills-based, argues Crowley, the field will continue to compromise itself and its ability to theorize what writing can or should be.

Sidney Dobrin (2011) makes a similar, if more forceful, argument throughout his book *Postcomposition*, which criticizes "the field's intellectual focus upon (writing) subjects and the teaching and management of those subjects rather than upon writing itself" (7). He argues that writing studies has created a "disciplinary bureaucratic structure in which subject management and production has unfolded as the central focus of the field" (59). He suggests that this focus on the subject (rather than writing itself) is a remnant of "the early neo-romantics who created student-centered thinking" (73); that is, the process and expressivist pedagogies of the 1970s that are often allied with the craft-as-technique position. The field is invested in this romantic understanding of writing, and subjectivity, argues Dobrin, since it has enabled writing studies to amass whatever meager institutional power it has been able to attain, specifically through the administration of writing programs, the required composition course, and the students and instructors that must be managed as a result. For Dobrin, a field centered around the teaching and administration of student subjects will never free itself from the skills-based view of writing that the contemporary university insists upon.

Such an identity is obviously a perilous one, as it restricts the kind of intellectual labor deemed appropriate for the discipline, and, accordingly, limits its position within the university. One need not look beyond composition's labor practices to find evidence of how this craft-as-technique perspective actively undermines the field. When writing is understood as mere technique, it is very easy to see writing instruction as nonintellectual work that doesn't require any particular expertise or experience. As Strickland (2011) explains, "Insofar as required writing is identified with 'mechanical' correctness, it is regarded as menial labor" (37–38). Accordingly, graduate students and contingent faculty are routinely assigned the work of teaching first-year composition, even with little training, support, or interests in the broader field of writing studies.[3] What's more, this skills-based understanding of writing tends to reproduce gendered and raced divisions of labor, even within the already-vulnerable ranks of graduate instructors and contingent faculty: Because writing instruction is seen as simply imparting the skills necessary to undertake the "real work" of the university, it is further marginalized and relegated to the most precarious laborers, particularly women and people of color (Schell 1998; Strickland 2011). The cycle becomes self-perpetuating: when writing is taught by such low-status instructors, the discipline itself is "reduced to a set of 'skills' that, once learned, can free people to move on to allegedly more complex forms of intellectual work" (Mayers 2007, 95), thus again consigning writing studies to its humble institutional role as purveyor of basic techniques.

The field's continued reliance on such writing-as-technique arguments comes at a steep cost, particularly as neoliberal values of efficiency and professionalism continue to influence the university. Bruce Horner (2007) expresses this fear bluntly, noting that arguments that reduce the field to its value in the neoliberal market only further devalue our work. Defending the discipline on the grounds "that composition teaching does in fact impart objective 'skills' that will have the same use wherever they are employed . . . contribute[s] to the low status of composition as mere preparatory 'service' work more properly the task of high schools, or, at best, two-year colleges," he argues (173). Shari Stenberg (2015)—who, unlike Dobrin, Crowley, and Horner, does not see the field as necessarily complicit in its own denigration—shares these same concerns about the consequences of an instrumentalist view of writing: "In a view of education as job training," she writes, "writing becomes a masterable, commodified skill whose purpose is deployment in the workplace . . . there is little tolerance for learning processes that entail engagement of (an often recursive) process, collaboration and dialogue among learners and reflection—in other words, exactly the kind of learning research in composition and rhetoric promotes" (8). While scholars may disagree about the degree to which the field itself is responsible for the kind of skills-based view of writing that has and will, in all likelihood, continue to be valued by the university, the reality is that such a view (a view that implies craft-as-technique) threatens to undermine the disciplinary legitimacy of writing studies. An overly simplistic sense of craft or techne only reinforces the already widespread (if misguided) view that writing, and writing instruction, is simply a matter of mastering a series of grammar rules or technical procedures, and, consequently, relegates the field to a bureaucratic rather than intellectual function within the university. Accepting a view of craft-as-technique, in short, dooms writing studies as a discipline to a mere managerial role, one whose only function is the imparting of a narrow set of skills to student subjects.

I agree with scholars like Young and Pender, who argue that the field's knowledge claims, and its disciplinary legitimacy, depend on its ability to position itself as a techne. However, we should be cautious that our justifications for disciplinary expertise do not rely on or perpetuate reductive understandings of techne that too closely resemble technique. That is exactly why, I argue, we must return to craft: embracing craft—in the rich, rhetorical sense I have argued for throughout this book—can help the field articulate itself as a multifaceted techne. Fueled by the embodied, lived labor of mêtis and the contingent, emergent fluidity of kairos, the craft knowledge of techne highlights how agential intra-actions can both sustain and undo power relationships craft—as techne, not technique—frames rhetoric as an inventional, contingent process: As techne, rhetoric can only emerge from deeply situated, material entanglements. Approaching techne as craft not only signals rhetoric's social, material, and generative capacities, but it can also chart a sustainable future for the field.

Grounding techne in craft is critical, I argue, because craft is uniquely positioned to present alternate models of writing, writerly subjectivity, and the identity of the discipline itself. Indeed, the few contemporary writing studies scholars who have explored craft in recent years tend to value it precisely because of its ability to articulate the complex work of the discipline within institutional contexts that might otherwise render the field as merely concerned with mechanical correctness. Mayers' aforementioned book argues that an expansive understanding of craft can create a durable and potent alliance between the fields of creative writing and writing studies (thus drastically changing the landscape of many English departments), while Prins (2012) suggests that the field embrace craft because it "both engages and extends many practices common to FYC [first-year composition]" such as "the social, historical, and material contexts of composers and users; the materiality of tools, technologies and texts, and we might differently engage those tools and technologies; and the social and ethical implications of the texts we produce" (159). More pointedly, Robert Johnson (2010) directly situates "the field of writing studies as a craft domain" (674), arguing that craft might provide a coherent disciplinary identity for the field. While I agree with these scholars that craft might offer a disciplinary identity to the sometimes-patchwork and still-maturing field of writing studies, this is not the only reason we ought to embrace a return to craft. Instead, I suggest that it's worth considering how craft, as a concept, can ground both the institutional and intellectual work of the field.

It is time, then, that the field give craft its due, and embrace craft as a foundational framework for our activities as theorists, teachers, and practitioners of writing, particularly as a means to combat the creeping influence of a skills-focused neoliberal university on the discipline. Embracing this version of craft refuses simplistic skills-oriented framings of our discipline and works to articulate a broader intellectual agenda for the field. Craft, in other words, can serve not merely as a productive metaphor for writing and rhetorical practices, but for the practices of the discipline itself. This is an especially important move given the very real exigences facing writing studies. In a moment when more and more scholars are expressing concerns about the field's position in the neoliberal university, it is crucial that writing studies resist reductive definitions of craft that position writing as mere mechanics in favor of a more capacious, rhetorically significant sense of craft.

A CRAFT AGENDA

Despite craft's unusual history within the field, it still has plenty to offer writing studies. While even an implicit endorsement of the craft-as-technique position threatens to circumscribe the kind of scholarly inquiries that it is possible for writing studies to undertake, and the kind of disciplinary identity that it is able to create as a result, I suggest that a reclamation of craft—one that frames composing as a material practice that emerges through the assembling of various human and nonhuman agents—can productively inform the future of the field. Specifically, because the concept of craft agency directs our attention to both the material conditions in which we make and the material agents with which we make, I argue that it can help to define a robust theoretical, political, and ethical future for the field. Fully embracing the reciprocal ethics of entanglement that characterizes craft agency necessitates a continual awareness of the material conditions in which we—teachers, scholars, and administrators—labor, and also provides a means of imagining how to remake them, especially emphasizing the importance of working with other agents. To close, then, I will briefly outline some of the ways craft agency might inform our disciplinary practices more broadly.

On the conceptual level, craft agency forces writing studies to move beyond its focus on subjectivity that has, as Dobrin and Crowley argue, hamstrung the field. They both suggest that as long as the discipline remains committed to its instrumental, managerial position within the university, it will also be devoted to a romantic and profoundly limited view of subjectivity that privileges the "subject as generator/producer/originator of writing" (Dobrin 2011, 78). In other words, because writing studies is so invested in the production and even control of subjects (as demonstrated through its bureaucratic institutional role), it tacitly endorses the idea that individual subjects exist independent from the material intra-actions that make rhetoric possible. This position is manifestly incompatible with craft agency, which refuses to see rhetoric or writing as the result of sovereign subjects and instead attributes it to materially specific human and nonhuman agentic assemblages. An embrace of craft agency, then, demands a profound disciplinary shift, one that adjusts writing studies' attention away from subjectivity and toward agency; that is, away from individual subjects and toward the intra-actions that give rise to rhetorical agency. A move from subjectivity to agency will thus equip the field to resist the romantic, self-determined subject that is too often conflated (unfairly or not) with overly simplistic, skills-based definitions of craft and instead move toward the complex techne of craft agency.

Such a refocusing will not be easy, as it raises difficult questions about the field's values, both as an intellectual and institutional enterprise. How, for example, might we reconcile writing studies' managerial functions when we refuse to accede to the neoliberal contention that writing is a commodifiable skill that results from autonomous, independent subjects? What kind of pedagogies might emerge as a result of this move toward a more ecological, relational understanding of rhetorical agency? And what kind of scholarly inquiries might be possible when we recalibrate our understandings of rhetorical agency? I cannot pretend to have all the answers to such questions, but I do want to call attention to how an embrace of craft agency can help the field more clearly articulate its ethical obligations as well as its political commitments. The techne of craft agency, I suggest, can provide a foundation from which the field can interrogate and reimagine its disciplinary practices.

A reconsideration of practice is in fact a necessary consequence of a new materialist perspective, explains Boyle (2016). Practice—like rhetoric itself—is seen not as an isolated moment of action but instead "as an ongoing series of mediated encounters" (534); practice is not a discrete *doing* but a continual process of *becoming*. Ethics, from this perspective, is a question of "develop[ing] *good practices*" (548; emphasis original), practices that are geared "toward serial encounters with a variety of different relations" (551). Our disciplinary practices, then, might be thought of as "composing [the] habits, dispositions, and orientations" (549) that in turn compose the field. Such a rethinking of practice is in fact especially urgent for the field of writing studies, which has always been especially invested in practice (most notably through its unwavering focus on writing pedagogy). Craft agency asks writing studies to interrogate its practices, and the intra-actions that those practices make possible. By this measure, craft agency follows the same trajectory as Dobrin's call to shift our disciplinary focus from subjectivity to agency, or Stenberg's (2015) "located agency": rather than focusing on the subject—which too often serves the needs of a naive neoliberal individualism—a shift to craft agency directs attention to the material conditions and intra-actions that make the field possible. Like Stenberg's "located agency," "the aim is not simply to articulate the self but to reflect on one's responsibility to others as a result of one's location, to ask how connections and alliances can be created as a consequence of this articulation" (119). In these conditions, learning, teaching, and writing are anything but an individual experience or action; rather, they all depend on "connection with and responsibility to others" (122). Craft agency takes these arguments a step further by locating ethics in "good practices" that are attuned to the specificity of agents' material locations and that take responsibility for the entanglements that form in those locations. At the disciplinary level, then, this would mean thinking about how our disciplinary practices might create the reciprocal ethics of entanglement that makes political change possible.

Although some may fear that a shift from subjectivity to agency would pose a threat to political action, denying "either the possibility or the value of subjectivity" just as "many marginalized others have only relatively recently acquired subjectivity" (Dobrin 2011, 76), I suggest that such concerns mistakenly attribute political action to individual subjects. Rather, as I have shown throughout this book, any political outcome results from specific material intra-actions among emplaced and embodied human and nonhuman agents. To ascribe political change to a singular rhetor is to ignore the deeply networked nature of power itself. The expansive, intra-active nature of craft agency is not at odds with political change; it is instead prerequisite for it. As a field, then, it is worth understanding how our practices work to "mobilize alliances with various people, technologies, discourses, environments, and so forth" (Gries 2019, 338), ultimately reinforcing existing power structures or disassembling them.

Concretely, craft agency would inform our disciplinary work at all levels: the pedagogical, the administrative, and the scholarly. While I don't agree with Dobrin's assessment that the field must break free from its "neurosis of pedagogy" (2011, 28)—indeed, craft agency's interest in "good practice" would instead demand continued critical attention to pedagogy—or necessarily support arguments for the abolition of the required composition course, I do support the larger implication inherent in both these positions that conceiving of writing, or the teaching of writing, as a merely mechanical or instrumental enterprise seriously limits the future of the field. Resorting to the neoliberal, skills-based language of craft-as-technique to defend ourselves (both to the university as a whole and within our own professional discourses) only undermines our intellectual and disciplinary possibilities. Yet, a full embrace of craft agency in our pedagogies, administrative activities, and scholarly work helps the field articulate a cohesive identity that is grounded in the political and ethical considerations that are inherent to craft agency.

Pedagogically speaking, a move to craft agency would explicitly reject subject-focused or skills-based views of writing instruction and instead insist that students explore the rhetorical and political effects of materiality. That is, a craft pedagogy would be particularly attentive to the bodies, the locations, and the tools that enable writing and rhetoric and would ask teachers and students alike to consider the relationships that enable or constrain their rhetorical activities, both within the classroom and beyond. Gries (2019) articulates one possible manifestation of a craft pedagogy in her article "Writing to Assemble Publics," where she argues for "a pedagogical approach that puts student-led assemblage and activation of publics at the center of its curriculum" (330). This approach follows a common public rhetoric pedagogy of asking students "to invent social activist campaigns in response to self-identified concerns" (331), but it does so while also enacting the new materialist perspective that rhetoric is an ongoing, material, collective process. That is, Gries asks her students to "think about rhetoric as the assembling of various entities that assemble bodies into collective action" (333). Throughout her article, Gries details how students were able to assemble vibrant, diverse publics, thus demonstrating how "rhetorical agency is a distributed affair and that rhetorical responsibility demands mobilizing alliances in generative and ethically conscious ways" (337).

Rivers (2016) outlines a pedagogy that is rooted in a similar desire to highlight rhetoric as an intra-active, material *doing* in his article "Geocomposition in Public Rhetoric and Writing Pedagogy." Here, Rivers explores the materiality of rhetoric specifically through place, as he uses geocaching to "physically move students into and through the public places around them in order to explore these places as a function of rhetorical activity and to cultivate such activity in return" (577). Students both located and composed their own geocaches in and around St. Louis, which invited them to "[develop] an embodied situational awareness of public space while cultivating the rhetorical skills to navigate and negotiate that space with others" (579). Like Gries, Rivers's pedagogy seeks to reframe rhetoric as a thoroughly material process of intra-active becoming while also remaining attentive to its political possibilities. In both these examples, students are asked to develop practices that place their bodies in relation to others (be it other human bodies, physical locations, or specific technologies or tools) and to imagine how those bodies might intra-act together to create change—practices all essential to the work of craft agency.

One other especially important location of craft pedagogy can also be found in the field's numerous discussions of multimodality. One of the most salient is the intensely multimodal approach outlined by Shipka (2011) in her book *Toward a Composition Made Whole*. Shipka argues for a robust understanding of multimodality, one that does not conflate "terms like *multimodal, intertextual, multimedia*" with digital (7, emphasis original). That is, Shipka offers a vision of multimodality that seeks to highlight the unique rhetorical affordances of *all* modes and argues that our pedagogies should do that same. Accordingly, she writes, "what matters is not simply that students learn to produce specific kinds of texts. . . . Rather, what is crucial is that students leave their courses exhibiting a more nuanced awareness of the various choices they make, or fail to make, throughout the process of producing a text and to carefully consider the effect those choices might have on others" (84–85). Shipka's goal of "creating courses that provide students with opportunities to forge new connections, to work in highly flexible ways, and to become increasingly cognizant of the ways texts provide shape for and take shape from the contexts in which they are produced, circulated, valued, and responded to" (84) is highly consistent with craft agency: it recognizes that composing is a situated, intra-active process that both creates and is created by larger rhetorical assemblages.

Adopting a similar belief in the unique affordances of multimodality are Alexander and Rhodes (2014), who, throughout their book *On Multimodality*, argue against any kind of multimodal pedagogy that "serve[s] the rhetorical ends of writing and more print-based composing" (19). They follow Shipka in advocating for an "approach to new and multimedia . . . [that becomes] cognizant of the rich rhetorical capabilities of new media so that students' work with those media is enlivened, provoked, and made substantive" (19). In particular, they value multimodality's capacities to "play with excess, with the dis-composed, with possibilities of communication and rhetorical affects and effects that take us far beyond the reasonable, the rational, the composed" (24); these capacities "offer us potentially whole new ways to experience the world" (60). Like Shipka, then, Alexander and Rhodes see in multi-modality the possibility to (re)arrange the material entanglements that make the world. A robustly multimodal pedagogy that follows the work of Shipka and Alexander and Rhodes (as well as several others, such as Anne Wysocki [2005] or Sheridan, Ridolfo, and Michel [2012])[4] is one means of enacting craft agency in the classroom, as it asks students to recognize and reflect on their entanglements with human and nonhuman others, especially emphasizing the outcomes those intra-actions might engender.

What all of these pedagogies have in common is that they encourage students to identify and interrogate the many agents that make writing possible in the hopes of (re)making rhetorical assemblages; they are, in other words, craft pedagogies that seek to foster the ethics of entanglement I have argued for throughout this book. Yet, it may also be worth centering craft more explicitly in our classrooms, both in the metaphorical sense of craft-as-techne described above, as well as the literal sense of crafted objects and processes. To draw just one example from this book, classroom examinations of craftivism might enable instructors and students alike to reflect on the material affordances and consequences of specific rhetorical tools and technologies, especially as they may or may not work to create more equitable, ethical assemblages. Yarn bombing, for instance, productively foregrounds the materiality of rhetoric—in this case, through the intra-actions of yarn, knitters, places, and objects—but it also highlights how certain agentic assemblages might exclude particular agents or outcomes. Who or what is precluded when yarn bombing practices appropriate graffiti culture without any recognition of its roots primarily in communities of color? We might then challenge students to imagine or even produce craftivist campaigns themselves, which would encourage them to participate in the construction of materially rich assemblages that also seek to reorient power in just and ethical ways. Whether or not explicitly centered in craft, however, a pedagogy of craft agency not only draws attention to the unique materiality of each composing student body, but also encourages awareness of the many other actors—course management software, campus architecture, uncomfortable desks, the coffee students sip while writing—that make any rhetorical act possible and asks students to imagine how they might participate in the (re)assembling of more ethical rhetorical outcomes.

At the administrative level, craft agency would dictate that we both build and support the kind of craft pedagogies described above while remaining vigilant to the ways in which the managerial aspects of administration tend to privilege subjectivity over agency and thus can slip into a simplistic craft-as-technique, instrumental view of writing. A craft approach to administration would thus fashion itself as a techne in the most robust sense: as a situated, flexible praxis. Because, as Atwill (1998) reminds us, techne "resists identification with a normative subject" (48), any administrative work grounded in craft agency would be focused not on the management or disciplining of individual subjects—be they teachers or students—but on assembling ethically-attentive, politically viable networks of rhetorical making. As the Women's March illustrates, creating flexible coalitions depends upon recognizing a broad array of co-constitutive material while also acknowledging the material specificity of those actors. These are the same coalitions that are essential to making any administrative endeavor successful. As such, craft may be especially instructive to WPA or other administrators who seek to reorient power within the assemblages they occupy in more equitable ways.

Consider, for example, how such an administrative philosophy might address the field's persistent and pernicious labor issues: because craft agency foregrounds the intra-active, material practices of making in which all rhetorical activity (including the teaching of writing) participates, it provides both a justification for and a roadmap to collective action as a means of transforming the ruthless labor practices that currently dominate the teaching of writing. Craft agency in this context follows the calls laid out in the 2016 Indianapolis Resolution, which addresses some of the field's most pressing labor exigences, most notably our continued reliance on (and, often, exploitation of) contingent faculty. This collaboratively authored document "calls on our professional organizations and their members to commit actively to labor equity" (Cox et al. 2016, 43), specifically challenging the field to "draw explicit attention to the reality that material conditions are teaching and learning conditions—that current labor conditions undervalue the intellectual demand on teaching, restrict resources such as technology and space to contract faculty, withhold conditions for shared and fair governance, and perpetuate unethical hiring practices—as the central pedagogical and labor issue of our time" (40). Craft agency responds to these demands by making visible the material assemblages produced by our disciplinary labor practices, and, importantly, recognizing that they are not fixed but instead always in process and up for negotiation. Meaningful, lasting changes do not result from the work of a single actor (even an especially significant one like a WPA) but emerges only from "solidarity," as the authors of the Indianapolis Resolution note (53). Resisting the neoliberal university's embrace of the "academic prescription, economic and management thinking, and subject-driven approaches" (Dobrin 2011, 94) that only work to constrain composition, and the majority of its labor force, within the lowliest of positions within the academy, will thus depend on our ability to harness "the power of coalition work" (Cox et al. 2016, 62). Individual administrators, then, should consider how they might foster labor practices that are based in a reciprocal ethics of entanglement, such as adopting the mechanisms for documenting labor conditions recommended by the Indianapolis Resolution.

Another example of how craft agency might play out in an administrative context can be found in the work of Asao B. Inoue (2019), who also calls attention to the question of labor through this proposal to move to labor-based contract grading. He notes that because "all grading and assessment exist within systems that uphold singular, dominant standards that are racist, and White supremacist" (3), labor-based contract grading attempts to make assessment practices more equitable, "offer[ing] students in writing classrooms the chance not just to redirect the way power moves in the classroom, but to critique power" (305). Inoue's argument not only foregrounds the (material) bodies that labor in our classrooms, but it also highlights how that labor exists with broader "assessment ecologies" (24). That is, Inoue asks us to rethink assessment not as the evaluation of singular student subjects, but as the practices that produce student agency within broader institutional assemblages. While Inoue's argument is located for the most part in localized classroom assessment, it is easy to imagine how it might inform programmatic-level assessment practices, enacting craft agency at a broader scale by being attuned not only to the varied assemblages we, along with our students, inhabit, but how those assemblages often work to reproduce power inequities. In this case, Inoue's work highlights how the assessment ecologies we exist within and construct can work in service of white supremacy. Inoue's argument thus prompts WPAs and others working at the administrative level to consider how even our most basic or even mundane disciplinary practices might be reoriented in more equitable ways, producing and participating in more ethical assemblages.

Finally, the politics and ethics of craft agency I've outlined here would insist that our scholarship engage with the material consequences of our research. The arguments that comprise this book might be understood as one attempt to enact craft agency at the scholarly level, as I've sought to help the field articulate the ethical implications and political values inherent in new materialist accounts of rhetoric and rhetorical agency. Scholarship that takes craft agency seriously would reject any attempt at theorizing it and does not consider the material bodies at stake, particularly those who lack access to powerful agentic networks. By centering these bodies, their intra-actions, and their experiences, we can ensure our scholarship is attuned to the networks of power that govern rhetorical action and, ideally, will consider how to redistribute this power in more equitable ways.

Such work is ambitious, but it is certainly possible; indeed, there are notable instances of scholars enacting craft agency in their work. Dustin Edwards's (2020) article "Digital Rhetoric on a Damaged Planet" is one such example, as he asks us "to consider how the foundations of rhetoric in a networked world are inseparable from conditions of environmental, ecological, and cultural damage" (60). While Edwards' argument that "the material infrastructures of the internet and connected platforms and devices are tangled up with lands, waters, energies, and histories that are often unseen, unfelt, or unacknowledged in our everyday lives" (60) is significant in terms of how we theorize rhetoric, I want to highlight how Edwards's work exemplifies craft agency. He challenges us—not just as scholars but as humans responsible, in some part, for the digital damage he traces—to make and dwell with stories of that damage, stories that "travel . . . into our classrooms, communities, and scholarship, collecting new thinking partners and tending to different sets of relations along the way" (69). Edwards calls on us to recognize who and what we make with, encouraging us to reorient our scholarly practices toward the kind of ethical intra-actions that drive craft agency.

Andrea Riley-Mukavetz's (2020) argument for a "relational scholarly practice" is another excellent example of craft agency at work. This approach asks writing studies scholars "to develop a series of respectful and reciprocal practices to other agents and beings where we (re: human actors) are not at the center of this constellated network but just one aspect of the web" (546), specifically through "developing a relationship with Indigenous intellect" (548). Riley-Mukavetz enacts the practice she advocates through storytelling, narrating her complicated relationship with snakes. As she reflects on several often-fearful encounters with snakes, Riley-Mukavetz seeks to "[develop] a relationship to the land through an Indigenous orientation [in order to] further understand how the colonial past and the paracolonial present impact our writing" (562). Importantly, Riley-Mukavetz's land-based method is also attentive to the material specificity of the body, as it asks us to reflect on how our bodies shape, and are shaped by, the lands on which we dwell. The vulnerability—and concurrent commitment to better understanding the various relationships that shape our embodied, emplaced experiences—that characterizes Riley-Mukavetz's "relational scholarly practice" is exactly the kind of difficult work craft agency demands of us, even if such work has perhaps not been valued by traditional disciplinary and institutional structures.

There are of course a number of additional ways craft agency might shape our scholarly practices, but to close, I want to focus on one ostensibly small but meaningful practice: citation. As I discussed in chapter 1, citational assemblages can be both powerful and exclusionary. Sara Ahmed (2017) has likened citation to both "memory" (15) and "bricks: the materials through which, from which, we create our dwellings" (16). While Ahmed is writing specifically about feminist citation, I think her point might also prompt reflection about citation practices more broadly. Whose thinking do we privilege in our scholarship? What does that mean for the kind of claims we can make or the work we can do? What kind of agential entanglements do we make visible—and which do we obscure—as we construct citational assemblages? For those of us working with new materialist rhetorics, we might recall the prolonged and repeated elision of Indigenous knowledges. As Clary-Lemon (2019) asks, "What might it look like if every new materialist scholar, as a matter of etiquette and decorum, alluded to connections with, instead of distance from, Indigenous work—or allowed the possibility to see themselves as mistaken" (sec. 4, para. 4)? We might also consider the nonhumans who make out scholarship possible, such as the land we write on, the bodies we write from, the software we write with, or the animals we write alongside.[5] A craft agency approach to citation and knowledge production would recognize the power inequities within the assemblages that simultaneously create and are created by a discipline and would seek to develop practices that productively and ethically reorient that power. We should consider, then, not just our citational practices as writers and researchers but our capacities as reviewers, editors, and advisors.[6] Working to foster more meaningful, more ethical, citational intra-actions within our scholarship is undoubtedly the kind of practice that craft agency seeks.

Across all the wide-ranging disciplinary practices I've highlighted here—our pedagogical, administrative, and scholarly work—is an implicit or explicit attention to the craft knowledge of techne. As I've argued in this chapter, figuring our disciplinary work as an inventive, entangled practice is essential for the continued growth and health of the field. Indeed, it is this uniquely generative nature that defines that field, claims Cooper (2019), in her book *The Animal Who Writes*: "Writing and teaching writing," she notes, "is all about possibilities for what could be" (234). As a discipline, that is, we are fundamentally invested in making the world anew, again and again; we are, in short, a craft discipline. Understanding writing and rhetoric as craft practices that structure our political and ethical lives both within and beyond the classroom allows us to chart an ambitious intellectual agenda that remains attentive to the many nonhuman, material agents that work alongside us to craft, to make, and to be.

NOTES

INTRODUCTION: RHETORIC IN THE MAKING

1. According to Plant (1997), doctors tried many treatments before Lovelace adopted what she called an "opium system." Plant notes that "this was supposed to bring her down, but it only added to her volatility" (29).

CHAPTER 1: CRAFT AGENCY

1. These theorists, and the many others who represent new materialism, hail from varied, if related, schools such as object-oriented ontology and actor-network theory. I collapse them here, even as I acknowledge the risks in doing so, in order to sketch out the broad contours of the larger material turn I am interested in exploring (especially as it has been taken up in writing studies).
2. Claire Colebrook argues that this kind of Marxist-informed materialist feminist perspective asks us to "both recognize how bodily life has unfolded historically to produce certain relations, and [to] acknowledge that freedom from those relations requires recognition of our materiality" (2008, 63). For more detailed explanations of materialist feminism, see the work of scholars such as Christine Delphy, Martha E. Gimenez, and Rosemary Hennessy.
3. Standpoint theorists including Donna Haraway, Sandra Harding, Nancy Hartsock, and Patricia Hill Collins have argued that because we experience the world (and the world experiences us) through our bodies, embodied experience shapes not only what and how we *know* but what and how we *are*.
4. Gries's (2015) iconographic tracking method is one notable example of a new materialist methodology of symmetry in action. To illustrate, Gries traces the circulation, transformation, and various rhetorical functions of the 2008 Obama Hope campaign poster as it came into contact with various human and nonhuman actors. Through her symmetrical analysis, Gries shows how a methodology focused on mapping intra-actions between humans and nonhumans—rather than the actions of a singular human actor—can offer a view of rhetoric that underscores its dynamic, ecological nature and accounts for the dynamic, co-constitutive nature of rhetorical actors.
5. Powell et al. (2014) are careful to note that "not all cultural rhetorics scholarship is decolonial" but emphasize decolonial thought as central to their work in cultural rhetorics because of its ability to "[work] towards building a world in which many worlds coexist" (sec. 2, n. 15).
6. I am aware that I may be creating a false dichotomy between feminist and Indigenous thinking here. Of course, there are significant overlaps between these two knowledge traditions, even if, as Maile Arvin, Eve Tuck, and Angie Morill note, mainstream feminism is still overwhelmingly white and thus needs to *recognize the persistence of Indigenous concepts and epistemologies, or ways of knowing"* (Arvin, Tuck, and Morrill 2013, 21; emphasis original). My distinction between feminist and Indigenous thinking here is accordingly not meant to perpetuate the exclusion of Indigenous knowledges from

feminist scholarship but instead reflects how these two knowledge traditions are most commonly taken up specifically in rhetorical studies.

7.   It's important to note that I'm using the plural feminist rhetorics deliberately so as to stress the vibrancy and multiplicity inherent in this scholarship. Feminism has never been a static belief system, methodology, or movement, which is why many increasingly prefer to use *feminisms* instead. The plural centers attention on the historical origins and general goals of feminist thought while also providing space for the contradictions and disruptions that are crucial to any living, changing movement. Likewise, my use of "feminist rhetorics" here reflects my desire to recognize the many positions, concerns, and investments of feminist rhetoricians, even while necessarily eliding some of the variation that characterizes this scholarship.

8.   Sennett, notably, does not fall within the feminist scholarly reconsideration of craft. In his influential book *The Craftsman*, Sennett's otherwise detailed and compelling description of craft does not engage deeply with craft's very gendered history. Thus, while I value his account of "crafts*man*ship" (my emphasis), especially because of how it centers process, it is necessarily limited.

CHAPTER 2: CRAFTING HISTORY, CRAFTING RHETORIC

1.   The story of Penelope also highlights craft's protective abilities, especially in the context of sexual violence, notes Jennifer Lin LeMesurier (2019). She suggests that Penelope's constant weaving was in fact an expressive of *mêtic* intelligence meant "to postpone [the] inevitable takeover of her body as property" (147).

2.   Consider, for example, the "industrial institutes" that emerged after the Civil War. Meant "to educate former slaves," writes Anna M. Fariello (2011), they "formed a parallel educational system in which handiwork played a central role . . . schools such as Tuskegee echoed Ruskin in their emphasis on handwork as a significant aspect of the learning experience" (30). In these schools, she notes, "classes in wood, metal, textiles, and leather were common" because of their perceived moral qualities as well as their potential as income-generating trades (30).

3.   Groeneveld focuses on third-wave feminist 'zines specifically, but there is plenty of evidence that there is significant overlap between third-wave feminism more generally and the resurgence of craft practices. One particularly relevant example is the Stitch 'n' Bitch phenomenon of the early 2000s. In 2003, Debbie Stoller, the founding editor of the feminist magazine *BUST*, published her knitting handbook *Stitch 'n' Bitch*, which not only contained cheeky knitting instructions and patterns such as the "Wonder Woman Bikini" and "Umbilical Cord" baby hat, but also had a section specifically devoted to finding and creating knitting communities. This book, and the groups it inspired, not only sought to reclaim a largely dismissive term but also positioned crafting communities as explicitly feminist (Chansky 2010; Minahan and Cox 2007; Turney 2009).

4.   In addition to its status as a national craft retailer, Hobby Lobby is perhaps best known for its role in the 2014 Supreme Court case *Burwell v. Hobby Lobby*. In this case, Hobby Lobby argued against an Affordable Care Act mandate that employer insurance cover birth control, citing concerns that the law violated its corporate "religious freedom." In a 5–4 decision, the court ruled in Hobby Lobby's favor, finding that "closely-held for-profit businesses . . . in which the owners have clear religious beliefs" need not provide coverage for certain kinds of contraception, such as the "morning-after pill" or IUDs (Mears and Cohen 2014).

5.   Wace's argument may not at first glance seem immediately relevant, given that his article was published in 1948. However, many rhetoric scholars (and students)

continue to rely on translations produced prior to 1948. The well-used second edition of Patricia Bizzell and Bruce Herzberg's *Rhetorical Tradition* (2001), for example, includes a translation of Plato's *Gorgias*—which includes a reference to textile work—that was produced in 1925.

6. This "new classicist" (Young 1980) approach to *techne* was important to the development of the field of writing studies because it positioned writing as knowable and thus teachable. For a more detailed discussion on the disciplinary significance of *techne*, see chapter 6.

CHAPTER 3: CRAFTIVISM AND THE MATERIAL SPECIFICITY OF RHETORICAL ACTION

1. Betsy Greer (2007) is typically credited with coining the term "craftivism" around 2003, although she acknowledges that others began using this term around the same time.

2. Yarn bombing is the mode of craftivism that has received the most scholarly attention, which is likely why is has also received the most criticism; these criticisms, however, generally hold across most craftivist practices, given the overwhelmingly white, middle-class makeup of the craftivist community as a whole.

3. The Missing and Murdered Indigenous Women (#MMIW) movement began among Canadian First Nations families and has since spread across North America with the goal of highlighting (and ultimately ending) the staggering rates of violence faced by Indigenous women. While it is difficult to get a clear picture of the scope of the crisis, some data are available. The Centers for Disease Control (2019) reports that homicide is the third leading cause of death among Indigenous women and girls ages 1–19, and the sixth leading cause of death among Indigenous women ages 20–44, while the National Institute of Justice (2016) found that nearly 85 percent of Indigenous women experience violence in their lifetime.

4. The law in question required "physicians who perform abortions to have admitting privileges at a nearby hospital and [required] abortion clinics in the state to have facilities comparable to an ambulatory surgical center" ("Whole Women's Health" n.d.). The Supreme Court found these provisions to be unconstitutional, thus frustrating similar anti-abortion efforts in other states.

5. For more on empathy in writing studies, see, in addition to Leake, Blankenship (2019), Fleckenstein (2009), Lindquist (2004), Lynch (1998), as well as Micciche (2005, 2007).

6. Originally introduced by Sonja K. Foss and Cindy L. Griffin, "invitational rhetoric" denotes a specific approach to rhetorical practice that is meant to offer "an invitation to understanding as a means to create a relationship rooted in equality, immanent value, and self-determination. Invitational rhetoric constitutes an invitation to the audience to enter the rhetor's world and to see it as the rhetor does" (Foss and Griffin 1995, 5). While my use of the term here is not meant to invoke Foss and Griffin's phrase specifically, it is intended to highlight the reciprocity the process they name suggests.

CHAPTER 4: MANIFESTING MATERIAL RELATIONSHIPS ONLINE THROUGH RAVELRY

1. It is difficult to offer a precise gender breakdown of Ravelry users. However, one researcher (who has conducted perhaps the broadest survey of Ravelry's users)

estimates it is roughly 96 percent women (Van Dam 2018). My research—and the reality that knitting and crochet are still strongly gendered—confirms that the site (at the very least) skews heavily female. Ravelry thus attracts a large number of women regularly: as of March 2020, Ravelry reported around 125 monthly page views, with roughly one million of its users active in the prior month. The site also reported a surprisingly loyal userbase, noting that "half of the very first 10,000 people who signed up for Ravelry way back in 2007 used the site during [the week of March 1, 2020]" (Ravelry 2020).

2.   There is a bit of debate around the question of what ancient textile practices count as "true" knitting. Many Egyptian knit artifacts, often described as "Coptic knitting," were produced by a different one-needle process that is usually seen as the predecessor to contemporary two-needle knitting (Hamilton-Brown 2017; Van Strydonk, De Moore, and Benazeth 2004). However, these technical differences are less relevant to my goal here of tracing knitting's *cultural* history.

3.   After obtaining IRB approval, I contacted Ravelry site administrators to ask how I might go about recruiting participants. The site administrator I contacted (using Ravelry's private messaging feature) informed me that the site did not permit research recruitment through the general forums. I was, however, welcome to contact individual groups and seek permission to recruit through their group forums. I sought and received permission to recruit in one of Ravlery's most popular groups, *Miscellaneous* (with 857 members) as well as two smaller groups to which I already belonged, *The Knitting Rhetoricians* and *MU Knit and Crochet*. I asked interview and survey participants about their experiences as knitters and as Ravelers, focusing on the Ravelry community as well as its interface. However, recruiting through the forums also likely resulted in a skewed sample, attracting participants who are at least somewhat active in various groups, which may not be representative of all or even most Ravelry users.

4.   I have used pseudonyms for interview participants.

5.   During an episode of the *Fiber Beat* podcast, co-founder Jessica Forbes explains that the company "[tries] not to ask too much information, because we're definitely not of a Facebook model of, like, mining for information" (Wade 2011).

6.   To be clear, Ravelry's policy does not ban *supporters* of Trump or his administration; it only bans users from posting content that supports Trump or his administration. Still, the ban prompted many Trump supporters to leave the site and even inspired the creation of new rival websites such as Fiberkind and Freedom Knits, where Trump-related fiber content is freely shared (Basu 2020).

7.   Pattern and material (such as yarn or needles) sales, along with minimal fiber-based advertising, keep Ravelry functioning from a financial standpoint: The site takes a cut of these sales to fund itself.

8.   Photos are important across the digital knitting world beyond Ravelry, but their use has been criticized for perpetuating a "white aesthetic." One knitter of color explained that on spaces like Instagram, popular photographs "focus[ed] on the knitting, not the person doing the knitting, which made it easier to forget what that person looked like. And sometimes, when followers were reminded, they showed their prejudice" (Saxena 2019). On Ravelry, however, bodies are frequently featured in project photos (especially for objects meant to be worn), even if the photos may perpetuate this "white aesthetic" in other ways.

9.   Of the 46 responses to an open-ended question asking about Ravelry's community, 41 participants—nearly 90 percent—had only positive reactions.

10.   In the pattern database, for example, the "language" search parameter shows twenty different languages for knitting patterns alone, with more than 230,000 patterns available in languages other than English.

11.   These events—formerly called the "Ravelympics"—have been popular since 2008, but after receiving a cease-and-desist notice from the US Olympic Committee accusing the site of copyright violation in 2012, the name "Ravellenic Games" was adopted instead (Midgette 2012).

CHAPTER 5: THE WOMEN'S MARCH, DIGITAL-MATERIAL ASSEMBLAGES, AND EMBODIED DIFFERENCE

1.   Mariella Mosthof (2017) notes that this new name also, intentionally or not, calls back to another well-known, Black-led protest, the 1963 March on Washington, which famously featured Martin Luther King Jr.'s "I Have a Dream Speech."

2.   Anne Graefer, Allaina Kilby, and Inger-Lise Kalviknes Bore explored the widespread use of grotesque humor in Women's March signs. They noted the presence of signs that deprecated Trump's body, relied on fecal or bodily waste humor, or that employed otherwise vulgar or offensive language or imagery, and suggest the presence of these kind of signs "[provide] an effective intervention in the dominant regime by allowing unheard voices to be heard and to respond to the issues they face" (Graefer, Kilby, and Bore 2018, 19). Signs at WMAL proved no exception, as some featured ostensibly vulgar language (like "Fuck the Patriarchy," or "Bitches Get Stuff Done") while others made use of bodily waste humor (a protester carrying a sign reading "Don't PEE on my rights" while also sporting a yellow umbrella) in order to offer a physical marker to the perceived grotesque spectacle of the presidential inauguration that took place just the day before.

3.   Biesecker specifically targets Karlyn Kohrs Campbell's groundbreaking 1989 anthology *Man Cannot Speak for Her*, which features (mainly) the rhetorical performances of individual women. Biesecker charges that Campbell uncritically adopts an individualist point of view. In a response essay, Campbell (1993) accepts this charge, writing, "The rhetorical efforts of women were, with some exceptions, created by individual women, those of men, by individual men" (155). However, given Campbell's (2005) later description of rhetorical agency as "communal" (3)—a definition I discuss in more detail in chapter 1—it is likely that her understanding of rhetoric as an individualist endeavor has evolved.

CHAPTER 6: RESCUING CRAFT FOR WRITING STUDIES

1.   It is hard not to recall Plato's famous dismissal of rhetoric as "cookery" in *Gorgias* (463b-c) here. While Plato's repudiation of rhetoric as knack (or craft) rather than an art is meant to undermine it, Elbow embraces this metaphor, seeing it as a way of demystifying the practice of writing.

2.   Expressivism is a fraught designation, and it is not my intention in this necessarily reductive overview to argue for either the limitations or virtues of expressivism. Generally speaking, though, expressivism posits that good writing emerges, at least in part, from the internal experiences of writers. Macrorie (2009), for example, locates good writing within the "honest" (299) and "authentic" (313) rendering of individual experiences, while Elbow claims that "writing calls on the ability to create words and ideas out of yourself" (7), describing invention as the process of "finding words in your head and putting them down on a blank piece of paper" (14). Expressivism was accused of representing a "naiveté about the status of 'individual imagination' and 'personal voice'" that ignores "the nature of language as a social practice" (Knoblach 1988, 132). However, an ongoing and lively debate

surrounding expressivism persists, with its defenders arguing that "expressivist bashing" (O'Donnell 1996, 423) ignores expressivism's potential to encourage "a thoughtful exploration of the social origins and positions of students" (Sumpter 2016, 343).

3.   It is difficult to provide exact data on who is teaching composition courses, but Jill Gladstein and Brandon Fralix's *National Census of Writing* perhaps comes closest to quantifying instructor demographics, even if its response rates are relatively low (Gladstein and Fralix 2013). The data do suggest, however, that most first-year composition courses are not taught by tenured or tenure-track composition specialists: Across 412 responses from four-year institutions, for example, 331 (80%) of responses noted that none of its sections of first-year composition courses were staffed by tenured or tenure-track writing studies faculty in the 2011–12 academic year.

4.   One particularly interesting exploration of multimodal pedagogies is found in Jason Palmeri's (2012) book *Remixing Composition*, which outlines the sometimes occluded but nevertheless rich history of multimodal composing in composition. Palmeri advocates a pedagogy very much in line with the multimodal approaches I outline here—one that, in his words, asks "students to employ multiple forms of composing to critically rehear and resee the world . . . to increase the likelihood that they will come to recognize and attempt to transform the unjust material hierarchies of race, class, gender, sexuality, and ability" (159). However, what is most relevant to my work in this chapter is Palmeri's tracing of multimodality throughout the earliest days of composition. Notably, the traces of multimodality he locates—such as Ray Kytle's 1972 *Comp Box*, which provided "students a box of *unbound* photocopied materials as well as an author's guide that explains the ways that students might draw upon the materials (cutting, pasting, rearranging, adding, deleting) to make their own texts" (103; emphasis original)—are almost all recognizably craft practices.

5.   For a fascinating account of how scholars already perform such work through the genre of acknowledgment sections, see Laura Micciche's (2017) *Acknowledging Writing Partners*. While acknowledgments may be dismissed as either "narcissistic" or "mundane" (21), I share Micciche's belief that they "enact a sophisticated theory of writing partnerships" (25).

6.   Carrie Mott and Daniel Cockayne, writing from the specific disciplinary location of geography, offer some concrete suggestions on this front that can inform the work of any scholar seeking to cultivate ethical citational assemblages (Mott and Cockayne 2017). They recommend that researchers engage in citation counting as a way to gauge (if imprecisely) how the identities of authors cited may reify exclusionary disciplinary power structures. They also suggest that researchers intentionally seek out nonacademic sources that may be more accessible to authors marginalized within academia. Additionally, they encourage academic journals and editors to develop citation policies that require authors to participate in more equitable citation practices.

REFERENCES

5.4 Million and Counting. n.d. "About." *Facebook*. Accessed November 23, 2021. https://www.facebook.com/5point4million/about.

Adsanatham, Chanon. 2018. "Bloody Rhetoric and Civic Unrest: Rhetorical Aims of Human Blood Splashing in the 2010 Thai Political Revolt." *Advances in the History of Rhetoric* 21 (3): 271–292. https://doi.org/10.1080/15362426.2018.1526546.

Ahmed, Sara. 2017. *Living a Feminist Life*. Durham: Duke University Press.

Alaimo, Stacy. 2008. "Trans-Corporeal Feminisms and the Ethical Space of Nature." In *Material Feminisms*, edited by Stacy Alaimo and Susan Hekman, 237–264. Bloomington: Indiana University Press.

Alaimo, Stacy. 2010. "The Naked Word: The Trans-Corporeal Ethics of the Protesting Body." *Women & Performance: A Journal of Feminist Theory* 20, no. 1 (March): 15–36. https://doi.org/10.1080/07407701003589253.

Alexander, Jonathan, and Jacqueline Rhodes. 2014. *On Multimodality: New Media in Composition Studies*. Urbana, IL: Conference on College Composition and Communication/National Council of Teachers of English.

Anderson, Joyce Rain. 2018. "Walking with Relatives: Indigenous Bodies of Protest." In *Unruly Rhetorics: Protest, Persuasion, Publics*, edited by Jonathan Alexander, Susan C. Jarratt, and Nancy Welch, 45–59. Pittsburgh: University of Pittsburgh Press.

Arola, Kristin L. 2010. "The Design of Web 2.0: The Rise of the Template, The Fall of Design." *Computers and Composition* 27, no. 1 (March): 4–14. https://doi.org/10.1016/j.compcom.2009.11.004.

Arola, Kristin L., and Adam Arola. 2017. "An Ethics of Assemblage: Creative Repetition and the 'Electric Pow Wow.'" In *Assembling Composition*, edited by Kathleen Blake Yancey and Stephen J. McElroy, 204–221. Urbana, IL: Conference on College Composition and Communication/National Council of Teachers of English.

Arvin, Maile, Eve Tuck, and Angie Morrill. 2013. "Decolonizing Feminism: Challenging Connections between Settler Colonialism and Heteropatriarchy." *Feminist Formations* 25, no. 1 (Spring): 8–34. https://doi.org/10.1353/ff.2013.0006.

Atwill, Janet. 1998. *Rhetoric Reclaimed: Aristotle and the Liberal Arts Tradition*. Ithaca, NY: Cornell University Press.

Banks, Adam J. 2006. *Race, Rhetoric, and Technology: Searching for Higher Ground*. Mahwah, NJ: Lawrence Erlbaum.

Banks, William P. 2003. "Written Through the Body: Disruptions and 'Personal' Writing." *College English* 66, no. 1 (September): 21–40.

Barad, Karen. 2007. *Meeting the Universe Halfway: Quantum Physics and the Entanglement of Matter and Meaning*. Durham, NC: Duke University Press.

Barkham, Patrick. 2011. "Nazis, Needlework and My Dad." *The Guardian*, September 2, 2011. https://www.theguardian.com/lifeandstyle/2011/sep/03/tony-casdagli-father-stitching-nazis.

Barlyn, Suzanne. 2018. "Strap on the FitBit: John Hancock to Sell Only Interactive Life Insurance." *Reuters*, September 19, 2018. https://www.reuters.com/article/us-manulife-financi-john-hancock-lifeins/strap-on-the-fitbit-john-hancock-to-sell-only-interactive-life-insurance-idUSKCN1LZ1WL.

https://doi.org/10.7330/9781646422555.c007

Barnett, Scot. 2015. "Rhetoric's Nonmodern Constitution: Techne, Phusis, and the Production of Hybrids." In *Thinking with Bruno Latour in Rhetoric and Composition*, edited by Paul Lynch and Nathaniel Rivers, 81–96. Carbondale: Southern Illinois University Press.

Barnett, Scot, and Casey Boyle. 2016 "Introduction: Rhetorical Ontology, or, How to Do Things with Things." In *Rhetoric, Through Everyday Things*, edited by Scot Barnett and Casey Boyle, 1–14. Tuscaloosa: University of Alabama Press.

Basu, Tanya. 2020. "How a Ban on Pro-Trump Patterns Unraveled the Online Knitting World." *MIT Review*, March 6, 2020. https://www.technologyreview.com/s/615325/ravelry-banon-pro-trump-patterns-unraveled-the-online-knitting-world-censorship-free/.

Behar, Katherine. 2016. *Object-Oriented Feminism*. Minneapolis: University of Minnesota Press.

Bellower, Hannah, and Scarlett Berrones. 2015. "The 'Hatting' of the Clock: Crafting Juniata's Knitting Community through Yarn Bombing the Clock Tower." *Harlot* 14. http://www.harlotofthearts.org/index.php/harlot/article/view/309/170.

Bennett, Jane. 2010. *Vibrant Matter: A Political Ecology of Things*. Durham, NC: Duke University Press.

Berlin, James. 1988. "Rhetoric and Ideology in the Writing Class." *College English* 50, no. 5 (September): 477–494.

Betlemidze, Mariam. 2015. "Mediatized Controversies of Feminist Protest: FEMEN and Bodies as Affective Events." *Women's Studies in Communication* 38 (4): 374–379. https://doi.org/10.1080/07491409.2015.1089103.

Biesecker, Barbara. 1992. "Coming to Terms with Recent Attempts to Write Women into the History of Rhetoric." *Philosophy and Rhetoric* 25 (2): 140–159.

Bishop, Wendy. 1990. *Released into Language: Options for Teaching Creative Writing*. Urbana, IL: National Council of Teachers of English.

Bizzell, Patricia, and Bruce Herzberg, eds. 2001. *The Rhetorical Tradition: Readings from Classical Times to the Present*. 2nd ed. Boston: Bedford/St. Martin's.

Black, Anthea, and Nicole Burisch. 2011. "Craft Hard Die Free: Radical Curatorial Strategies for Craftivism." In *Extra/Ordinary: Craft and Contemporary Art*, edited by Maria Elena Buszek, 204–221. Durham, NC: Duke University Press.

Black, Shannon. 2017. "KNIT+ RESIST: Placing the Pussyhat Project in the Context of Craft Activism." *Gender, Place & Culture* 24 (5): 696–710. https://doi.org/10.1080/0966369X.2017.1335292.

Blair, Carole, and Neil Michel. 2007. "The AIDS Memorial Quilt and the Contemporary Culture of Public Commemoration." *Rhetoric and Public Affairs* 10, no. 4 (Winter): 595–626. https://doi.org/10.1353/rap.2008.0024.

Blankenship, Lisa. 2019. *Changing the Subject: A Theory of Rhetorical Empathy*. Logan: Utah State University Press.

Boardman, Kathleen A., and Joy Ritchie. 1999. "Feminism in Composition: Inclusion, Metonymy, and Disruption." *College Composition and Communication* 5, no. 1 (June): 585–606.

Bogost, Ian. 2012. *Alien Phenomenology, or What It's Like to be a Thing*. Minneapolis: University of Minnesota Press.

Boothroyd, Sydney, Rachelle Bowen, Alicia Cattermole, Kenda Chang Swanson, Hanna Daltrop, Sasha Dwyer, Anna Gunn, et al. 2017. "(Re)Producing Feminine Bodies: Emergent Spaces Through Contestation in the Women's March on Washington." *Gender, Place & Culture* 24 (5): 711–721. https://doi.org/10.1080/0966369X.2017.1339673.

Borda, Jennifer L. 2002. "The Woman Suffrage Parades of 1910–1913: Possibilities and Limitations of an Early Feminist Rhetorical Strategy." *Western Journal of Communication* 66, no. 1 (Winter): 25–52. https://doi.org/10.1080/10570310209374724.

Bore, Inger-Lise Kalviknes, Anne Graefer, and Allaina Kilby. 2017. "This Pussy Grabs Back: Humour, Digital Affects and Women's Protest." *Open Cultural Studies* 1 (1): 529–540. https://doi.org/10.1515/culture-2017-0050.

Boyle, Casey. 2016. "Writing and Rhetoric and/as Posthuman Practice." *College English* 78, no. 6 (July): 532–554.

Boyle, Casey, James J. Brown, and Steph Ceraso. 2018 "The Digital: Rhetoric Behind and Beyond the Screen." *Rhetoric Society Quarterly* 48 (3): 251–259. https://doi.org/10.1080/02773945.2018.1454187.

Bratich, Jack Z. 2010. "The Digital Touch: Craft-work as Immaterial Labour and Ontological Accumulation." *ephemera* 10 (3/4): 303–318.

Bratich, Jack Z., and Heidi M. Brush. 2011. "Fabricating Activism: Craft-Work, Popular Culture, Gender." *Utopian Studies* 22 (1): 233–260.

Bray, Tim. 2009. "Ravelry." *Ongoing* (blog). September 2, 2009. http://www.tbray.org/ongoing/When/200x/2009/09/02/Ravelry.

Brewer, Sierra, and Lauren Dundes. 2018. "Concerned, Meet Terrified: Intersectional Feminism and the Women's March." *Women's Studies International Forum* 69 (July–August): 49–55. https://doi.org/10.1016/j.wsif.2018.04.008.

Buchanan, Lindal. 2005. *Regendering Delivery: The Fifth Canon and Antebellum Women Rhetors.* Carbondale: Southern Illinois University Press.

Burgess, Helen, Krystin Gollihue, and Stacey Pigg. 2018. "The Fates of Things." *Enculturation* 29. http://enculturation.net/fates.

Burns, Katelyn. 2017. "How 'Pussy Hats' Made Me Feel Excluded—and Then Welcomed—at The Women's March." *Medium,* January 23, 2017. https://medium.com/the-establishment/how-pussy-hats-made-me-feel-excluded-and-then-welcomed-at-the-women-s-march-ef11dae19c54.

Campbell, Colin. 2005. "The Craft Consumer: Culture, Craft and Consumption in a Postmodern Society." *Journal of Consumer Culture* 5 (1): 23–42. https://doi.org/10.1177/1469540505049843.

Campbell, Karlyn Kohrs. 1993. "Biesecker Cannot Speak for Her Either." *Philosophy and Rhetoric* 26 (2): 153–159.

Campbell, Karlyn Kohrs. 2005. "Agency: Promiscuous and Protean." *Communication and Critical/Cultural Studies* 2, no. 1 (March): 1–19. https://doi.org/10.1080/1479142042000332134.

Carlson, Erin Brock. 2020. "Embracing a Metic Lens for Community-Based Participatory Research in Technical Communication." *Technical Communication Quarterly* 29 (4): 1–19. https://doi.org/10.1080/10572252.2020.1789745.

Carr, Chantel, and Chris Gibson. 2016. "Geographies of Making: Rethinking Materials and Skills for Volatile Futures." *Progress in Human Geography* 4 (3): 297–315. https://doi.org/10.1177/0309132515578775.

Castells, Manuel. 2012. *Networks of Outrage and Hope: Social Movements in the Internet Age.* Cambridge, UK: Polity Press.

Centers for Disease Control. 2019. *Leading Causes of Death—Females—Non-Hispanic American Indian or Alaska Native—United States, 2017.* https://www.cdc.gov/women/lcod/2017/nonhispanic-native/index.htm.

Chalmers, Jamie. 2014. "Don't Get Angry, Get Cross-Stitch!" In *Craftivism: The Art and Craft of Activism,* edited by Betsy Greer. Kindle ed. Vancouver, Canada: Arsenal Pulp Press.

Chansky, Ricia A. 2010. "A Stitch in Time: Third-Wave Feminist Reclamation of Needled Imagery." *The Journal of Popular Culture* 43 (4): 681–700.

Chávez, Karma R. 2011. "Counter-Public Enclaves and Understanding the Function of Rhetoric in Social Movement Coalition-Building." *Communication Quarterly* 59, no. 1 (January–March): 1–18. https://doi.org/10.1080/01463373.2010.541333.

Chenoweth, Erica, and Jeremy Pressman. 2017. "This is What we Learned by Counting the Women's Marches." *Washington Post,* February 7, 2017. https://www.washingtonpost

.com/news/monkey-cage/wp/2017/02/07/this-is-what-we-learned-by-counting-the-womens-marches/?noredirect=on&utm_term=.13259f194579.

CheyOnna. 2017. "On Why Knitting Can Be Part of the Struggle for Black Liberation." *The Yarn Mission* (blog), August 15, 2017. http://theyarnmission.com/part-one-on-why-knitting-can-be-part-of-the-struggle-for-black-liberation/.

Chira, Susan, and Yamiche Alcindor. 2017. "Defiant Voices Flood U.S. Cities as Women Rally for Rights." *New York Times*, January 21, 2017. https://www.nytimes.com/2017/01/21/us/women-march-protest-president-trump.html.

Cho, Sumi, Kimberlé Crenshaw, and Leslie McCall. 2013. "Toward a Field of Intersectionality Studies: Theory, Application, and Praxis." *Signs* 38, no. 4 (Summer): 785–810. https://doi.org/10.1086/669608.

Christensen, Henrik Serup. 2011. "Political Activities on the Internet: Slacktivism or Political Participation by Other Means?" *First Monday* 16, no. 2 (February). https://firstmonday.org/article/view/3336/2767.

Clark, Nicole. 2019. "The Real Reason Ravelry's Ban on White Supremacy is Surprising." *Vice*, June 25, 2019. https://www.vice.com/en_us/article/xwnp4a/the-real-reason-ravelrys-ban-on-white-supremacy-is-surprising.

Clary-Lemon, Jennifer. 2019. "Gifts, Ancestors, and Relations: Notes Towards an Indigenous New Materialism." *Enculturation* 30. http://enculturation.net/gifts_ancestors_and_relations.

Close, Samantha. 2018. "Knitting Activism, Knitting Gender, Knitting Race." *International Journal of Communication* 12:867–889.

Cocker, Emma. 2017. "Weaving Codes/Coding Weaves: Penelopean Mêtis and the Weaver-Coder's Kairos." *Textile* 15 (2): 124–141. https://doi.org/10.1080/14759756.2017.1298233.

Colebrook, Claire. 2008. "On Not Becoming Man: The Materialist Politics of Unactualized Potential." In *Material Feminisms*, edited by Stacy Alaimo and Susan Hekman, 52–84. Bloomington: Indiana University Press.

Connors, Robert J. 1985. "Mechanical Correctness as a Focus in Composition Instruction." *College Composition and Communication* 36, no. 1 (February): 61–72.

Coole, Diana, and Samantha Frost. 2010. "Introducing the New Materialisms." In *New Materialisms: Ontology, Agency, and Politics*, edited by Diana Coole and Samantha Frost, 1–43. Durham, NC: Duke University Press.

Cooper, Marilyn M. 2011. "Rhetorical Agency as Emergent and Enacted." *College Composition and Communication* 62, no. 3 (February): 420–449.

Cooper, Marilyn M. 2019. *The Animal Who Writes: A Posthumanist Composition*. Pittsburgh: University of Pittsburgh Press.

Corbett, Edward P. J. 1969. "The Rhetoric of the Open Hand and the Rhetoric of the Closed Fist." *College Composition and Communication* 20, no. 5 (December): 288–296.

Costin, Cathy Lynn. 2015. "Craft Specialization." In *The International Encyclopedia of Human Sexuality*, edited by Patricia Whelehan and Anne Bolin, 270–274. Malden, MA: Wiley-Blackwell.

Cox, Annica, Timothy R. Dougherty, Seth Kahn, Michelle LaFrance, and Amy Lynch-Biniek. 2016. "The Indianapolis Resolution: Responding to Twenty-First-Century Exigencies/Political Economies of Composition Labor." *College Composition and Communication* 68, no. 1 (September): 38–67.

Coyle, Kat. 2016. "The Pussyhat Project Knit Pattern." *Ravelry*, November 2016. https://www.ravelry.com/patterns/library/pussyhat-project.

Craftivist Collective. 2013. "Craftivism Ingredient #3: Building Relationships Through Craft." *Craftivist Collective* (blog), July 10, 2013. https://craftivist-collective.com/blog/2013/07/an-ingredient-of-our-craftivism-recipe-building-relationships-through-craft/.

Crawford, Alan. 1997. "Ideas and Objects: The Arts and Crafts Movement in Britain." *Design Issues* 13, no. 1 (Spring): 15–26.

Crenshaw, Kimberlé. 1989. "Demarginalizing the Intersection of Race and Sex: A Black Feminist Critique of Antidiscrimination Doctrine, Feminist Theory and Antiracist Politics." *University of Chicago Legal Forum* 139–167.

Croeser, Sky, and Tim Highfield. 2014. "Occupy Oakland and #oo: Uses of Twitter Within the Occupy Movement." *First Monday* 19, no. 3 (March). https://firstmonday.org/article/view/4827/3846.

Crowley, Sharon. 1998. *Composition in the University: Historical and Polemical Essays*. Pittsburgh: University of Pittsburgh Press.

"Cunt Fling-Ups!" 2013. *Craft Cartel* (blog). http://craftcartel.com/cunt-fling-ups/.

Cushman, Ellen. 1996. "The Rhetorician as an Agent of Social Change." *College Composition and Communication* 47, no. 1 (February): 7–28.

Cushman, Ellen, Rachel Jackson, Annie Laurie Nichols, Courtney Rivard, Amanda Moulder, Chelsea Murdock, David M. Grant, and Heather Brook Adams. 2019. "Decolonizing Projects: Creating Pluriversal Possibilities in Rhetoric." *Rhetoric Review* 38 (1): 1–22. https://doi.org/10.1080/07350198.2019.1549402.

Dawkins, Nicole. 2011. "Do-It-Yourself: The Precarious Work and Postfemininst Politics of Handmaking (in) Detroit." *Utopian Studies* 22 (2): 261–284. https://doi.org/10.5325/utopianstudies.22.2.0261.

deCerteau, Michel. 2011. *The Practice of Everyday Life*. Translated by Steven Rendall. 3rd ed. Berkeley: University of California Press.

DeLuca, Kevin Michael. 1999. "Unruly Arguments: The Body Rhetoric of Earth First!, Act Up, and Queer Nation." *Argumentation and Advocacy* 36, no. 1 (Summer): 9–21. https://doi.org/10.1080/00028533.1999.11951634.

Detienne, Marcel, and Jean-Pierre Vernant. 1991. *Cunning Intelligence in Greek Culture and Society*. Translated by Janet Lloyd. Chicago: University of Chicago Press.

Dobrin, Sidney I. 2011. *Postcomposition*. Carbondale: Southern Illinois University Press.

Dobrin, Sidney I., ed. 2015. *Writing Posthumanism, Posthuman Writing*. Anderson, SC: Parlor Press.

Dolmage, Jay. 2006. "'Breathe Upon Us an Even Flame': Hephaestus, History, and the Body of Rhetoric." *Rhetoric Review* 25 (2): 119–140. https://doi.org/10.1207/s15327981rr2502_1.

Dolmage, Jay. 2009. "Metis, Mêtis, Mestiza, Medusa: Rhetorical Bodies across Rhetorical Traditions." *Rhetoric Review* 28 (1): 1–28. https://doi.org/10.1080/07350190802540690.

Dubisar, Abby M. 2015. "Embodying and Disabling Antiwar Activism: Disrupting YouTube's 'Mother's Day for Peace.'" *Rhetoric Review* 34 (1): 56–73. https://doi.org/10.1080/07350198.2015.976305.

Duffy, John. 2017. "The Good Writer: Virtue Ethics and the Teaching of Writing." *College English* 79, no. 3 (January): 229–250.

Dupere, Katie. 2017. "These Barbed Wire Dreamcatchers Help Support the Resistance at Standing Rock." *Mashable*, January 30, 2017. https://mashable.com/article/standing-rock-barbed-wire-dreamcatchers/.

Ede, Lisa, Cheryl Glenn, and Andrea Lunsford. 1995. "Border Crossings: Intersections of Rhetoric and Feminism." *Rhetorica: A Journal of the History of Rhetoric* 13, no. 4 (November): 401–442. https://doi.org/10.1525/rh.1995.13.4.401.

Edwards, Clive. 2006. "'Home Is Where the Art Is': Women, Handicrafts and Home Improvement, 1750–1900." *Journal of Design History* 19, no. 1 (Spring): 11–21. https://doi.org/10.1093/jdh/epk002.

Edwards, Dustin. 2020. "Digital Rhetoric on a Damaged Planet: Storying Digital Damage as Inventive Response to the Anthropocene." *Rhetoric Review* 39 (1): 59–72. https://doi.org/10.1080/07350198.2019.1690372.

Elbow, Peter. 1973. *Writing Without Teachers*. New York: Oxford University Press.

Endres, Danielle, and Samantha Senda-Cook. 2011. "Location Matters: The Rhetoric of Place in Protest." *Quarterly Journal of Speech* 97 (3): 257–282. https://doi.org/10.1080/00335630.2011.585167.

Ewalt, Joshua P. 2016. "The Agency of the Spatial." *Women's Studies in Communication* 39 (2): 137–140. https://doi.org/10.1080/07491409.2016.1176788.

Fariello, Anna M. 2011. "Making and Naming: The Lexicon of Studio Craft." In *Extra/Ordinary: Craft and Contemporary Art*, edited by Maria Elena Buszek, 23–42. Durham, NC: Duke University Press.

Feliz, Julia. 2017. "An Open Letter to the Craftivism Movement." *Medium*, August 20, 2017. https://medium.com/@jd.feliz/an-open-letter-to-the-craftivism-movement-816ccb285b0.

Fishman, Stephen M., and Lucille Parkinson McCarthy. 1992. "Is Expressivism Dead?" *College English* 54, no. 6 (October): 647–661.

Fleckenstein, Kristie S. 2005. "Cybernetics, Ethos, and Ethics: The Plight of the Bread-and-Butter-Fly." *JAC* 25 (2): 323–346.

Fleckenstein, Kristie S. 2009. *Vision, Rhetoric, and Social Action in the Composition Classroom.* Carbondale: Southern Illinois University Press.

Fleitz, Elizabeth. 2015. "Material." *Peitho* 18, no. 1 (Fall/Winter): 34–38.

Flynn, Elizabeth A., Patricia Sotirin, and Ann Brady. 2012. "Introduction: Feminist Rhetorical Resilience—Possibilities and Impossibilities." In *Feminist Rhetorical Resilience*, edited by Elizabeth A. Flynn, Patricia Sotirin, and Ann Brady, 1–29. Logan: Utah State University Press.

Foss, Sonja K. 1996. "Re-sourcement as Emancipation: A Case Study of Ritualized Sewing." *Women's Studies in Communication* 19 (1): 55–76.

Foss, Sonja K., and Cindy L. Griffin. 1995. "Beyond Persuasion: A Proposal for an Invitational Rhetoric." *Communications Monographs* 62, no. 1 (March): 2–18. https://doi.org/10.1080/03637759509376345.

Franke-Ruta, Garance. 2017. "More Than 1 in 100 Americans Marched against Donald Trump on Saturday, Say Political Scientists." *Yahoo News*, January 22, 2017. https://www.yahoo.com/news/more-than-1-in-100-americans-marched-against-donald-trump-saturday-say-political-scientists-231429458.html.

Freelon, Deen, Charlton McIlwain, and Meredith Clark. 2018. "Quantifying the Power and Consequences of Social Media Protest." *New Media & Society* 20 (3): 990–1011. https://doi.org/10.1177/1461444816676646.

Fuegi, John, and Jo Francis. 2003. "Lovelace & Babbage and the Creation of the 1843 'Notes.'" *IEEE Annals of the History of Computing* 25, no. 4, (October–December): 16–26. https://doi.org/10.1109/MAHC.2003.1253887.

Gabriel, Teshome, and Fabian Wagmister. 1997. "Notes on Weavin' Digital: T(h)inkers at the Loom." *Social Identities* 3 (3): 333–344. https://doi.org/10.1080/13504639751943.

Gade, Emily Kalah. 2017. "Why the Women's March May Be the Start of a Serious Social Movement." *The Washington Post*, January 30, 2017. https://www.washingtonpost.com/news/monkey-cage/wp/2017/01/30/why-the-womens-march-may-be-the-start-of-a-serious-social-movement/?noredirect=on&utm_term=.c1fc6a8e093e.

Gauntlett, David. 2012. *Making is Connecting: The Social Meaning of Creativity, from DIY and Knitting to YouTube and Web 2.0.* Cambridge, UK: Polity Press.

Geerts, Evelien, and Iris Van der Tuin. 2013. "From Intersectionality to Interference: Feminist Onto-Epistemological Reflections on the Politics of Representation." *Women's Studies International Forum* 41, no. 3 (November–December): 172–178. https://doi.org/10.1016/j.wsif.2013.07.013.

Geisler, Cheryl. 2005. "Teaching the Post-Modern Rhetor: Continuing the Conversation on Rhetorical Agency." *Rhetoric Society Quarterly* 35 (4): 107–113. https://doi.org/10.1080/02773940509391324.

Gelang, Marie. 2013. "Kairos, the Rhythm of Timing." In *Off Beat: Pluralizing Rhythm*, edited by Jan Hein Hoogstad and Birgitte Stougaard Pedersen, 89–101. New York: Rodopi.

Gelt, Jessica. 2017. "Shepard Fairey Explains His 'We the People' Inauguration Protest Posters." *Los Angeles Times*, January 20, 2017. https://www.latimes.com/entertainment /arts/la-et-cm-shepard-fairey-inauguration-20170119-story.html.

Gibson, Chris. 2016. "Material Inheritances: How Place, Materiality, and Labor Process Underpin the Path-Dependent Evolution of Contemporary Craft Production." *Economic Geography* 92 (1): 61–86. https://doi.org/10.1080/00130095.2015.1092211.

Gladstein, Jill, and Brandon Fralix. 2013. *The National Census of Writing*. writingcensus .swarthmore.edu.

Goggin, Maureen Daly. 2002. "An 'Essamplaire Essai' on the Rhetoricity of Needlework Sampler-Making: A Contribution to Theorizing and Historicizing Rhetoricial Praxis." *Rhetoric Review* 21 (4): 309–338. https://doi.org/10.1207/S15327981RR2104_1.

Goggin, Maureen Daly. 2009. "Fabricating Identity: Janie Terrero's 1912 Embroidered English Suffrage Signature Hankerchief." In *Women and Things, 1750–1950: Gendered Material Strategies*, edited by Maureen Daly Goggin and Beth Fowkes Tobin, 18–42. Burlington, VT: Ashgate.

Goggin, Maureen Daly. 2015. "Joie de Fabriquer: The Rhetoricity of Yarn Bombing." *Peitho* 17, no. 2 (Spring/Summer): 145–171.

Goggin, Maureen Daly, and Beth Fowkes Tobin. 2009. "Introduction: Materializing Women." In *Women and Things, 1750–1950: Gendered Material Strategies*, edited by Maureen Daly Goggin and Beth Fowkes Tobin, 1–14. Burlington, VT: Ashgate.

Gökarıksel, Banu, and Sara Smith. 2017. "Intersectional Feminism beyond U.S. Flag Hijab and Pussy Hats in Trump's America." *Gender, Place & Culture* 24 (5): 628–644. https:// doi.org/10.1080/0966369X.2017.1343284.

Gradea, Adriana Cordali. 2014. "Embroidered Feminist Rhetoric in Andrea Dezső's *Lessons from My Mother*." *Rhetoric Review* 33 (3): 219–243. https://doi.org/10.1080/07350198 .2014.917510.

Graefer, Anne, Allaina Kilby, and Inger-Lise Kalviknes Bore. 2018. "Unruly Women and Carnivalesque Countercontrol: Offensive Humor in Mediated Social Protest." *Journal of Communication Inquiry* 43 (2): 171–193. https://doi.org/10.1177/0196859918800485.

Grant, David M. 2017. "Writing Wakan: The Lakota Pipe as Rhetorical Object." *College Composition and Communication* 69, no.1 (September): 61–86.

Greer, Betsy. 2007. "Craftivism Definition." *Craftivism* (blog). http://craftivism.com /definition/.

Greer, Betsy. 2008. *Knitting for Good!* Boston: Trumpeter Books.

Greer, Betsy. 2011. "Whats and Whys." *Craftivism* (blog), June 20, 2011. http://craftivism .com/blog/whats-and-whys-and-craftivism-meets-parliament/.

Greer, Betsy. 2014a. "Knitting Craftivism: From My Sofa to Yours." In *Craftivism: The Art and Craft of Activism*, edited by Betsy Greer. Kindle ed. Vancouver: Arsenal Pulp Press.

Greer, Betsy. 2014b. "Interview with Craft Cartel (Rayna Fahey and Casey Jenkins)." In *Craftivism: The Art and Craft of Activism*, edited by Betsy Greer. Kindle ed. Vancouver: Arsenal Pulp Press.

Greer, Betsy. 2014c. "Interview with Maria Molten of NCAA Net Works." In *Craftivism: The Art and Craft of Activism*, edited by Betsy Greer. Kindle ed. Vancouver: Arsenal Pulp Press.

Greer, Betsy. 2014d. "Interview with Sarah Corbett of the Craftivist Collective." In *Craftivism: The Art and Craft of Activism*, edited by Betsy Greer. Kindle ed. Vancouver: Arsenal Pulp Press.

Greer, Betsy. 2014e. "Interview with Varvara Guljajeva and Mar Canet." In *Craftivism: The Art and Craft of Activism*, edited by Betsy Greer. Kindle ed. Vancouver: Arsenal Pulp Press.

Greer, Betsy. 2015a. "Craft and Privilege, Part 2: Redefining what Crafty and Creative Mean." *Craftivism* (blog), April 8, 2015. http://craftivism.com/blog/craft-and-privilege -part-2-redefining-what-crafty-and-creative-means/.

Greer, Betsy. 2015b. "Craft and Privilege, Part 3: Looking at our Legacy." *Craftivism* (blog), April 16, 2015. http://craftivism.com/blog/craft-and-privilege-part-3-looking-at-our -legacy/.

Gregory, Jill, April Lewton, Stephanie Schmidt, Diane "Dani" Smith, and Mark Mattern. 2002. "Body Politics with Feeling: The Power of the Clothesline Project." *New Political Science* 24 (3): 433–448. https://doi.org/10.1080/0739314022000005455.

Gries, Laurie. 2011. "Agential Matters: Tumbleweed, Women-Pens, Citizen-Hope, and Rhetorical Actancy." In *Ecology, Writing Theory, and New Media*, edited by Sidney I. Dobrin, 67–91. New York: Routledge.

Gries, Laurie. 2015. *Still Life with Rhetoric: A New Materialist Approach for Visual Rhetorics.* Logan: Utah State University Press.

Gries, Laurie E. 2019. "Writing to Assemble Publics: Making Writing Activate, Making Writing Matter." *College Composition and Communication* 70, no. 3 (February): 327–355.

Groeneveld, Elizabeth. 2010. "'Join the knitting revolution': Third-Wave Feminist Magazines and the Politics of Domesticity." *Canadian Review of American Studies* 40 (2): 259–277. https://doi.org/10.1353/crv.2010.0006.

Grosz, Elizabeth A. 1994. *Volatile Bodies: Toward a Corporeal Feminism.* Bloomington: Indiana University Press.

Guilbeault, Douglas, and Samuel Woolley. 2016. "How Twitter Bots are Shaping the Election." *The Atlantic*, November 1, 2016. https://www.theatlantic.com/technology/arch ive/2016/11/election-bots/506072/.

Haas, Angela M. 2007. "Wampum as Hypertext: An American Indian Intellectual Tradition of Multimedia Theory and Practice." *Studies in American Indian Literatures* 19, no. 4 (Winter): 77–100. https://doi.org/10.1353/ail.2008.0005.

Hackney, Fiona. 2006. "Use Your Hands for Happiness: Home Craft and Make-do-and-Mend in British Women's Magazines in the 1920s and 1930s." *Journal of Design History* 19 (1): 24–38. https://doi.org/10.1093/jdh/epk003.

Hahner, Leslie. A., and Scott J. Varda. 2014. "Yarn Bombing and the Aesthetics of Exceptionalism." *Communication and Critical/Cultural Studies* 11, no. 4 (December): 301–321. https://doi.org/10.1080/14791420.2014.959453.

Håland, Evy Johanna. 2004. "Athena's Peplos: Weaving as a Core Female Activity in Ancient and Modern Greece." *Cosmos* 20:155–182.

Hallenbeck, Sarah. S. 2012. "Toward a Posthuman Perspective: Feminist Rhetorical Methodologies and Everyday Practices." *Advances in the History of Rhetoric* 15 (1): 9–27. https://doi.org/10.1080/15362426.2012.657044.

Hamilton, Inga. 2014. "Daily Narratives and Enduring Images: The Love Encased by Craft." In *Craftivism: The Art and Craft of Activism*, edited by Betsy Greer. Kindle ed. Vancouver: Arsenal Pulp Press.

Hamilton-Brown, Lorna. 2017. "Myth—Black People Don't Knit" (master's thesis, Royal College of Art).

Harlizius-Klück, Ellen. 2017. "Weaving as Binary Art and the Algebra of Pattern." *Textile* 15 (2): 176–197. https://doi.org/10.1080/14759756.2017.1298239.

Hawhee, Debra. 2004. *Bodily Arts: Rhetoric and Athletics in Ancient Greece.* Austin: University of Texas Press.

Hawk, Byron. 2004. "Toward a Post-Techne—Or, Inventing Pedagogies for Professional Writing." *Technical Communication Quarterly* 13 (4): 371–92. https://doi.org/10.1207/s15 427625tcq1304_2.

Hawk, Byron. 2007. *A Counter-history of Composition: Toward Methodologies of Complexity.* Pittsburgh: University of Pittsburgh Press.

Hawk, Byron, Chris Lindgren, and Andrew Mara. 2015. "Utopian Laptop Initiatives: From Technological Deism to Object-Oriented Rhetoric." In *Writing Posthumanism, Posthuman Writing*, edited by Sidney I. Dobrin, 192–213. Anderson, SC: Parlor Press.

Hayes, Shannon. 2010. *Radical Homemakers*. Richmondville, NY: Left to Write Press.

Hellstrom, Maria. 2013. "Knitting Ourselves into Being: The Case of Labour and Hip Domesticity on the Social Network ravelry.com" (master's thesis, Victoria University of Wellington).

Hess, Amanda. 2017. "How a Fractious Women's Movement Came to Lead the Left." *The New York Times Magazine*, February 7, 2017. https://www.nytimes.com/2017/02/07/magazine/how-a-fractious-womens-movement-came-to-lead-the-left.html?hp&action=click&pgtype=Homepage&clickSource=story-heading&module=second-column-region&region=top-news&WT.nav=top-news&_r=1.

"History of the Clothesline Project." n.d. *Clothesline Project*, Accessed October 10, 2018. http://www.theclotheslineproject.org/history.htm.

"History of the Quilt." n.d. *The AIDS Memorial Quilt*, Accessed August 24, 2018. https://www.aidsmemorial.org/quilt-history.

Holloway, S. T. 2018. "Why This Black Girl Will Not Be Returning to the Women's March." *Huffpost*, January 19, 2018. https://www.huffpost.com/entry/why-this-black-girl-will-not-be-returning-to-the-womens-march_n_5a3c1216e4b0b0e5a7a0bd4b.

"Home." n.d. *Craftivist Collective*, Accessed August 22, 2018. https://craftivist-collective.com/.

Horner, Bruce. 2007. "Redefining Work and Value for Writing Program Administration." *JAC* 27 (1–2): 163–184.

Inoue, Asao B. 2019. *Labor-Based Grading Contracts: Building Equity in the Compassionate Writing Classroom*. Fort Collins, CO: The WAC Clearinghouse.

Jack, Jordynn. 2009. "Acts of Institution: Embodying Feminist Rhetorical Methodologies in Space and Time." *Rhetoric Review* 28 (3): 285–303. https://doi.org/10.1080/07350190902958909.

Jefferies, Janis. 2016. "Crocheted Strategies: Women Crafting Their Own Communities." *Textile* 14 (1): 14–35. https://doi.org/10.1080/14759756.2016.1142788.

Johnson, Maureen, Daisy Levy, Katie Manthey, and Maria Novotny. 2015. "Embodiment: Embodying Feminist Rhetorics." *Peitho* 18, no. 1 (Fall/Winter): 39–44.

Johnson, Nan. 2002. *Gender and Rhetorical Space in American Life, 1866–1910*. Carbondale: Southern Illinois University Press.

Johnson, Robert R. 2010. "Craft Knowledge: Of Disciplinarity in Writing Studies." *College Composition and Communication* 61, no. 4 (June): 673–690.

Julier, Laura. 1994. "Private Texts and Social Activism: Reading the Clothesline Project." *English Education* 26, no. 4 (December): 249–259.

Kinneavy, James L. 2002. "Kairos in Classical and Modern Theory." In *Rhetoric and Kairos: Essays in History, Theory, and Praxis*, edited by Phillip Sipiora and James S. Baumlin, 58–76. Albany: State University of New York Press.

Kirsch, Gesa. 1999. *Ethical Dilemmas in Feminist Research: The Politics of Location, Interpretation, and Publication*. Albany: State University of New York Press.

Knoblach, C. H. 1988. "Rhetorical Constructions: Dialogue and Commitment." *College English* 50, no. 2 (February): 125–140.

Krugh, Michele. 2014. "Joy in Labour: The Politicization of Craft from the Arts and Crafts Movement to Etsy." *Canadian Review of American Studies* 44, no. 2 (Summer): 281–301. https://doi.org/10.3138/CRAS.2014.S06.

Kurlinkus, William Campbell. 2014. "Crafting Designs: An Archaeology of 'Craft' as God Term." *Computers and Composition* 33 (September): 50–67. https://doi.org/10.1016/j.compcom.2014.07.002.

Kurtyka, Faith. 2016. "We're Creating Ourselves Now: Crafting as Feminist Rhetoric in a Social Sorority." *Peitho* 18, no. 2 (Spring/Summer): 25–44.

Laposky, Issie. 2017. "The Women's March Defines Protest in the Facebook Age." *Wired*, January 21, 2017. https://www.wired.com/2017/01/womens-march-defines-protest-facebook-age/.

Larabee, Ann. 2017. "Pussy Hats as Social Movement Symbols." *The Journal of Popular Culture* 50 (2): 215–217. https://doi.org/10.1111/jpcu.12547.

Latour, Bruno. 2005. *Reassembling the Social: An Introduction to Actor-Network-Theory*. New York: Oxford University Press.

Leake, Eric. 2016. "Writing Pedagogies of Empathy: As Rhetoric and Disposition." *Composition Forum*, 34 (Summer). http://compositionforum.com/issue/34/empathy.php.

LeMesurier, Jennifer Lin. 2019. "Searching for Unseen Metic Labor in the Pussyhat Project." *Peitho* 22, no. 1 (Fall/Winter): 144–156.

Lemieux, Jamilah. 2017. "Why I'm Skipping the Women's March on Washington." *Colorlines* (blog), January 17, 2017. https://www.colorlines.com/articles/why-im-skipping-womens-march-washington-op-ed.

Levine, Faythe. 2014. "Craft: Embracing Empowerment and Equality." In *Craftivism: The Art and Craft of Activism*, edited by Betsy Greer. Kindle ed. Vancouver: Arsenal Pulp Press.

Lindquist, Julie. 2004. "Class Affects, Classroom Affectations: Working through the Paradoxes of Strategic Empathy." *College English* 67, no. 2 (November): 187–209.

Lou, Jackie Jia, and Adam Jaworski. 2016. "Itineraries of Protest Signage: Semiotic Landscape and the Mythologizing of the Hong Kong Umbrella Movement." *Journal of Language and Politics* 15 (5): 609–642. https://doi.org/10.1075/jlp.15.5.06lou.

Luckman, Susan. 2013. "The Aura of the Analogue in the Digital Age: Women's Crafts, Creative Markets, and Home-Based Labour after Etsy." *Cultural Studies Review* 19, no. 1 (March): 249–270.

Lundberg, Christian, and Joshua Gunn. 2005. "'Ouija Board, Are There Any Communications?' Agency, Ontotheology, and the Death of the Humanistic Subject, or, Continuing the ARS Conversation." *Rhetoric Society Quarterly* 35 (4): 83–105. https://doi.org/10.1080/02773940509391323.

Lynch, Dennis A. 1998. "Rhetorics of Proximity: Empathy in Temple Grandin and Cornel West." *Rhetoric Society Quarterly* 28 (1): 5–23. https://doi.org/10.1080/02773949809391110.

MacDonald, Anne. 1988. *No Idle Hands: The Social History of American Knitting*. New York: Ballatine Books.

Macrorie, Ken. 2009. "From Telling Writing." In *The Norton Book of Composition Studies*, edited by Susan Miller, 297–313. New York: Norton.

Manjoo, Farhad. 2011. "A Tight-Knit Community." *Slate*, July 6, 2011. http://www.slate.com/articles/technology/technology/2011/07/a_tightknit_community.html.

Marback, Richard. 2008. "Unclenching the Fist: Embodying Rhetoric and Giving Objects their Due." *Rhetoric Society Quarterly* 38, no. 1 (January): 46–65. https://doi.org/10.1080/02773940701779751.

Martinez Dy, Angela, Lee Martin, and Susan Marlow. 2014. "Developing a Critical Realist Positional Approach to Intersectionality." *Journal of Critical Realism* 13, no. 5 (October): 447–466. https://doi.org/10.1179/1476743014Z.00000000043.

Mason, Paul. 2017. "'Millions Have Done Something Together'—Why the Women's March Will Spark the Resistance." *The Guardian*, January 23, 2017. https://www.theguardian.com/world/2017/jan/23/millions-have-done-something-together-why-the-womens-march-will-spark-the-resistance.

Matchar, Emily. 2013. *Homeward Bound: Why Women Are Embracing the New Domesticity*. London: Simon and Schuster.

Mattingly, Carol. 2002. *Appropriate [ing] Dress: Women's Rhetorical Style in Nineteenth-Century America*. Carbondale: Southern Illinois University Press.

Mayer, Jane. 2018. "How Russia Helped Swing the Election for Trump." *The New Yorker*, October 1, 2018. https://www.newyorker.com/magazine/2018/10/01/how-russia-helped-to-swing-the-election-for-trump.

Mayers, Tim. 2007. *(Re)Writing Craft: Composition, Creative Writing, and the Future of English Studies*. Pittsburgh: University of Pittsburgh Press.

McCall, Leslie. 2005. "The Complexity of Intersectionality." *Signs* 30 (3): 1771–1800.

McCausland, Phil. 2017. "Peace, Positivity as Massive Women's March Makes Voices Heard in D.C." *NBC News*, January 21, 2017. https://www.nbcnews.com/news/us-news/peace-positivity-massive-women-s-march-make-voices-heard-d-n710356.

McIntyre, Megan. 2015. "Agency Matters." *Peitho* 18, no. 1 (Fall/Winter): 25–28.

Mears, Bill, and Tom Cohen. 2014. "Supreme Court Rules against Obama in Contraception Case." *CNN*, June 30, 2014. https://www.cnn.com/2014/06/30/politics/scotus-obamacare-contraception/index.html.

Metta, Marilyn. 2015. "Embodying Mêtis: The Braiding of Cunning and Bodily Intelligence in Feminist Storymaking." *Outskirts* 32. http://www.outskirts.arts.uwa.edu.au/volumes/volume-32/marilyn-metta.

Micciche, Laura R. 2005. "Emotions, Ethics, and Rhetorical Action." *JAC* 25 (1): 161–184.

Micciche, Laura R. 2007. *Doing Emotion: Rhetoric, Writing, Teaching*. Portsmouth, NH: Boynton/Cook.

Micciche, Laura R. 2014. "Writing Material." *College English* 76, no. 6 (July): 488–505.

Micciche, Laura R. 2017. *Acknowledging Writing Partners*. Fort Collins, CO: WAC Clearinghouse.

Midgette, Anne. 2012. "After Ravelry Blasts, Olympic Committee Learns Knitters Are a Social-Media Force." *The Washington Post*, June 27, 2012. https://www.washingtonpost.com/lifestyle/style/after-ravelry-blasts-olympic-committee-learns-knitters-are-a-social-media-force/2012/06/29/gJQApl7SCW_story.html?utm_term=.e594368372df.

Million Artist Movement. n.d. *Million Artist Movement*. https://millionartistmovement.com/.

Million Artist Movement. 2015. *Power Tree Tool Kit*. https://millionartistmovement.files.wordpress.com/2015/03/power-quilt-tool-kit.pdf.

Minahan, Stella, and Jule Wolfram Cox. 2007. "Stitch 'n' Bitch: Cyberfeminism, a Third Place, and the New Materiality." *Journal of Material Culture* 12 (1): 5–21. https://doi.org/10.1177/1359183507074559.

MMIWGQT Bead Project. n.d. *Cannupa Hanska*. http://www.cannupahanska.com/mmiwqtbeadproject.

Moore, Mandy, and Leanne Prain. 2009. *Yarn Bombing: The Art of Crochet and Knit Graffiti*. Vancouver: Arsenal Pulp Press.

Mosthof, Mariella. 2017. "If You're Not Talking about the Criticism Surrounding the Women's March, Then You're Part of the Problem." *Bustle*, January 30, 2017. https://www.bustle.com/p/if-youre-not-talking-about-the-criticism-surrounding-the-womens-march-then-youre-part-of-the-problem-33491.

Mott, Carrie, and Daniel Cockayne. 2017. "Citation Matters: Mobilizing the Politics of Citation Toward a Practice of 'Conscientious Engagement'." *Gender, Place & Culture* 24 (7): 954–973. https://doi.org/10.1080/0966369X.2017.1339022.

Mueller, Melissa. 2010. "Helen's Hands: Weaving for Kleos in the Odyssey." *Helios* 37 (1): 1–21.

Murray, Donald M. 1981. "Making Meaning Clear: The Logic of Revision." *Journal of Basic Writing* 3, no. 3 (Fall): 33–40.

Myzelev, Alla. 2009. "Whip Your Hobby into Shape: Knitting, Feminism and Construction of Gender." *Textile* 7 (2): 148–163. https://doi.org/10.2752/175183509X460065.

National Institute for Justice. 2016. "Five Things About Violence against American Indian and Alaska Native Women and Men." *National Institute for Justice*, November 30, 2016.

https://nij.ojp.gov/topics/articles/five-things-about-violence-against-american-indian
-and-alaska-native-women-and-men.

Neumayer, Christina, and Gitte Stald. 2014. "The Mobile Phone in Street Protest: Tex-
ting, Tweeting, Tracking, and Tracing." *Mobile Media & Communication* 2 (2): 117–133.
https://doi.org/10.1177/2050157913513255.

Niedderer, Kristina, and Katherine Townsend. 2018. "The Politics of Craft." *Craft Research*
9 (1): 3–7. https://doi.org/10.1386/crre.9.1.3_2.

Noble, Safiya Umoja. 2018. *Algorithms of Oppression: How Search Engines Reinforce Racism.*
New York: NYU Press.

O'Donnell, Thomas G. 1996. "Politics and Ordinary Language: A Defense of Expressivist
Rhetorics." *College English* 58, no. 4 (April): 423–439.

O'Farrell, Lauren. 2014. "How a Knitted Mouse Made Me a Craftivist." In *Craftivism: The
Art and Craft of Activism,* edited by Betsy Greer. Kindle ed. Vancouver: Arsenal Pulp
Press.

Oxford English Dictionary (OED). 2019. s.v. "rhetorical *(adj.),*" www.oed.com/view/Entry
/165181.

Palmeri, Jason. 2012. *Remixing Composition: A History of Multimodal Writing Pedagogy.* Carbondale: Southern Illinois University Press.

Parker, Rozsika. 1984. *The Subversive Stitch: Embroidery and the Making of the Feminine.* London: The Women's Press.

Parkins, Wendy. 2000. "Protesting Like a Girl: Embodiment, Dissent and Feminist Agency."
Feminist Theory 1 (1): 59–78.

Pender, Kelly. 2011. *Techne: from Neoclassicism to Postmodernism.* Anderson, SC: Parlor Press.

Penney, Joel, and Caroline Dadas. 2014. "(Re)Tweeting in the Service of Protest: Digital
Composition and Circulation in the Occupy Wall Street Movement." *New Media &
Society* 16 (1): 74–90. https://doi.org/10.1177/1461444813479593.

Pentney, Beth Ann. 2008. "Feminism, Activism, and Knitting: Are the Fibre Arts a Viable
Model for Feminist Political Action?" *thirdspace* 8, no. 1 (Summer). https://journals.sfu
.ca/thirdspace/index.php/journal/article/viewArticle/pentney/210.

Perl, Sondra. 1980. "Understanding Composing," *College Composition and Communication*
31, no. 4 (December): 363–369.

Pflugfelder, Ehren Helmut. 2015. "Is No One at the Wheel? Nonhuman Agency and Agen-
tive Movement." In *Thinking with Bruno Latour in Rhetoric and Composition,* edited by
Paul Lynch and Nathaniel Rivers, 115–131. Carbondale: Southern Illinois University
Press.

Plant, Sadie. 1997. *Zeros + Ones: Digital Women and the New Technoculture.* London: Fourth
Estate Press.

Plato. 1994. *Gorgias.* Translated by Robin Waterfield. New York: Oxford University Press.

Plocek, Keith. 2005. "Knitta, Please!" *Houston Press,* December 15, 2005. https://www
.houstonpress.com/news/knitta-please-6547197.

Pomykala, Kristin. 2017. "Snake(s)kin: The Intertwining Metis and Mythopoetics of Ser-
pentine Rhetoric." *Rhetoric Society Quarterly* 47 (3): 264–274. https://doi.org/10.1080
/02773945.2017.1309916.

Porter, James E. 1998. *Rhetorical Ethics and Internetworked Writing.* Greenwich, CT: Ablex
Publishing.

Porter, James E. 2009. "Recovering Delivery for Digital Rhetoric." *Computers and Composition* 26, no. 4 (December): 207–224. https://doi.org/10.1016/j.compcom.2009.09
.004.

Portwood-Stacer, Laura. 2013. *Lifestyle Politics and Radical Activism.* New York: Bloomsbury.

Powell, Katrina M, and Pamela Takayoshi. 2003. "Accepting the Roles Created for Us:
The Ethics of Reciprocity." *College Composition and Communication* 54, no. 3 (February):
394–422.

Powell, Malea, Daisy Levy, Andrea Riley-Mukavetz, Marilee Brooks-Gillies, Maria Novotny, and Jennifer Fisch-Ferguson. 2014. "Our Story Begins Here: Constellating Cultural Rhetorics." *Enculturation.* http://enculturation.net/our-story-begins-here.

Prins, Kristin. 2012. "Crafting New Approaches to Composition." In *Composing (Media) = Composing (Embodiment): Bodies, Technologies, Writing, the Teaching of Writing,* edited by Kristin L. Arola and Anne Frances Wysocki, 145–161. Logan: Utah State University Press.

Puar, Jasbir. 2012. "'I Would Rather Be a Cyborg than a Goddess' Becoming-Intersectional in Assemblage Theory." *philoSOPHIA* 2 (1): 49–66.

Pussyhat Project. n.d. "Our Story." *Pussyhat Project.* https://www.pussyhatproject.com/our -story.

Ramanathan, Lavanya. 2017. "Was the Women's March Just Another Display of White Privilege? Some Think So." *The Washington Post,* January 24, 2017. https://www.washing tonpost.com/lifestyle/style/was-the-womens-march-just-another-display-of-white-privi lege-some-think-so/2017/01/24/00bbdcca-e1a0-11e6-a547-5fb9411d332c_story.html ?utm_term=.6502eb38b974.

Ratcliffe, Krista. 2002. "Material Matters: Bodies and Rhetoric." *College English* 64, no. 5 (May): 613–623.

Ravelry. n.d. "About." *Ravelry.* https://www.ravelry.com/about.

Ravelry. 2014. "4 Million!" *Ravelry.* http://www.ravelry.com/about/fourmillion.

Ravelry. 2019. "New Policy." *Ravelry.* June 23, 2019. https://www.ravelry.com/content/no -trump.

Ravelry (@Ravelry). 2020. "We're coming up on 9 million registered users. This is a number that news outlets like to report but it's not a number that is meaningful to us. It tells you that a lot of people are curious about a knitting/crochet site. Here are some different numbers that describe Ravelry." Twitter, March 7, 2020. https://twitter.com /ravelry/status/1236432587024994309.

Ravenscroft, Alison. 2018. "Strange Weather: Indigenous Materialisms, New Materialism, and Colonialism." *Cambridge Journal of Postcolonial Literary Inquiry* 5, no. 3 (September): 353–370. https://doi.org/10.1017/pli.2018.9.

Reid, Alex. 2012. "What is Object-Oriented Rhetoric?" *Itineration.* http://tundra.csd.sc .edu/itineration/node/11.

Rhodes, Jacqueline. 2005. *Radical Feminism, Writing, and Critical Agency: From Manifesto to Modem.* Albany: State University of New York Press.

Rice, Jeff. 2016. *Craft Obsession: The Social Rhetorics of Beer.* Carbondale: Southern Illinois University Press.

Rickert, Thomas. 2013. *Ambient Rhetoric: The Attunements of Rhetorical Being.* Pittsburgh: University of Pittsburgh Press.

Riley-Mukavetz, Andrea. 2020. "Developing a Relational Scholarly Practice: Snakes, Dreams, and Grandmothers." *College Composition and Communication* 71, no. 4 (June): 545–565.

Rivers, Nathaniel A. 2016. "Geocomposition in Public Rhetoric and Writing Pedagogy." *College Composition and Communication* 67, no. 4 (June): 576–606.

Rivers, Nathaniel A., and Ryan P. Weber. 2011. "Ecological, Pedagogical, Public Rhetoric." *College Composition and Communication* 63, no. 2 (December): 187–218.

Roberts, L. J. 2014. "Making Mirrors: Craft Tactics in the Age of Ongoing AIDS." In *Craftivism: The Art and Craft of Activism,* edited by Betsy Greer. Kindle ed. Vancouver: Arsenal Pulp Press.

Robertson, Kirsty. 2011. "Rebellious Doilies and Subversive Stitches: Writing a Craftivist History." In *Extra/Ordinary: Craft and Contemporary Art,* edited by Maria Elena Buszek, 184–203. Durham, NC: Duke University Press.

Rohan, Liz. 2004. "I Remember Mamma: Material Rhetoric, Mnemonic Activity, and One Woman's Turn-of-the-Twentieth-Century Quilt." *Rhetoric Review* 23 (4): 368–287. https://doi.org/10.1207/s15327981rr2304_5.

Rose-Redwood, CindyAnn, and Reuben Rose-Redwood. 2017. "'It Definitely Felt Very White': Race, Gender, and the Performative Politics of Assembly at the Women's March in Victoria, British Columbia." *Gender, Place & Culture* 24 (5): 645–654. https://doi .org/10.1080/0966369X.2017.1335290.

Rosiek, Jerry Lee, and Jimmy Snyder. 2020. "Narrative Inquiry and New Materialism: Stories as (not Necessarily Benign) Agents." *Qualitative Inquiry* 26 (10): 1151–1162. https://doi.org/1077800418784326.

Rosiek, Jerry Lee, Jimmy Snyder, and Scott L. Pratt. 2020. "The New Materialisms and Indigenous Theories of Non-Human Agency: Making the Case for Respectful Anti-Colonial Engagement." *Qualitative Inquiry* 26 (3–4): 331–346. https://doi.org/10 .1177/1077800419830135.

Royster, Jacqueline Jones. 2000. *Traces of a Stream: Literacy and Social Change among African American Women.* Pittsburgh: University of Pittsburgh Press.

Royster, Jacqueline Jones, and Gesa E. Kirsch. 2012. *Feminist Rhetorical Practices: New Horizons for Rhetoric, Composition, and Literacy Studies.* Carbondale: Southern Illinois University Press.

Rumsey, Suzanne Kesler. 2009. "Heritage Literacy: Adoption, Adaptation, and Alienation of Multimodal Literacy Tools." *College Composition and Communication* 60, no. 3 (February): 573–586.

Sasson-Levy, Orna, and Tamar Rapoport. 2003. "Body, Gender, and Knowledge in Protest Movements: The Israeli Case." *Gender & Society* 17, no. 3 (June): 379–403. https://doi .org/10.1177/0891243203251729.

Saxena, Jaya. 2019. "The Knitting Community is Reckoning with Racism." *Vox,* February 25, 2019. https://www.vox.com/the-goods/2019/2/25/18234950/knitting-racism -instagram-stories?fbclid=IwAR30Y8rCt2P-Q88lokv13LPQ_KcLSk6CcGykyX-A2oKb Wx2kED1jcaqFno4.

Schell, Eileen E. 1998. "The Costs of Caring: 'Feminism' and Contingent Women Workers in Composition Studies." In *Feminism and Composition Studies: In Other Words,* edited by Susan C. Jarratt and Lynn Worsham, 74–93. New York: Modern Language Association.

Schulz, Karsten A. 2017. "Decolonizing Political Ecology: Ontology, Technology and 'Critical' Enchantment." *Journal of Political Ecology* 24:125–143.

Sennett, Richard. 2008. *The Craftsman.* New Haven, CT: Yale University Press.

Shamus, Kristen Jordan. 2018. "Pink Pussyhats: The Reason Feminists are Ditching Them." *Detroit Free Press,* January 10, 2018. https://www.freep.com/story/news/2018/01/10 /pink-pussyhats-feminists-hats-womens-march/1013630001/.

Sheridan, David, Jim Ridolfo, and Anthony J. Michel. 2012. *The Available Means of Persuasion: Mapping a Theory and Pedagogy of Multimodal Public Rhetoric.* Anderson, SC: Parlor Press.

Shipka, Jody. 2011. *Toward a Composition Made Whole.* Pittsburgh: University of Pittsburgh Press.

Significant Seams. 2012. "The E17 Neighbourhood Quilt." *Significant Seams,* March 5, 2012. http://significantseams.org.uk/the-e17-neighbourly-quilt-have-you-started-your -patch/.

Singleton, Benedict. 2014. "On Craft and Being Crafty" (PhD diss., Northumbria University).

Sipiora, Phillip. 2002. "Introduction." In *Rhetoric and Kairos: Essays in History, Theory, and Praxis,* edited by Phillip Sipiora and James S. Baumlin, 1–22. Albany: State University of New York Press.

Sloan, Jeanette. 2018. "Black People Do Knit & The Diversknitty Conversation." *Jeanette Sloan* (blog), October 17, 2018. https://jeanettesloan.wordpress.com/2018/10/17 /black-people-do-knit-the-diversknitty-conversation/.

Sohan, Vanessa Kraemer. 2015. "'But a Quilt Is More': Recontextualizing the Discourse(s) of the Gee's Bend Quilts." *College English* 77, no. 4 (March): 294–316.

Solis, Marie. 2017. "Women of Color Are Being Blamed for Dividing the Women's March—and It's Nothing New." *Mic*, January 21, 2017. https://www.mic.com/articles /166202/women-of-color-are-being-blamed-for-dividing-the-women-s-march-and-it-s -nothing-new#.fLus1Q4gu.

"Solo Work." n.d. *Margarita Cabrera*, https://www.margaritacabrera.com/portafolio/solo -work/.

Spinuzzi, Clay. 2015. "Symmetry as a Methodological Move." In *Thinking with Bruno Latour in Rhetoric and Composition*, edited by Paul Lynch and Nathaniel Rivers, 23–39. Carbondale: Southern Illinois University Press.

Stenberg, Shari J. 2015. *Repurposing Composition: Feminist Interventions for a Neoliberal Age*. Logan: Utah State University Press.

Stormer, Nathan, and Bridie McGreavy. 2017. "Thinking Ecologically About Rhetoric's Ontology: Capacity, Vulnerability, and Resilience." *Philosophy & Rhetoric* 50 (1): 1–25.

Strickland, Donna. 2011. *The Managerial Unconscious in the History of Composition Studies*. Carbondale: Southern Illinois University Press.

Strycharz, Heather. 2014. "Sewing Voices: The Arpilleristas and the Women of the Adithi Collective." In *Craftivism: The Art and Craft of Activism*, edited by Betsy Greer. Kindle ed. Vancouver: Arsenal Pulp Press.

Sukrita. 2019. "On Ravelry's Trump Ban." *Unfinished Object* (blog), June 26, 2019. https:// www.unfinishedobject.com/blog/on-ravelrys-trump-ban.

Sumpter, Matthew. 2016. "Shared Frequency: Expressivism, Social Constructionism, and the Linked Creative Writing-Composition Class." *College English* 78, no. 4 (March): 340–361.

Sundberg, Juanita. 2014. "Decolonizing Posthumanist Geographies." *Cultural Geographies* 21 (1): 33–47. https://doi.org/10.1177/1474474013486067.

TallBear, Kim. 2015. "An Indigenous Reflection on Working beyond the Human/Not Human." *GLQ: A Journal of Lesbian and Gay Studies* 21 (2–3): 230–235.

TEDx Talks. 2013. "How a Piece of Fabric Can Change the World: Sarah Corbett at TEDx-Brixton." Uploaded on October 23, 2013. YouTube video, 20:40 min. https://www .youtube.com/watch?v=Zf9ahnpDGqo.

Tetreault, Laura. 2019. " 'White Women Voted for Trump': The Women's March on Washington and Intersectional Feminist Futures." *Computers and Composition Online* (March 2019). http://cconlinejournal.org/techfem_si/01_Tetreault/index.html.

Textile Arts Center. 2016. "5.4 Million and Counting Project Update!" http://textilearts center.com/blog/5-4-million-and-counting-project-update/.

Tobin, Lad. 1989. "Bridging Gaps: Analyzing our Students' Metaphors for Composing." *College Composition and Communication* 40, no. 4 (December): 444–458.

Todd, Zoe. 2016. "An Indigenous Feminist's Take on the Ontological Turn: 'Ontology' is Just Another Word for Colonialism." *Journal of Historical Sociology* 29, no. 1 (March): 4–22. https://doi.org/10.1111/johs.12124.

Tomlinson, Barbara. 1986. "Cooking, Mining, Gardening, Hunting: Metaphorical Stories Writers Tell about Their Composing Processes." *Metaphor and Symbolic Activity* 1 (1): 57–79. https://doi.org/10.1207/s15327868ms0101_4.

Tomlinson, Barbara. 1988. "Tuning, Tying, and Training Texts: Metaphors for Revision." *Written Communication* 5 (1): 58–81. https://doi.org/10.1177/0741088388005001003.

Towns, Armond R. 2018. "Black 'Matter' Lives." *Women's Studies in Communication* 41 (4): 349–358. https://doi.org/10.1080/07491409.2018.1551985.

Trapani, William C., and Chandra A. Maldonado. 2018. "Kairos: On the Limits to Our (Rhetorical) Situation." *Rhetoric Society Quarterly* 48 (3): 278–286. https://doi.org/10 .1080/02773945.2018.1454211.

Tufekci, Zeynep. 2017. *Twitter and Tear Gas: The Power and Fragility of Networked Protest*. New Haven, CT: Yale University Press.

Tufekci, Zeynep, and Christopher Wilson. 2012. "Social Media and the Decision to Participate in Political Protest: Observations from Tahrir Square." *Journal of Communication* 62,
no. 2: 363–379. https://doi.org/10.1111/j.1460-2466.2012.01629.

Turney, Joanne. 2009. *The Culture of Knitting*. New York: Berg.

Twitter Data (@TwitterData). 2017. "In the past 24 hours, there have been 11.5 million
#WomensMarch Tweets sent around the world." Twitter, January 21, 2017. https://
twitter.com/TwitterData/status/823041638369034245.

Van Dam, Andrew. 2018. "This Researcher Studied 400,000 Knitters and Discovered
What Turns a Hobby into a Business." *Washington Post*, November 14, 2018. https://
www.washingtonpost.com/business/2018/11/14/how-an-economist-found-an-ideal
-dataset-inside-facebook-knitting/.

Van Strydonck, Mark, Antoine De Moor, and Dominique Benazeth. 2004. "C14 Dating
Compared to Art Historical Dating of Roman and Coptic Textiles from Egypt." *Radio-
carbon* 46 (1): 231–244.

Vollers, Anna Claire. 2017. "Thousands Parade Through Birmingham Streets for Alabama
Women's March." *AL.com*, January 21, 2017. https://www.al.com/news/birmingham
/2017/01/thousands_parade_through_birmi.html.

Vopat, Carole Gottlieb. 1976. "Fiction 100: An Anthology of Short Stories [Review]." *College
Composition and Communication* 27, no. 1 (February): 85–88.

Wace, Alan J. B. 1948. "Weaving or Embroidery?" *American Journal of Archaeology* 52, no. 1
(January–March): 51–55.

Wade, Michael. 2011. "Ravel-ution." In *Fiber Beat*, September 7, 2011, podcast, MP3 audio,
http://fiberbeat.blogspot.com/2011/09/fiber-beat-episode-22-ravel-ution.html.

Wallace, Jacqueline. 2012. "Yarn Bombing, Knit Graffiti and Underground Brigades: A
Study of Craftivism and Mobility." *Journal of Mobile Media* 6 (3). http://wi.mobilities
.ca/yarn-bombing-knit-graffiti-and-underground-brigades-a-study-of-craftivism-and
-mobility/.

Wallace, Tim, and Alicia Parlapiano. 2017. "Crowd Scientists Say Women's March in Washington Had 3 Times as Many People as Trump's Inauguration." *New York Times*, January 22, 2017. https://www.nytimes.com/interactive/2017/01/22/us/politics/womens
-march-trump-crowd-estimates.html.

West, Catherine. 2014. "Giving Voice through Craftivism." In *Craftivism: The Art and Craft of
Activism*, edited by Betsy Greer. Kindle ed. Vancouver: Arsenal Pulp Press.

White, Eric Charles. 1987. *Kaironomia: On the Will-to-Invent*. Ithaca, NY: Cornell University
Press.

"Whole Women's Health v. Hellerstedt." n.d. *SCOTUSblog* (blog). https://www.scotusblog
.com/case-files/cases/whole-womans-health-v-cole/.

Wildermuth, Susan, Corey B. Davis, Edward Frederick, and Josh Bolton. 2014. "Sign, Sign,
Everywhere a Sign: An Analysis of the Argument, Target and Content of Protest Signs
Displayed During the Wisconsin Budget Repair Bill/Act 10 Protests of 2011." *American
Communication Journal* 16, no. 1 (Summer): 15–35.

Willey, Angela. 2016. "A World of Materialisms: Postcolonial Feminist Science Studies and
the New Natural." *Science, Technology, & Human Values* 4 (6): 991–1014. https://doi.org
/10.1177/0162243916658707.

Women's March. 2017. *Guiding Vision and Definition of Principles*. https://static1.squarespace
.com/static/5c3feb79fcf7fdce5a3c790b/t/5c433e85c2241ba6b9353fce/15479107
89489/2019%2BUnity%2BPrinciples.pdf.

Women's March (@womensmarch). 2017. "Download #WomensMarch guide!" Twitter,
January 21, 2017. https://twitter.com/womensmarch/status/822816097145655296.

Wortham, Jenna. 2017. "Who Didn't Go to the Women's March Matters More Than Who
Did." *New York Times Magazine*, January 24, 2017. https://www.nytimes.com/2017/01
/24/magazine/who-didnt-go-to-the-womens-march-matters-more-than-who-did.html.

Wrenn, Corey. 2019. "Pussy Grabs Back: Bestialized Sexual Politics and Intersectional Failure in Protest Posters for the 2017 Women's March." *Feminist Media Studies* 19 (6): 803–821. https://doi.org/10.1080/14680777.2018.1465107.

Wysocki, Anne Frances. 2005. "awaywithwords: On the Possibilities in Unavailable Designs." *Computers and Composition* 22 (1): 55–62. https://doi.org/10.1016/j.compcom.2004.12 .011.

Yarn Mission. n.d. "About Us." *The Yarn Mission.* Accessed July 23, 2020. http://theyarn mission.com/about-us-2/.

Young, Richard E. 1980. "Arts, Crafts, Gifts, and Knacks: Some Disharmonies in the New Rhetoric." *Visible Language* 14 (4): 341–350.

Zylinska, Joanna. 2014. *Minimal Ethics for the Anthropocene.* Ann Arbor, MI: Open Humanities Press. http://dx.doi.org/10.3998/ohp.12917741.0001.001.

INDEX

ABOUT THE AUTHOR

Leigh Gruwell is an assistant professor of English at Auburn University where she teaches undergraduate and graduate courses in writing and rhetoric. Her research centers on digital, feminist, and new materialist rhetorics as well as composition pedagogy and research methodologies and has previously been published in *Computers and Composition, Composition Forum,* and *Present Tense.*